Praise for *Juniper QFX10000 Series*

"Juniper QFX10000 balances functionality and expense in a unique proposition not found in merchant silicon."

—*Joel Jaeggli, operations and management area director, IETF*

"With a fundamental shift in the delivery and consumption of network functions, the QFX10000 provides flexible configurations for any modern data center."

—*Anthony Burke, Architect, VMware*

"This book is an invaluable resource useful for any network engineer looking to understand the finer details of the Juniper QFX10000, which is immensely helpful to our work at Twitter."

—*Tim Hoffman, lead backbone engineer, Twitter*

"Gain valuable insights on architecting data center networks, which are backed by concrete examples."

—*Brian Tam, network lead, Uber*

"This is simply one of the best guides on modern datacenter architecture, presented in a pragmatic and understandable way."

—*Sargun Dhillon, senior lead, Mesosphere*

"The Juniper QFX10000 has new silicon plus a new memory architecture that eliminates bottlenecks. Want to make the most of what Juniper has created? You need this book."

—*Ethan Banks, cofounder, Packet Pushers*

Juniper QFX10000 Series
A Comprehensive Guide on Building Next-Generation Data Centers

Douglas Richard Hanks, Jr.

Beijing · Boston · Farnham · Sebastopol · Tokyo

Juniper QFX10000 Series

by Douglas Richard Hanks, Jr.

Printed in the United States of America.

Published by O'Reilly Media, Inc., 1005 Gravenstein Highway North, Sebastopol, CA 95472.

O'Reilly books may be purchased for educational, business, or sales promotional use. Online editions are also available for most titles (*http://safaribooksonline.com*). For more information, contact our corporate/institutional sales department: 800-998-9938 or *corporate@oreilly.com*.

Editors: Brian Anderson and Courtney Allen	**Indexer:** Wendy Catalano
Production Editor: Melanie Yarbrough	**Interior Designer:** David Futato
Copyeditor: Octal Publishing Inc.	**Cover Designer:** Randy Comer
Proofreader: Jasmine Kwityn	**Illustrator:** Douglas Richard Hanks, Jr.

August 2016:   First Edition

Revision History for the First Edition

2016-07-25:   First Release

See *http://oreilly.com/catalog/errata.csp?isbn=9781491922255* for release details.

978-1-491-92225-5

[LSI]

This book is dedicated to the awesome teams at Juniper Networks that made the Juniper QFX10000 possible. I've learned and grown so much in my career by being part of the JDI team tasked with bringing these new switches to market. It's been challenging both from a technical and business point of view. It's such an honor to be part of the team creating and inventing the latest technology.

Thank you,

Doug

Table of Contents

Preface

This new book is a little shorter than my previous books on the Juniper MX and Juniper QFX5100. That's because I want to focus on what's new instead of just writing about the same things in a different way. This book will focus mainly on a few key new technologies: hardware and software architecture of the Juniper QFX510000 and Ethernet VPN (EVPN).

For a while, Juniper had a product gap in its switching portfolio: a high-density, feature-rich data center switch. The Juniper QFX10000 family of switches fills this gap in spades. It has been the most anticipated switch in the company's history. Juniper spared no expense when designing this new device. As of this writing, it comes packed to the brim with features, including full Multiprotocol Label Switching (MPLS), insane logical scale, and the most 40GbE and 100GbE ports.

The Juniper QFX10000 switch was designed from the ground up to solve some serious problems. Obviously it's a spine switch, but you're also able to use it in many different use cases across several different verticals. Here are some examples:

- Service provider
  - High-scale Ethernet/IP spine switch
  - Segment routing core switch
- Internet exchange
  - Core or edge/access switch
- Public/private cloud
  - High-scale Clos Fabric or spine switch
- Enterprise
  - Junos Fusion aggregate device
  - Standard Ethernet/IP spine switch

— Collapsed spine switch and edge router

The Juniper QFX10000 also takes virtualization to heart: under the hood, it uses Linux and KVM to virtualize the network operating system (Junos) to reap all the benefits of virtualization, such as snapshots and In-Service Software Upgrades (ISSU).

This book is going to show you, step by step, how to build a better network by using the Juniper QFX10000 Series—it's such a versatile platform that you can place it in the fabric, spine, or edge of any type of network and provide instant value. The Juniper QFX10000 was designed to be a network virtualization beast. You can choose between six different networking technologies and support overlay networking directly in hardware with no performance loss.

No Apologies

I'm an avid reader of technology books, and I always get a bit giddy when a new book is released because I can't wait to read it and learn more about a specific technology. However, one trend I have noticed is that every networking book tends to regurgitate the basics over and over. There are only so many times you can force yourself to read about spanning tree, the split-horizon rule, or OSPF LSA types. One of the goals of this book is to introduce new and fresh content that hasn't been published before.

I made a conscious decision to keep the technical quality of this book very high; this created a constant debate as to whether to include primer or introductory material in the book to help refresh a reader's memory with certain technologies and networking features. In short, here's what I decided:

Spanning tree and switching
> Spanning tree and switching is covered in great detail in every JNCIA and CCNA book on the market. If you want to learn more about spanning tree or switching, check out *Junos Enterprise Switching* (O'Reilly, 2009), or *CCNA ICND2 Official Exam Certification Guide*, Second Edition (Cisco Press, 2007).

Routing protocols
> There are various routing protocols such as OSPF and IS-IS used throughout this book in case studies. No introductory chapters are included for IS-IS or OSPF, and it's assumed that you are already familiar with these protocols. If not, you can learn more by checking out *Junos Enterprise Routing*, Second Edition (O'Reilly, 2011) or *Juniper Networks Certified Internet Expert Study Guide* (*http://juni.pr/ 29MlVUK*) by Juniper Networks.

Multichassis Link Aggregation (MC-LAG)

Ah, MC-LAG, we meet again. If you want to learn more about MC-LAG, read *Juniper QFX5100* (O'Reilly, 2014) or *Juniper MX Series*, Second Edition (O'Reilly, 2016).

Quality of Service

Classifiers, schedulers, and drop profiles. Oh my! Read *Juniper MX Series*, Second Edition.

IP fabrics

Read *Juniper QFX5100*. There's plenty of stuff in there.

After many hours of debate, I decided that I should defer to other books when it comes to introductory material and keep the content of this book at an expert level. I expect that you already have your JNCIE or CCIE (or you're well on your way) and will enjoy the technical quality of this book. If you're just getting started out, I want to share a list of existing books that are widely respected within the networking community that you might find more helpful:

- *Juniper MX Series*, Second Edition (O'Reilly)—the best book out of the bunch, no bias right?
- *Juniper QFX5100 Series* (O'Reilly)
- *Junos Enterprise Routing*, Second Edition (O'Reilly)
- *Junos Enterprise Switching* (O'Reilly)
- *QoS-Enabled Networks* (Wiley & Sons)
- *MPLS-Enabled Applications*, Third Edition (Wiley & Sons)
- *Network Mergers and Migrations* (Wiley)
- *Juniper Networks Certified Internet Expert* (Juniper Networks)
- *Juniper Networks Certified Internet Professional* (Juniper Networks)
- *Juniper Networks Certified Internet Specialist* (Juniper Networks)
- *Juniper Networks Certified Internet Associate* (Juniper Networks)
- *CCIE Routing and Switching*, Fourth Edition (Cisco Press)
- *Routing TCP/IP*, volumes 1 and 2 (Cisco Press)
- *OSPF and IS-IS* (Addison-Wesley)
- *OSPF: Anatomy of an Internet Routing Protocol* (Addison-Wesley)
- *The Art of Computer Programming* (Addison-Wesley)
- *TCP/IP Illustrated*, volumes 1, 2, and 3 (Addison-Wesley)
- *UNIX Network Programming*, volumes 1 and 2 (Prentice Hall PTR)

- *Network Algorithmics: An Interdisciplinary Approach to Designing Fast Networked Devices* (Morgan Kaufmann)

What's in This Book?

This book was written for network engineers, by network engineers. The ultimate goal of this book is to share with the reader the logical underpinnings of the Juniper QFX10000. Each chapter represents a specific vertical within the Juniper QFX10000 and will provide enough depth and knowledge to provide you with the confidence to implement and design new architectures for your network using the Juniper QFX10000 series.

Here's a short summary of the chapters and what you'll find inside:

Chapter 1, Juniper QFX10000 Hardware Architecture

Learn all about the new Juniper silicon that powers all of the Juniper QFX10000 switches. This includes all of the fixed switches and modular chassis and line cards.

Chapter 2, QFX10000 Software Architecture

A lot has changed since vanilla Junos. Everything is virtualized and uses these newfangled DevOps tools.

Chapter 3, Next-Generation Internet Exchange Architecture Case Study

I took a hard right turn and went off the beaten path in this chapter. Learn about how to take a particular use case and break down the requirements into simple building blocks. Learn how to apply the requirements against a set of technologies to make the best architecture decisions. I then break down the architecture into engineering and design trade-offs that are critical to implementing a solid production network.

Chapter 4, Performance and Scale

All of these features are great, but you need to know the performance and scaling attributes. No problem. Let's take a deep-dive into the control plane and data plane and explore both the physical and logical performance and scaling abilities of the Juniper QFX10000. You're going to love what you see.

Chapter 5, Junos Fusion

Heeeelp. I need the Easy Button. Learn how to build an Ethernet fabric based on IEEE 802.1BR using the Juniper QFX10000 and QFX5000 Series. Everything is plug and play with a single point of management. No need to worry about routing protocols and other things within the data center.

Chapter 6, Ethernet VPN

EVPN is the latest and greatest thing. Think L3VPN, but for Layer 2. There are a lot of ins and outs with this new protocol. I break it down bit by bit and explain how each function works and compare the various options so that you can see the engineering trade-offs. We'll close the chapter out with a nice case study.

Each chapter includes a set of review questions based on the topics that are covered in the respective chapter, all designed to get you thinking about what you've just read and digested. If you're not in the certification mode, the questions will provide a mechanism for critical thinking, potentially prompting you to locate other resources to further your knowledge.

As with most deep-dive books, you will be exposed to a variety of hidden, Junos Shell, and even MPC-level VTY commands performed after forming an internal connection to a PFE component. And as always, the standard disclaimers apply.

In general, a command being hidden indicates that the feature is not officially supported in that release. Such commands should only be used in production networks after consultation with Juniper Networks Technical Assistance Center (JTAC). Likewise, the shell is not officially supported or documented. The commands available can change, and you can render a router unbootable with careless use of a shell commands. The same holds true for PFE component–level shell commands, often called VTY commands.

The hidden and shell commands that are used in this book were selected because they were the only way to illustrate certain operational characteristics or the results of complex configuration parameters.

Again, hidden and shell commands should be used only under JTAC guidance; this is especially true when dealing with a router that is part of a production network.

You have been duly warned.

Conventions Used in This Book

The following typographical conventions are used in this book:

Italic

Indicates new terms, URLs, email addresses, filenames, file extensions, pathnames, directories, and Unix utilities

`Constant width`

Indicates commands, options, switches, variables, attributes, keys, functions, types, classes, namespaces, methods, modules, properties, parameters, values, objects, events, event handlers, XML tags, HTML tags, macros, the contents of files, and the output from commands

Constant width bold
Shows commands and other text that should be typed literally by the user, as well as important lines of code

Constant width italic
Shows text that should be replaced with user-supplied values

 This icon signifies a tip, suggestion, or general note.

 This icon indicates a warning or caution.

Comments and Questions

Please address comments and questions concerning this book to the publisher:

O'Reilly Media, Inc.
1005 Gravenstein Highway North
Sebastopol, CA 95472
800-998-9938 (in the United States or Canada)
707-829-0515 (international or local)
707-829-0104 (fax)

We have a web page for this book, where we list errata, examples, and any additional information. You can access this page at *http://bit.ly/juniperqfx10000-series.*

To comment or ask technical questions about this book, send email to *bookquestions@oreilly.com.*

For more information about our books, courses, conferences, and news, see our website at *http://www.oreilly.com.*

Find us on Facebook: *http://facebook.com/oreilly*

Follow us on Twitter: *http://twitter.com/oreillymedia*

Watch us on YouTube: *http://www.youtube.com/oreillymedia*

Safari® Books Online

 *Safari Books Online* is an on-demand digital library that delivers expert content in both book and video form from the world's leading authors in technology and business.

Technology professionals, software developers, web designers, and business and creative professionals use Safari Books Online as their primary resource for research, problem solving, learning, and certification training.

Safari Books Online offers a range of plans and pricing for enterprise, government, education, and individuals.

Members have access to thousands of books, training videos, and prepublication manuscripts in one fully searchable database from publishers like O'Reilly Media, Prentice Hall Professional, Addison-Wesley Professional, Microsoft Press, Sams, Que, Peachpit Press, Focal Press, Cisco Press, John Wiley & Sons, Syngress, Morgan Kaufmann, IBM Redbooks, Packt, Adobe Press, FT Press, Apress, Manning, New Riders, McGraw-Hill, Jones & Bartlett, Course Technology, and hundreds more. For more information about Safari Books Online, please visit us online.

CHAPTER 1

Juniper QFX10000 Hardware Architecture

There's always something a little magical about things that are developed and made in-house. Whether it's a fine Swiss watch with custom movements or a Formula 1 race car, they were built for one purpose: to be the best and perform exceptionally well for a specific task. I always admire the engineering behind such technology and how it pushes the limits of what was previously thought impossible.

When Juniper set out to build a new aggregation switch for the data center, a lot of time was spent looking at the requirements. Three things stood out above the rest:

High logical scale
> New data center architectures such as collapsing the edge and aggregation tiers or building large hosting data centers require a lot of logical scale such as the number of host entries, route prefixes, access control lists (ACL), and routing instances.

Congestion control
> Given the high density of 40/100GbE ports and collapsing the edge and aggregation tiers into a single switch, a method for controlling egress congestion was required. Using a mixture of Virtual Output Queuing (VOQ) and large buffers guarantees that the traffic can reach its final destination.

Advanced features
> Software-Defined Networks (SDNs) have changed the landscape of data center networking. We are now seeing the rise of various tunneling encapsulations in the data center such as Multiprotocol Label Switching (MPLS) and Virtual Extensible LAN (VXLAN). We are also seeing new control-plane protocols such as Open vSwitch Database Management Protocol (OVSDB) and Ethernet VPN (EVPN). If you want to collapse the edge into the aggregation switch, you also need all of the WAN encapsulations and protocols.

Combining all three of these requirements into a single switch is difficult. There were no off-the-shelf components available to go build such a high-performance and feature-rich switch. Juniper had to go back to the whiteboard and design a new network processer specifically for solving the switching challenges in the modern data center.

This is how the new Juniper Q5 network processor was born.

Network Processors

Network processors are just a type of application-specific integrated circuit (ASIC). There is a very large range of different types of ASICs that vary in functionality, programmability, and speed, as shown in Figure 1-1.

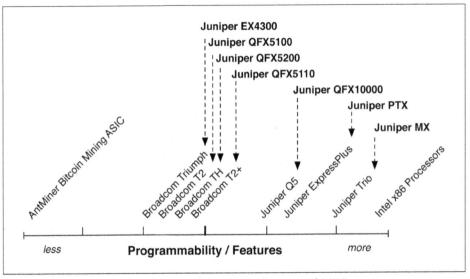

Figure 1-1. Line graph of programmability versus features of ASICs

There are many factors to consider in an ASIC. At a high level, it's easy to classify them in terms of programmability. For example, if all you need to do is mine Bitcoins, the AntMiner ASIC does this very well. The only downside is that it can't do anything else beyond mine Bitcoins. On the flip side, if you need to perform a wide range of tasks, an Intel x86 processor is great. It can play games, write a book, check email, and much more. The downside is that it can't mine Bitcoins as fast as the AntMiner ASIC, because it isn't optimized for that specific task.

In summary, ASICs are designed to perform a specific task very well, or they are designed to perform a wide variety of tasks but not as fast. Obviously there is a lot of area between these two extremes, and this is the area into which most of the network processors fall. Depending on the type of switch, it will serve a specific role in the network. For example, a top-of-rack (ToR) switch doesn't need all of the features and speed of a spine or core switch. The Juniper ToR switches fall more toward the left of the graph, whereas the Juniper QFX10000, Juniper PTX, and Juniper MX are more toward the right. As you move from the spine of the network into the edge and core, you need more and more features and programmability.

Another important attribute to consider is the amount of logical scale and packet buffer. Depending on the type of switch and use case, you might need more or less of each. Generally, ToR switches do not require a lot of scale or packet buffer. Spine switches in the data center require a lot more logical scale because of the aggregation of the L2 and L3 addressing. The final example is that in the core and backbone of the network, all of the service provider's customer addressing is aggregated and requires even more logical scale, which is made possible by the Juniper MX, as illustrated in Figure 1-2.

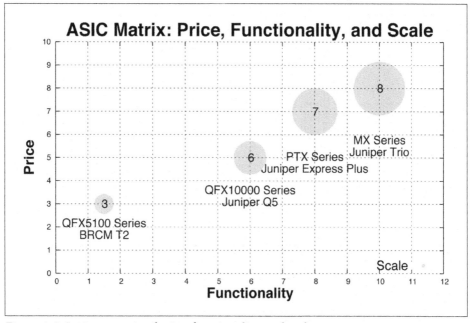

Figure 1-2. Juniper matrix of price, functionality, and scale

The goal of the QFX10000 was to enable the most common use cases in the fabric and spine of the data center. From a network processor point of view, it was obvious it needed to bridge the gap between Broadcom T2 and Juniper Trio chipsets. We needed more scale, buffer, and features than was available in the Broadcom T2 chipset, and less than the Juniper Trio chipset. Such a combination of scale, features, and buffer wasn't available from existing merchant silicon vendors, so Juniper engineers had to create this new chipset in-house.

The Juniper Q5 Processor

The Juniper Q5 network processor is an extremely powerful chipset that delivers high logical scale, congestion control, and advanced features. Each Juniper Q5 chip is able to process 500Gbps of full duplex bandwidth at 333 million packets per second (Mpps). There are three major components to the Juniper Q5 chipset (Figure 1-3):

- Front panel ports
- Packet processing
- Fabric interfaces

The front panel ports are the ports that are exposed on the front of the switch or line card for production use. Each Juniper Q5 chip can handle up to 5x100GbE, 12x40GbE, or 48x10GbE ports.

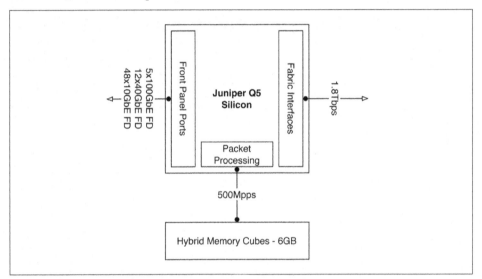

Figure 1-3. Juniper Q5 chipset architecture

The packet processing is able to handle up to 500 Mpps within a single chip so that packets can be looped back through the chipset for additional processing. The overall chip-to-chip packet processing is able to handle 333 Mpps. For example, the Juniper QFX10002-72Q switch has a total of six Juniper Q5 chips, which brings the total system processing power to 2 billion packets per second (Bpps).

The Juniper Q5 chipsets have been designed to build very dense and feature-rich switches with very high logical scale. Each switch is built using a multichip architecture; traffic between Juniper Q5 chips are *cellified* and sprayed across a switching fabric.

Front Panel Ports

Each Juniper Q5 chip is tri-speed; it supports 10GbE, 40GbE, and 100GbE. As of this writing, the IEEE still hasn't ratified the 400GbE MAC so the Juniper Q5 chip is unable to take advantage of 400GbE. However, as soon as the 400GbE MAC is ratified, the Juniper Q5 chip can be quickly programmed to enable the 400GbE MAC.

Packet Processing

The heart of the Juniper Q5 chipset is the packet processor. The packet processor is responsible for inspecting the packet, performing lookups, modifying the packet (if necessary), and applying ACLs. The chain of actions the packet processor performs is commonly referred to as the pipeline.

The challenge with most packet processors is that the packet processing pipeline is fixed in nature. This means that the order of actions, what can be done, and performance is all very limited. A limited packet processing pipeline becomes a challenge when working with different packet encapsulations. For example, think about all of the different ways a VXLAN packet could be processed:

- Applying an ACL before or after the encapsulations or decapsulation
- Requiring multiple destination lookups based on inner or outer encapsulations
- Changing from one encapsulation to another, such as VXLAN to MPLS

The Juniper Q5 chipset was designed to solve these challenges from the beginning. The key is creating a flexible packet processing pipeline that's able to process packets multiple ways at any stage through the pipeline without a loss in performance. Figure 1-4 illustrates this pipeline.

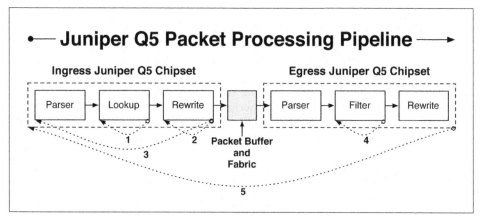

Figure 1-4. The Juniper Q5 packet processing pipeline

The Juniper Q5 packet processing pipeline is divided into two parts: the *ingress* and *egress* chipsets. The Juniper Q5 chipsets communicate with one another through a fabric that is interconnected to every single Juniper Q5 chipset. The ingress chipset is mainly responsible for parsing the packet, looking up its destination, and applying any type of tunnel termination and header rewrites. The egress chipset is mainly responsible for policing, counting, shaping, and quality of service (QoS). Notice Figure 1-4 has five loopbacks throughout the pipeline. These are the flexible *points of recirculation* that are enabled in the Juniper Q5 chipset and which make it possible for the Juniper QFX10000 switches to handle multiple encapsulations with rich services. Let's walk through each of these recirculation points, including some examples of how they operate:

- There are various actions that require recirculation in the lookup block on the ingress Juniper Q5 chipset. For example, tunnel lookups require multiple steps: determine the Virtual Tunnel End-Point (VTEP) address, identify the protocol and other Layer 4 information, and then perform binding checks.

- The ingress Juniper Q5 chipset can also recirculate the packet through the rewrite block. A good example is when the Juniper QFX10000 switch needs to perform a pair of actions such as (VLAN rewrite + NAT) or (remove IEEE 802.1BR tag + VLAN rewrite).

- The packet can also be recirculated through the entire ingress Juniper Q5 chipset. There are two broad categories that require ingress recirculation: filter after lookup and tunnel termination. For example, ingress recirculation is required when you need to apply a loopback filter for host-bound packets or apply a filter to a tunnel interface.

- The egress Juniper Q5 chipset can perform multiple actions. For example, it can count packets, police packets, or apply software traps.

- Finally, the entire packet is able to recirculate through the entire ingress and egress Juniper Q5 packet processing pipeline multiple times, as well. The main purpose is to support multicast replication tree traversal.

The Juniper Q5 packet processing pipeline is a very powerful and flexible mechanism to enable rich tunnel services, packet filtering, multicast, network services, and QoS. The pipeline is programmable and can be upgraded through each Juniper software release to support new features and further increase performance and efficiency.

Fabric Interfaces

Each Juniper Q5 chipset has a set of fabric interfaces that are used to connect it to a Juniper fabric chip that lets it have full bisectional bandwidth to every other Juniper Q5 chipset within the switch, as depicted in Figure 1-5.

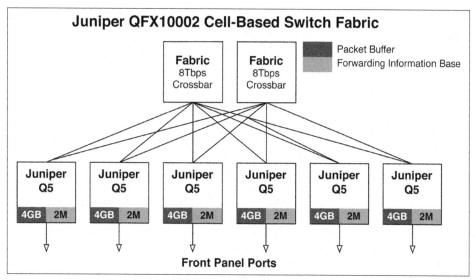

Figure 1-5. Juniper QFX10002 cell-based switching fabric

The Juniper QFX10002-72Q has a total of six Juniper Q5 chipsets to support the 72x40GbE interfaces. Each of the Juniper Q5 chipsets are connected together in a Clos topology using a pair of Juniper fabric chips that can each support up to 8Tbps of bandwidth. There are two major design philosophies when it comes to building a multiple chipset switch:

- Packet-based fabrics
- Cell-based fabrics

Packet-based fabrics are the easiest method to implement a multichip switch. It simply forwards all traffic between the chipsets as native IP. Both the front panel chips and fabric chips can utilize the same underlying chipset. However, the drawback is that packet-based fabrics are not very good at Equal-Cost Multipath (ECMP) and are prone to head-of-line blocking. This is because in a packet-based fabric, each chipset will fully transmit each packet—regardless of size—across the switch. If there are large or small flows, they will be hashed across the fabric chips according to normal IP packet rules. As you can imagine, this means that fat flows could be pegged to a single fabric chip and begin to overrun smaller flows. Imagine a scenario in which there are multiple chips transmitting jumbo frames to a single egress chip. It would quickly receive too much bandwidth and begin dropping packets. The end result is that ECMP greatly suffers and the switch loses significant performance at loads greater than 80 percent, due to the head-of-line blocking.

The alternative is to use a cell-based fabric, which uniformly partitions ingress packets into cells of the same size. For example, a 1000-byte packet could be split up into

16 different cells which have a uniform size of 64 bytes each. The advantage is that large IP flows are broken up into multiple cells that can be load balanced across the switching fabric to provide nearly perfect ECMP.

Traditionally, cells are fixed in size, which creates another problem in packing efficiency, often referred to as *cell tax*. Imagine a scenario in which there was a 65-byte packet, but the cell size was 64 bytes. In such a scenario, two cells would be required; the first cell would be full, whereas the second cell would use only one byte. To overcome this problem, the Juniper Q5 chipset cell size can vary depending on the overall load of the switch to achieve better packing efficiency. For example, as the overall bandwidth in the switch increases, the cell size can dynamically be increased to transmit more data per cell. The end result is that a cell-based fabric offers nearly perfect ECMP and can operate at 99 percent capacity without dropping packets.

The Juniper Q5 chipset uses a cell-based fabric with variable cell sizes to transmit data among the different Juniper Q5 chipsets. Each model of the QFX10000 switches uses the cell-based fabric technology, including the fixed QFX10002 switches.

Juniper QFX10002 fabric walk-through

Let's take a look at some of the detailed information about the fabric from the command line on the QFX10002. Keep in mind that the Juniper QFX10002; can have either one or two fabric chips, and either three or six Packet Forwarding Engines (PFEs). For example, the QFX10002-36Q has three PFEs with a single fabric chip; and the QFX10002-72Q has two fabric chips and six PFEs as shown in Figure 1-5. The reason for this is that the QFX10002-36Q is exactly half the size of the QFX10002-72Q, so it requires exactly half the number of resources.

In the following QFX10002 examples, we'll execute all the commands from a Juniper QFX10002-72Q that has two fabric chips and six PFEs.

Let's begin by verifying the number of fabric chips:

```
dhanks@qfx10000-02> show chassis fabric plane-location local
-----------Fabric Plane Locations-------------
SIB           Planes
0             0   1
```

Now let's get more detailed information about each fabric chip:

```
dhanks@qfx10000-02> show chassis fabric sibs
Fabric management SIB state:
SIB #0  Online
    FASIC #0 (plane 0) Active
        FPC #0
            PFE #0  : OK
            PFE #1  : OK
            PFE #2  : OK
            PFE #3  : OK
```

```
        PFE #4  : OK
        PFE #5  : OK
FASIC #1 (plane 1) Active
    FPC #0
        PFE #0  : OK
        PFE #1  : OK
        PFE #2  : OK
        PFE #3  : OK
        PFE #4  : OK
        PFE #5  : OK
```

Now we can begin to piece together how the PFEs are connected to the two fabric chips. Use the following command to see how they're connected:

```
dhanks@qfx10000-02> show chassis fabric fpcs local
Fabric management FPC state:
FPC #0
    PFE #0
        SIB0_FASIC0 (plane  0)   Plane Enabled, Links OK
        SIB0_FASIC1 (plane  1)   Plane Enabled, Links OK
    PFE #1
        SIB0_FASIC0 (plane  0)   Plane Enabled, Links OK
        SIB0_FASIC1 (plane  1)   Plane Enabled, Links OK
    PFE #2
        SIB0_FASIC0 (plane  0)   Plane Enabled, Links OK
        SIB0_FASIC1 (plane  1)   Plane Enabled, Links OK
    PFE #3
        SIB0_FASIC0 (plane  0)   Plane Enabled, Links OK
        SIB0_FASIC1 (plane  1)   Plane Enabled, Links OK
    PFE #4
        SIB0_FASIC0 (plane  0)   Plane Enabled, Links OK
        SIB0_FASIC1 (plane  1)   Plane Enabled, Links OK
    PFE #5
        SIB0_FASIC0 (plane  0)   Plane Enabled, Links OK
        SIB0_FASIC1 (plane  1)   Plane Enabled, Links OK
```

As you can see, each PFE has a single connection to each of the fabric chips. The Juniper QFX10002 uses an internal Clos topology of PFEs and fabric chips to provide non-blocking bandwidth between all of the interfaces as shown in Figure 1-5.

The Juniper QFX10000 Series

The Juniper QFX10000 family is often referred to as the Juniper *QFX10K* Series. At a high-level, there are four switches (see Figure 1-6):

- Juniper QFX10002-36Q
- Juniper QFX10002-72Q
- Juniper QFX10008
- Juniper QFX10016

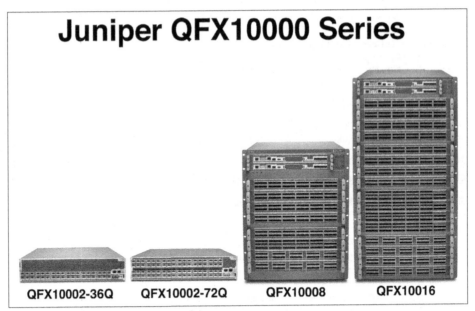

Figure 1-6. Juniper QFX10000 Series lineup

The Juniper QFX10002 model is a compact 2RU switch that comes in two port densities: 36 ports and 72 ports. The Juniper QFX10008 and QFX10016 are modular chassis switches with 8 and 16 slots, respectively.

The great thing about the Juniper QFX10K Series is that the only differences between the switches are simply the port densities. You lose no features, buffer, or logical scale between the smallest Juniper QFX10002-36Q and the largest Juniper QFX10016. Simply choose the port scale that meets your requirements; you don't need to worry about sacrificing logical scale, buffer, or feature sets.

The Juniper QFX10K was designed from the ground up to support large-scale web, cloud and hosting providers, service providers, and Enterprise companies. The Juniper QFX10K will most commonly be found in the spine, core, or collapsed edge of a data center switching network.

Juniper QFX10K Features

The Juniper QFX10K was designed from the ground up to solve some of the most complicated challenges within the data center. Let's take a look at some of the basic and advanced features of the Juniper QFX10K.

Layer 2

- Full Layer 2 switching with support for up to 32,000 bridge domains.

- Full spanning tree protocols
- Support for the new EVPN for control plane–based learning with support for multiple data-plane encapsulations.
- Support for virtual switches; these are similar to Virtual Routing and Forwarding (VRF) instances, but specific to Layer 2. For example, you can assign a virtual switch per tenant and support overlapping bridge domain IDs.

Layer 3

- Full IP routing and feature-rich Junos routing protocols: Open Shortest Path First (OSPF), Intermediate System–to–Intermediate System (IS-IS), and Multi-protocol Border Gateway Protocol (MP-BGP).
- Support for a large number of Virtual Routing and Forwarding (VRF) routing tables.

Tunnel encapsulations

- Virtual Extensible LAN (VXLAN)
- VXLAN Operations, Administration, and Maintenance (OAM): traceroute and ping
- Generic Routing Encapsulation (GRE)

MPLS

- MPLS-over-MPLS: L3VPN and EVPN
- MPLS-over-UDP: L3VPN and EVPN
- MPLS OAM: traceroute and ping
- LDP, RSVP, LDP-over-RSVP, traffic engineering, and auto-bandwidth
- Fast Reroute (FRR)
- Node and link protection
- MPLS flow and entropy labels
- Auto policing

Network services

- Full QoS: multifield classifiers, behavior aggregates, schedulers, drop profiles, and rewrite tools

- VoQ architecture to prevent head-of-line (HOL) blocking
- Precision time protocol (PTP) with v1588 support using an oven-baked oscillator

Automation and programmability

- Linux operating system that's completely open for customization
- Support for Linux KVM, Containers (LXC), and Docker
- Full NETCONF and YANG support for configuration changes
- Full JSON API for configuration changes
- Support for Apache Thrift for control-plane and data-plane changes
- Support for OpenStack and CloudStack orchestration
- Support for VMware NSX virtual networking
- Support for Chef and Puppet
- Native programming languages such as Python with the PyEZ library
- Zero-Touch Provisioning (ZTP)

Traffic analytics

- Microburst detection
- High-frequency and real-time traffic statistics streaming in multiple output formats, including Google ProtoBufs
- Network congestion correlation
- ECMP-aware traceroute and ping
- Application-level traffic statistics using Cloud Analytics Engine (CAE)
- Traffic analytics with time stamping.

 As of this writing, some of the traffic analytics tools are roadmap features. Check with your Juniper accounts team or on the Juniper website (*http://www.juniper.net*) for more information.

Juniper QFX10K Scale

The Juniper QFX10K is built for scale. There are some attributes such as firewall filters and MAC addresses that are able to distribute state throughout the entire switch on a per-PFE basis. The PFE is simply a Juniper-generic term for a chipset, which in the case of the Juniper QFX10K is the Juniper Q5 chipset. For example, when it comes to calculating the total number of firewall filters, there's no need to have a copy of the same firewall filter in every single Juniper Q5 chip; this is because firewall filters are generally applied on a per-port basis. However, other attributes such as the Forwarding Information Base (FIB) need to be synchronized across all PFEs, and cannot benefit from distributing the state across the entire system. Table 1-1 lists all of the major physical attributes as well as many of the commonly used logical scaling numbers for the Juniper QFX10000 family.

Table 1-1. Juniper QFX10000 logical scaling numbers

Attribute	QFX10K2-36Q	QFX10K2-72Q	QFX10008	QFX10016
Switch throughput	2.88Tbps	5.76Tbps	48Tbps	96Tbps
Forwarding capacity	1 Bpps	2 Bpps	16 Bpps	32 Bpps
Max 10GbE	144	288	1,152	2,304
Max 40GbE	36	72	288	576
Max 100GbE	12	24	240	480
MAC	256K	512K	1M*	1M*
FIB	256K IPv4 and 256K IPv6—upgradable to 2M			
RIB	10M prefixes			
ECMP	64-way			
IPv4 multicast	128K			
IPv6 multicast	128K			
VLANs	16K			
VXLAN tunnels	16K			
VXLAN endpoints	8K			
Filters	8K per PFE			
Filter terms	64K per PFE			
Policers	8K per PFE			
Vmembers	32K per PFE			
Subinterfaces	16K			
BGP neighbors	4K			
ISIS adjacencies	1K			
OSPF neighbors	1K			
GRE tunnels	4K			
LDP sessions	1K			
LDP labels	128K			
MPLS labels	128K			
BFD clients (300 ms)	1K			
VRF	4K			

Keep in mind that the scaling numbers for each of the Juniper QFX10K switches can change in the future with software releases. Table 1-1 represents a snapshot in time as of Junos 15.1X53-D10.

 The listed scaling numbers are accurate as of Junos 15.1X53-D10. Each new version of Junos will bring more features, scale, and functionality. For the latest scaling numbers, go to Juniper's website (*http://www.juniper.net*) or contact your account team.

Juniper QFX10002-36Q

The Juniper QFX10002-36Q (Figure 1-7) is the baby brother to the Juniper QFX10002-72Q; the Juniper QFX10002-36Q simply has half the number of ports. However, do not let its little size fool you; it packs a ton of switching power in a massive punch.

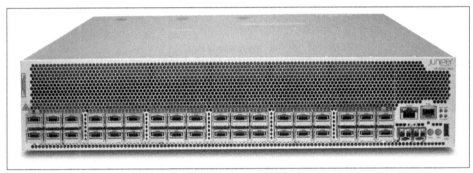

Figure 1-7. The Juniper QFX10002-36 switch

As with all members of the Juniper QFX10000 family, the Juniper Q5 chipset powers the QFX10002-36Q and gives it amazing port density, logical scale, bandwidth delay buffer, and a massive feature set. Let's take a quick look at the port options of the Juniper QFX10002-36Q:

- 36x40GbE (QSFP28)
- 12x100GbE (QSFP28)
- 144x10GbE (SFP+)

Right out of the box, the Juniper QFX10002-36Q offers tri-speed ports: 10GbE, 40GbE, and 100GbE. The 10GbE ports require that you use a break-out cable, which results in 4x10GbE ports for every 40GbE port. However, to support a higher speed port, you need to combine together three 40GbE ports to support a single 100GbE port. This means that two adjacent 40GbE ports will be disabled to support a 100GbE port.

Role

The Juniper QFX10002-36Q is designed primarily as a spine switch to operate in the aggregation and core of the network, as shown in Figure 1-8.

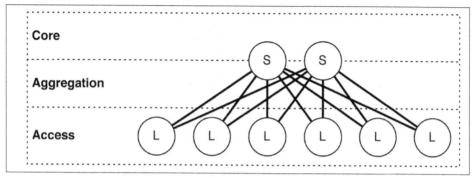

Figure 1-8. Juniper QFX10002-36S as a spine switch in network topology

In Figure 1-8, the "S" refers to the spine switch, and the "L" refers to the leaf switch; this is known as a *spine-and-leaf* topology. We have taken a traditional, tiered data center model with core, aggregation, and access and superimposed the new spine and leaf topology.

The Juniper QFX10002-36Q has enough bandwidth and port density, in a small environment, to collapse both the traditional core and aggregation functions. For example, a single pair of Juniper QFX10002-36Q switches using Juniper QFX5100-48S as leaf switches results in 1,727x10GbE interfaces with only 6:1 over-subscription. Of course, you can adjust these calculations up or down based on the over-subscription and port densities required for your environment.

Expanding the example, Figure 1-9 illustrates how the edge routers and servers connect into the spine and leaf architecture. The Juniper QFX10002-36Q is shown as S1 and S2, whereas Juniper QFX5100 switches are shown as L1 through L4. The connections between the spine and leaf are 40GbE, whereas the connections from the spine to the edge are 100GbE. In the case of the edge tier, the assumption is that these devices are Juniper MX routers. Finally, the hosts connect into the leaf switches by using 10GbE.

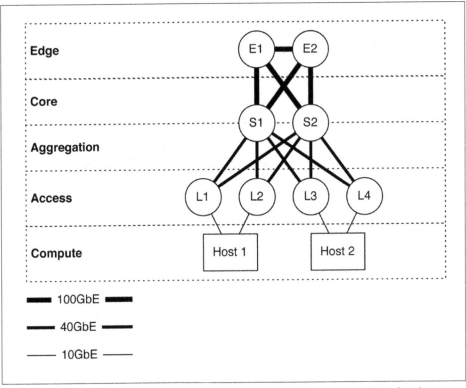

Figure 1-9. The Juniper QFX10002-36Q in multiple tiers in a spine-and-leaf architecture

Attributes

Table 1-2 takes a closer look at the most common attributes of the Juniper QFX10002-36Q. You can use it to quickly find physical and environmental information.

Table 1-2. Juniper QFX10002-36Q attributes

Attribute	Value
Rack units	2
System throughput	2.88Tbps
Forwarding capacity	1 Bpps
Built-in interfaces	36xQSFP+
Total 10GbE interfaces	144x10GbE
Total 40GbE interfaces	36x40GbE
Total 100GbE interfaces	12x100GbE
Airflow	Airflow In (AFI) or Airflow Out (AFO)
Typical power draw	560 W

Attribute	Value
Maximum power draw	800 W
Cooling	3 fans with N + 1 redundancy
Total packet buffer	12 GB
Latency	2.5 μs within PFE or 5.5 μs across PFEs

The Juniper QFX10002-36Q packs an amazing amount of bandwidth and port density in a very small 2RU form factor. As denoted by the model number, the Juniper QFX10002-36Q has 32 built-in 40GbE interfaces that you can break out into 4x10GbE each, or you can turn groups of three into a single 100GbE interface, as demonstrated in Figure 1-10.

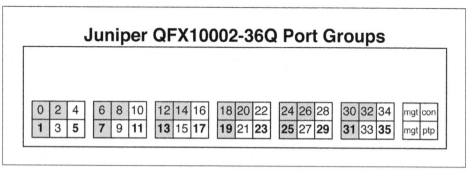

Figure 1-10. Juniper QFX10002-36Q port groups

Each port group consists of three ports. For example, ports 0, 1, and 2 are in a port group; ports 3, 4, and 5 are in a separate port group. Port groups play a critical role on how the tri-speed interfaces can operate. The rules are as follows:

10GbE interfaces
> If you decide to break out a 40GbE interface into 4x10GbE interfaces, it must apply to the entire port group. The configuration must be applied only to the first interface of the port group. For example, to break out interface et-0/0/1 into 4x10GbE, you first must identify what port group it belongs to, which in this case is the first port group. The next step is to determine which other interfaces are part of this port group; in our case, it's et-0/0/0, et-0/0/1, and et-0/0/2. To break out interface et-0/0/1, you need to set the configuration of interface et-0/0/0 to support channelized interfaces. The reason for this is that interface et-0/0/0 is the first interface in the port group to which et-0/0/1 belongs. In summary, all interfaces within that port group will be broken out into 4x10GbE interfaces. That means you must break out et-0/0/0, et-0/0/1, and et-0/0/2 into 4x10GbE interfaces.

40GbE interfaces
> By default, all ports are 40GbE. No special rules here.

100GbE interfaces

Only a single interface within a port group can be turned into 100GbE. If you enable 100GbE within a port group, the other two ports within the same port group are disabled and cannot be used. Figure 1-10 illustrates which ports within a port group are 100GbE-capable by showing the interface name in **bold**. For example, the interface 1 in the first port group supports 100GbE, whereas interfaces 0 and 2 are disabled. In the second port group, interface 5 supports 100GbE, whereas interfaces 3 and 4 are disabled.

You configure tri-speed interface settings on a per–port group basis. For example, port group 1 might support 12x10GbE and port group 2 might support a single 1x100GbE interface. Overall, the system is very flexible in terms of tri-speed configurations.

Management panel

The Juniper QFX10002-36 is split into two functional areas (Figure 1-11): the port panels and management panel.

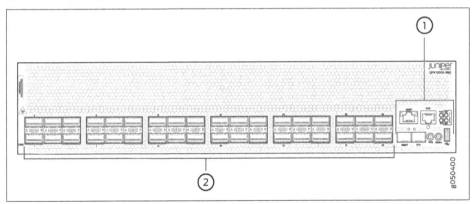

Figure 1-11. Juniper QFX10002-36Q management panel (1) and port panel (2)

Figure 1-12 presents an enlarged view of the management panel.

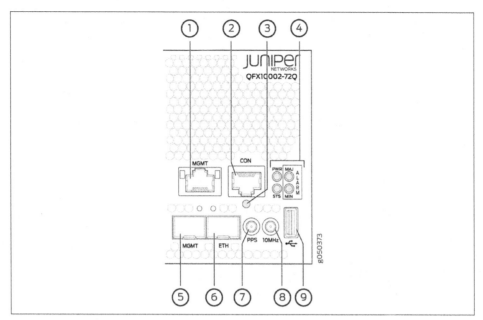

Figure 1-12. Juniper QFX10002 management panel components

The management panel is full of the usual suspects to physically manage the switch and provide external storage. Let's go through them one by one:

1. em0-RJ-45 (1000BASE-T) management Ethernet port (MGT).

2. RJ-45 console port (CON) that supports RS-232 serial connections.

3. Reset button. To reset the entire switch except the clock and FPGA functions, press and hold this button for five seconds.

4. Status LEDs.

5. em1-SFP management Ethernet port (MGT).

6. PTP Ethernet-SFP (1000BASE-T) port (ETH).

7. 10 Hz pulses-per-second (PPS) Subminiature B (SMB) connector for input and output measuring the time draft from an external grandmaster clock.

8. 10 MHz SMB timing connector.

9. USB port for external storage and other devices.

There are two management ports on a QFX10002 that have LEDs whose purpose is to indicate link status and link activity (see Figure 1-13). These two ports, located on the management panel next to the access ports, are both labeled MGMT. The top management port is for 10/100/1000 BASE-T connections and the lower port is for 10/100/1000 BASE-T and small-form pluggable (SFP) 1000 BASE-X connections.

The copper RJ45 port has separate LEDs for status and activity. The fiber SFP port has a combination link and activity LED.

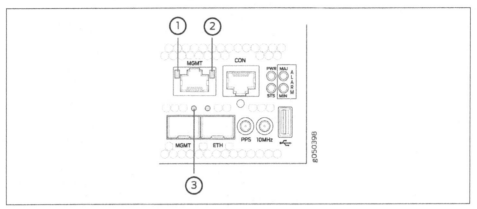

Figure 1-13. Juniper QFX10002 management port LEDs

Table 1-3 list the LED status representations.

Table 1-3. Management port LEDs on Juniper QFX10002

LED	Color	State	Description
Link/activity	Off	Off	No link established, fault, or link is down.
	Yellow	Blinking	Link established with activity.
Status	Off	Off	Port speed is 10M or link is down.
	Green	On	Port speed is 1000M.

Figure 1-14 shows additional chassis status LEDs on the right side of the switch indicate the overall health of the switch; this includes faults, power, and general status.

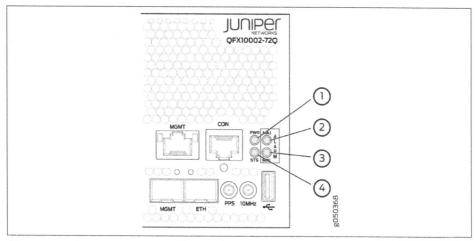

Figure 1-14. Juniper QFX10002 chassis status LEDs

Table 1-4 lists what the chassis status LEDs indicate.

Table 1-4. Juniper QFX10002 chassis status LEDs

Name	Color	State	Description
PWR-Alarm	Off	Off	Powered off
	Green	On	Powered on
	Yellow	Blinking	Power fault
STA-Status	Off	Off	Halted or powered off
	Green	On	Junos loaded
	Green	Blinking	Beacon active
	Yellow	Blinking	Fault
MJR-Major alarm	Off	Off	No alarms
	Red	On	Major alarm
MIN-Minor alarm	Off	Off	No alarms
	Yellow	On	Minor alarm

FRU Panel

Figure 1-15 shows the rear of the QFX10002, where you will find the Field Replaceable Units (FRUs) for power and cooling.

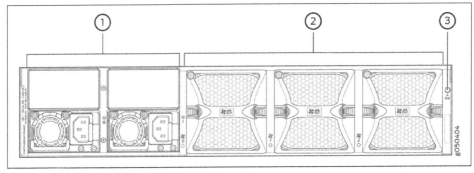

Figure 1-15. Juniper QFX10002-36Q FRU panel

Let's inspect each element in more detail:

1. AC or DC power supplies. The QFX10002-36Q has two power supplies. The QFX10002-72Q has four power supplies.

2. Reversible fans. Supports AFI and AFO.

3. Electrostatic discharge (ESD) connector.

Walk around the Juniper QFX10002

Let's take a quick tour of the Juniper QFX10002. We just went through all of the status LEDs, alarms, management ports, and FRUs. Now let's see them in action from the command line.

To see if there are any chassis alarms, use the following command:

```
dhanks@qfx10000-02> show chassis alarms
2 alarms currently active
Alarm time                 Class  Description
2016-01-11 00;07:28 PST   Major  PEM 3 Not Powered
2016-01-11 00;07:28 PST   Major  PEM 2 Not Powered
```

To see the overall operating environment, use the **show chassis environment** command, as demonstrated here:

```
dhanks@qfx10000-02> show chassis environment
Class Item                      Status     Measurement
Power FPC 0 Power Supply 0      OK
      FPC 0 Power Supply 1      OK
      FPC 0 Power Supply 2      Present
      FPC 0 Power Supply 3      Present
Temp  FPC 0 Intake Temp Sensor  OK        20 degrees C / 68 degrees F
      FPC 0 Exhaust Temp Sensor OK        28 degrees C / 82 degrees F
      FPC 0 Mezz Temp Sensor 0  OK        20 degrees C / 68 degrees F
      FPC 0 Mezz Temp Sensor 1  OK        31 degrees C / 87 degrees F
      FPC 0 PE2 Temp Sensor     OK        26 degrees C / 78 degrees F
```

```
              FPC 0 PE1 Temp Sensor          OK        26 degrees C / 78 degrees F
              FPC 0 PF0 Temp Sensor          OK        34 degrees C / 93 degrees F
              FPC 0 PE0 Temp Sensor          OK        26 degrees C / 78 degrees F
              FPC 0 PE5 Temp Sensor          OK        27 degrees C / 80 degrees F
              FPC 0 PE4 Temp Sensor          OK        27 degrees C / 80 degrees F
              FPC 0 PF1 Temp Sensor          OK        39 degrees C / 102 degrees F
              FPC 0 PE3 Temp Sensor          OK        27 degrees C / 80 degrees F
              FPC 0 CPU Die Temp Sensor      OK        30 degrees C / 86 degrees F
              FPC 0 OCXO Temp Sensor         OK        32 degrees C / 89 degrees F
Fans          FPC 0 Fan Tray 0 Fan 0         OK        Spinning at normal speed
              FPC 0 Fan Tray 0 Fan 1         OK        Spinning at normal speed
              FPC 0 Fan Tray 1 Fan 0         OK        Spinning at normal speed
              FPC 0 Fan Tray 1 Fan 1         OK        Spinning at normal speed
              FPC 0 Fan Tray 2 Fan 0         OK        Spinning at normal speed
              FPC 0 Fan Tray 2 Fan 1         OK        Spinning at normal speed
```

Using the show chassis environment, you can quickly get a summary of the power, temperatures, and fan speeds of the switch. In the preceding example, everything is operating correctly.

For more detail on the power supplies, use the following command:

```
dhanks@qfx10000-02> show chassis environment fpc pem
fpc0:
--------------------------------------------------------------------
FPC 0 PEM 0 status:
   State                     Online
   Temp Sensor 0             OK    22 degrees C / 71 degrees F
   Temp Sensor 1             OK    32 degrees C / 89 degrees F
   Temp Sensor 2             OK    34 degrees C / 93 degrees F
   Fan 0                     5096 RPM
   Fan 1                     6176 RPM
   DC Output        Voltage(V) Current(A)  Power(W)  Load(%)
                        12         30         360       55
FPC 0 PEM 1 status:
   State                     Online
   Temp Sensor 0             OK    24 degrees C / 75 degrees F
   Temp Sensor 1             OK    34 degrees C / 93 degrees F
   Temp Sensor 2             OK    34 degrees C / 93 degrees F
   Fan 0                     4800 RPM
   Fan 1                     5760 RPM
   DC Output        Voltage(V) Current(A)  Power(W)  Load(%)
```

Now, let's get more information about the chassis fans:

```
dhanks@qfx10000-02> show chassis fan
      Item                   Status   RPM    Measurement
      FPC 0 Tray 0 Fan 0     OK       5000   Spinning at normal speed
      FPC 0 Tray 0 Fan 1     OK       4400   Spinning at normal speed
      FPC 0 Tray 1 Fan 0     OK       5500   Spinning at normal speed
      FPC 0 Tray 1 Fan 1     OK       4400   Spinning at normal speed
      FPC 0 Tray 2 Fan 0     OK       5000   Spinning at normal speed
      FPC 0 Tray 2 Fan 1     OK       4400   Spinning at normal speed
```

Next, let's see what the routing engine in the Juniper QFX10002 is doing:

```
dhanks@qfx10000-02> show chassis routing-engine
Routing Engine status:
  Slot 0:
    Current state               Master
    Temperature                 20 degrees C / 68 degrees F
    CPU temperature             20 degrees C / 68 degrees F
    DRAM                        3360 MB (4096 MB installed)
    Memory utilization          19 percent
    5 sec CPU utilization:
      User                      12 percent
      Background                0 percent
      Kernel                    1 percent
      Interrupt                 0 percent
      Idle                      88 percent
    1 min CPU utilization:
      User                      10 percent
      Background                0 percent
      Kernel                    1 percent
      Interrupt                 0 percent
      Idle                      90 percent
    5 min CPU utilization:
      User                      9 percent
      Background                0 percent
      Kernel                    1 percent
      Interrupt                 0 percent
      Idle                      90 percent
    15 min CPU utilization:
      User                      9 percent
      Background                0 percent
      Kernel                    1 percent
      Interrupt                 0 percent
      Idle                      90 percent
    Model                       RE-QFX10002-72Q
    Serial ID                   BUILTIN
    Uptime                      5 days, 10 hours, 29 minutes, 29 seconds

    Last reboot reason          0x2000:hypervisor reboot
    Load averages:              1 minute   5 minute  15 minute
                                  0.08        0.03      0.01
```

Finally, let's get detailed temperature information about all of the PFEs and fabric chips in the chassis:

```
dhanks@qfx10000-02> show chassis sibs temperature-thresholds
                         Fan speed      Yellow alarm      Red alarm     Fire Shutdown
                        (degrees C)     (degrees C)      (degrees C)     (degrees C)
Item                    Normal  High   Normal  Bad fan   Normal  Bad fan   Normal
FPC 0 Intake Temp Sensor   30    65      65      65        70      70        75
FPC 0 Exhaust Temp Sensor  30    65      65      65        70      70        75
FPC 0 Mezz Temp Sensor 0   30    65      65      65        70      70        75
FPC 0 Mezz Temp Sensor 1   30    65      65      65        70      70        75
```

FPC 0 PE2 Temp Sensor	50	90	90	90	100	100	103
FPC 0 PE1 Temp Sensor	50	90	90	90	100	100	103
FPC 0 PF0 Temp Sensor	50	90	90	90	100	100	103
FPC 0 PE0 Temp Sensor	50	90	90	90	100	100	103
FPC 0 PE5 Temp Sensor	50	90	90	90	100	100	103
FPC 0 PE4 Temp Sensor	50	90	90	90	100	100	103
FPC 0 PF1 Temp Sensor	50	90	90	90	100	100	103
FPC 0 PE3 Temp Sensor	50	90	90	90	100	100	103
FPC 0 CPU Die Temp Sensor	50	90	90	90	100	100	103
FPC 0 OCXO Temp Sensor	50	90	90	90	100	100	103

Juniper QFX10002-72Q

Figure 1-16 shows the Juniper QFX10002-72Q, the workhouse of the fixed-switches. It's filled to the brim with 72x40GbE interfaces with deep buffers, high logical scale, and tons of features.

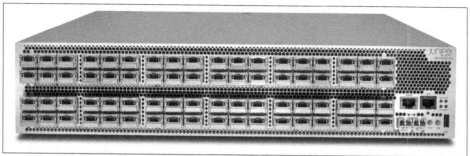

Figure 1-16. Juniper QFX10002-72Q switch

Again, the Juniper Q5 chipset powers the Juniper QFX10002-72Q, just like its little brother, the Juniper QFX10002-36Q. Let's take a quick look at the port options of the Juniper QFX10002-72Q:

- 72x40GbE (QSFP28)
- 24x100GbE (QSFP28)
- 288x10GbE (SFP+)

Right out of the box, the Juniper QFX10002-72Q offers tri-speed ports: 10GbE, 40GbE, and 100GbE. The 10GbE ports require that you use a break-out cable, which results in 4x10GbE ports for every 40GbE port. However, to support a higher speed port, you must combine 3 40GbE ports together to support a single 100GbE port. This means that two adjacent 40GbE ports will be disabled to support a 100GbE port.

Role

The Juniper QFX10002-72Q is designed primarily as a spine switch to operate in the aggregation and core of the network, as shown in Figure 1-17.

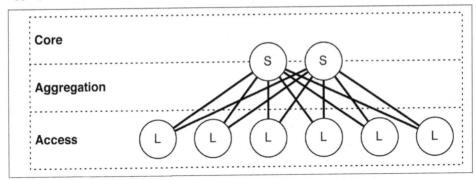

Figure 1-17. Juniper QFX10002-72S as a spine switch in network topology

In the figure, "S" refers to the spine switch, and "L" refers to the leaf switch (spine-and-leaf topology). We have taken a traditional, tiered data center model with core, aggregation, and access and superimposed the new spine and leaf topology.

The Juniper QFX10002-72Q has enough bandwidth and port density, in a small to medium-sized environment, to collapse both the traditional core and aggregation functions. For example, a single pair of Juniper QFX10002-72Q switches using Juniper QFX5100-48S as leaf switches results in 3,456x10GbE interfaces with only 6:1 over-subscription. Again, you can adjust these calculations up or down based on the over-subscription and port densities required for your environment.

Expanding the example, Figure 1-18 illustrates how the edge routers and servers connect into the spine-and-leaf architecture. The Juniper QFX10002-72Q is shown as S1 and S2, whereas Juniper QFX5100 switches are shown as L1 through L4. The connections between the spine and leaf are 40GbE, whereas the connections from the spine to the edge are 100GbE. In the case of the edge tier, the assumption is that these devices are Juniper MX routers. Finally, the hosts connect into the leaf switches by using 10GbE.

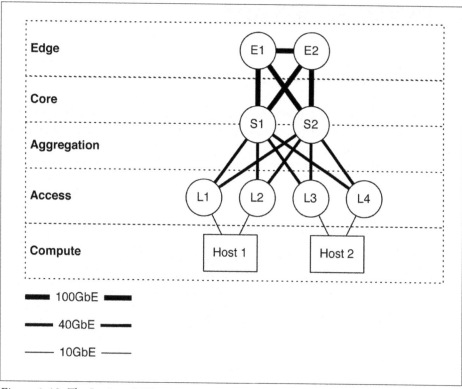

Edge

Core

Aggregation

Access

Compute

E1 — E2

S1 --- S2

L1   L2   L3   L4

Host 1   Host 2

━━━ 100GbE ━━━

━━ 40GbE ━━

── 10GbE ──

Figure 1-18. The Juniper QFX10002-72Q in multiple tiers in a spine-and-leaf architecture

Attributes

Let's take a closer look at the most common attributes of the Juniper QFX10002-72Q, which are presented in Table 1-5.

Table 1-5. Juniper QFX10002-72Q attributes

Attribute	Value
Rack units	2
System throughput	5.76Tbps
Forwarding capacity	2 Bpps
Built-in interfaces	72xQSFP+
Total 10GbE interfaces	288x10GbE
Total 40GbE interfaces	72x40GbE
Total 100GbE interfaces	24x100GbE
Airflow	AFI or AFO
Typical power draw	1,050 W

Attribute	Value
Maximum power draw	1,450 W
Cooling	3 fans with N + 1 redundancy
Total packet buffer	24 GB
Latency	2.5 µs within PFE or 5.5 µs across PFEs

The Juniper QFX10002-72Q packs an amazing amount of bandwidth and port density in a very small 2RU form factor. As denoted by the model number, the Juniper QFX10002-72Q has 72 built-in 40GbE interfaces, which you can break out into 4x10GbE each or you can turn groups of three into a single 100GbE interface, as depicted in Figure 1-19.

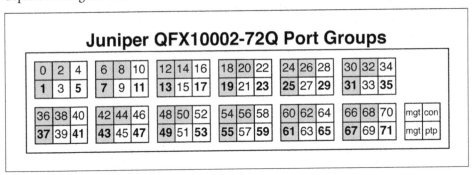

Figure 1-19. Juniper QFX10002-72Q port groups

Each port group consists of three ports. For example, ports 0, 1, and 2 are in a port group; ports 3, 4, and 5 are in a separate port group. Port groups play a critical role in how the tri-speed interfaces can operate. The rules are as follows:

10GbE interfaces

If you decide to break out a 40GbE interface into 4x10GbE interfaces, it must apply to the entire port group. The configuration must be applied only to the first interface of the port group. For example, to break out interface et-0/0/1 into 4x10GbE, you first must identify to which port group it belongs; in this case, it is the first port group. The next step is to determine which other interfaces are part of this port group; in our case, it's et-0/0/0, et-0/0/1, and et-0/0/2. To break out interface et-0/0/1, you need to set the configuration of interface et-0/0/0 to support channelized interfaces. The reason for this is because interface et-0/0/0 is the first interface in the port group to which et-0/0/1 belongs. In summary, all interfaces within that port group will be broken out into 4x10GbE interfaces. This means that you must break out et-0/0/0, et-0/0/1, and et-0/0/2 into 4x10GbE interfaces.

40GbE interfaces

By default, all ports are 40GbE. No special rules here.

100GbE interfaces

Only a single interface within a port group can be turned into 100GbE. If you enable 100GbE within a port group, the other two ports within the same port group are disabled and cannot be used. Figure 1-19 illustrates which ports within a port group are 100GbE-capable by showing the interface name in **bold**. For example, the interface 1 in the first port group supports 100GbE, whereas interfaces 0 and 2 are disabled. The second port group, interface 5 supports 100GbE, whereas interfaces 3 and 4 are disabled.

You configure tri-speed interface settings on a per–port group basis. For example, port group 1 might support 12x10GbE and port group 2 might support a single 100GbE interface. Overall, the system is very flexible in terms of tri-speed configurations.

Management/FRU panels

The management and FRU panels of the Juniper QFX10002-72Q are identical to the Juniper QFX10002-36Q, so there's no need to go over the same information. Feel free to refer back to "Juniper QFX10002-72Q" on page 25 for detailed information about the management and FRU panels.

Juniper QFX10008

The Juniper QFX10008 (Figure 1-20) is the smallest modular chassis switch in the Juniper QFX10000 Series. This chassis has eight slots for line cards and two slots for redundant routing engines. In the figure, the following line cards are installed, ordered top to bottom:

- QFX10000-36Q
- QFX10000-36Q
- QFX10000-36Q
- QFX10000-36Q
- QFX10000-36Q
- QFX10000-60S-6Q
- QFX10000-30C
- QFX10000-30C

Figure 1-20. The Juniper QFX10008 chassis switch

As always, the Juniper Q5 chipset powers the Juniper QFX10008 (likewise its little brother, the Juniper QFX10002). The only difference between the QFX10002 and QFX10008 is that the QFX10008 is modular and supports line cards and two physical routing engines. Otherwise, the features, scale, and buffer are the same. Some of the line cards have small differences in buffer speed, but we'll discuss that later in the chapter. In summary, the Juniper QFX10008 offers the same features, scale, and performance as the QFX10002, except it offers more ports due to its larger size and line-card options.

Role

The Juniper QFX10008 is designed as a spine switch to operate in the aggregation and core of the network, as shown in Figure 1-21.

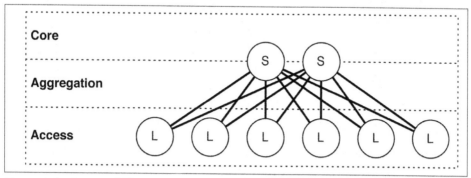

Figure 1-21. Juniper QFX10008 as a spine switch in a network topology

In Figure 1-21, the "S" refers to the spine switch, and the "L" refers to the leaf switch (spine-and-leaf topology). We have taken a traditional, tiered data center model with core, aggregation, and access and superimposed the new spine-and-leaf topology.

The Juniper QFX10008 has enough bandwidth and port density, in a medium to large-sized environment, to collapse both the traditional core and aggregation functions. For example, a single pair of Juniper QFX10008 switches using Juniper QFX5100-48S as leaf switches results in 13,824 10GbE interfaces with only 6:1 over-subscription. You can adjust these calculations up or down based on the over-subscription and port densities required for your environment.

Expanding the example, Figure 1-22 illustrates how the edge routers and servers connect into the spine-and-leaf architecture. The Juniper QFX10008 is shown as S1 and S2, whereas Juniper QFX5100 switches are shown as L1 through L4. The connections between the spine and leaf are 40GbE, whereas the connections from the spine to the edge are 100GbE. In the case of the edge tier, the assumption is that these devices are Juniper MX routers. Finally, the hosts connect into the leaf switches by using 10GbE.

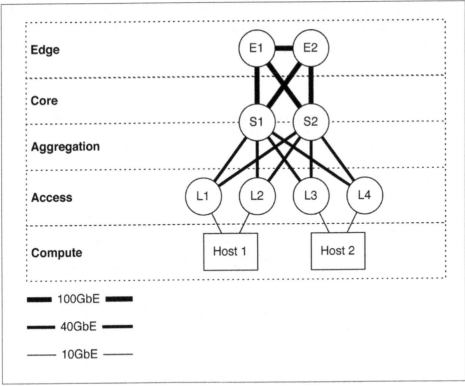

Figure 1-22. The Juniper QFX10008 in multiple tiers in a spine-and-leaf architecture

Attributes

Table 1-6 lists the most common attributes of the Juniper QFX10008.

Table 1-6. Juniper QFX10008 attributes

Attribute	Value
Rack units	13
Fabric capacity	96Tbps (system) and 7.2Tbps (slot)
Forwarding capacity	16 Bpps
Line card capacity	8
Routing engine capacity	2
Switching fabrics	6
Maximum 10GbE interfaces	1,152x10GbE
Maximum 40GbE interfaces	288x40GbE
Maximum 100GbE interfaces	240x100GbE
Airflow	Front-to-back
Typical power draw	1,659 W (base) and 2,003 W (redundant)

Attribute	Value
Reserved power	2,517 W (base) and 2,960 W (redundant)
Cooling	2 fan trays with 1 + 1 redundancy
Maximum packet buffer	96 GB
Latency	2.5 μs within PFE or 5.5 μs across PFEs

The Juniper QFX10008 is a very flexible chassis switch that's able to fit into smaller data centers and provide high logical scale, deep buffers, and tons of features.

Juniper QFX10016

The Juniper QFX10016 (Figure 1-23) is the largest spine switch that Juniper offers in the QFX10000 Series. It's an absolute monster weighting in at 844 lbs fully loaded and able to provide 288Tbps of fabric bandwidth at 32 Bpps.

There are not a lot of differences between the Juniper QFX10008 and QFX10016 apart from the physical scale. Thus, we'll make this section very short and highlight only the differences. Table 1-7 lists the most common attributes of the QFX10016.

Table 1-7. Juniper QFX10016 attributes

Attribute	Value
Rack units	21
Fabric capacity	288Tbps (system) and 7.2Tbps (slot)
Forwarding capacity	16 Bpps
Line card capacity	16
Routing engine capacity	2
Switching fabrics	6
Maximum 10GbE interfaces	2,304x10GbE
Maximum 40GbE interfaces	576x40GbE
Maximum 100GbE interfaces	480x100GbE
Airflow	Front-to-back
Typical power draw	4,232 W (base) and 4,978 W (redundant)
Reserved power	6,158 W (base) and 7,104 W (redundant)
Cooling	2 fan trays with 1 + 1 redundancy
Maximum packet buffer	192 GB
Latency	2.5 μs within PFE or 5.5 μs across PFEs

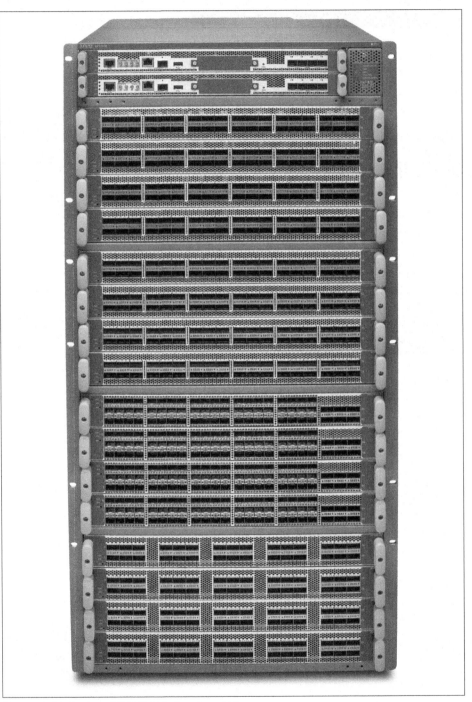

Figure 1-23. Juniper QFX10016 chassis switch

The Juniper QFX10008 shares the same line cards, power supplies, and routing engines/control boards with the larger Juniper QFX10016. The fan trays and switch fabric are different between the two Juniper QFX10000 chassis because of the physical height differences.

Juniper QFX10K Line Cards

As of this writing, there are three line cards for the Juniper QFX10000 chassis: QFX10000-36Q, QFX10000-30C, and the QFX10000-60S-6Q. Each line card is full line-rate and non-blocking. Also, each line card offers high logical scale with deep buffers.

Juniper QFX10000-36Q

The first line card has 36-port 40GbE interfaces, which is similar to the QFX10002-36Q, but in a line card form factor. The QFX10000-36Q line card (Figure 1-24) also supports 100GbE interfaces using port groups; we use the same method of disabling two out of three interfaces per port group. The QFX10000-36Q supports the following interface configurations:

- 144x10GbE interfaces
- 36x40GbE interfaces
- 12x100GbE interfaces
- Or any combination of per–port group configurations

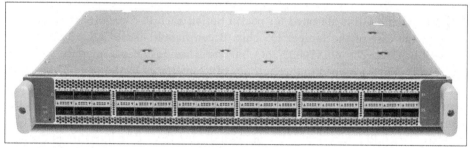

Figure 1-24. The Juniper QFX10000-36Q line card

The QFX10000-36Q has three PFEs that provide enough bandwidth, buffer, and high scale for all 36x40GbE interfaces, as shown in Figure 1-25.

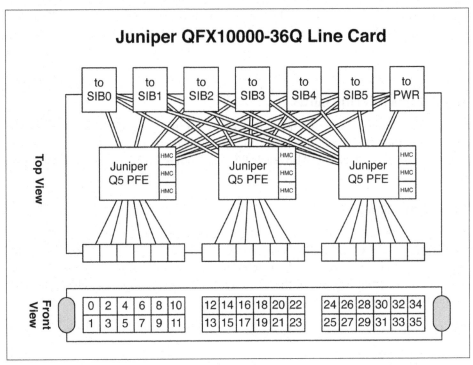

Figure 1-25. Juniper QFX10000-36Q architecture

Each of the PFEs have three 2 GB Hybrid Memory Cubes (HMCs), so each Juniper Q5 chip has a total 6 GB of memory. 2 GB of memory is allocated for hardware tables (FIB, etc.) and 4 GB is allocated for packet buffer. Each PFE handles a set of interfaces; in the case of the Juniper Q5 chip, it can handle 48x10GbE, 12x40GbE, or 5x100GbE ports. The QFX10000-36Q line card has 36x40GbE interfaces, so each Juniper Q5 chip is assigned to three groups of 12 interfaces, as shown in Figure 1-25. Each Juniper Q5 chip is connected in a full mesh to every single Switch Interface Board (SIB). Having a connection to each SIB ensures that the PFE is able to transmit traffic during any SIB failure in the system. There are actually many different connections from each PFE to a single SIB, but we'll discuss the SIB architecture in the next section. Each Juniper Q5 chip is connected to every other Juniper Q5 chip in the system; so regardless of the traffic profiles in the switch, everything is a single hop away.

Juniper QFX10000-30C

The next line card in the family is the QFX10000-30C, as shown in Figure 1-26. This is a native 30x100GbE QSFP28 line card, but also supports 30x40GbE in a QSFP+ form factor.

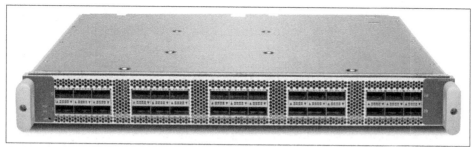

Figure 1-26. Juniper QFX10000-30C line card

Because of the large number of 100GbE interfaces, each QFX10000-C line card requires a total of six Juniper Q5 chips, as illustrated in Figure 1-27. If you recall, each Juniper Q5 chip can handle up to 5x100GbE interfaces. The double-lines in the figure represent the Q5-to-SIB connection, whereas the single lines represent an interface-to-Q5 connection.

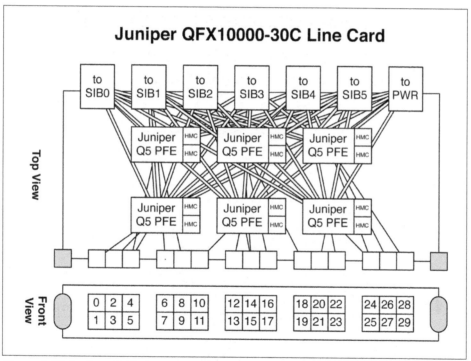

Figure 1-27. Juniper QFX1000-30C architectureJuniper QFX10000-60S-6Q

The third line card is the QFX10000-60S-6Q (Figure 1-28), which supports 60x10GbE and 6x40GbE. You can also enable 2x100GbE interfaces by disabling two out of the three interfaces per port group.

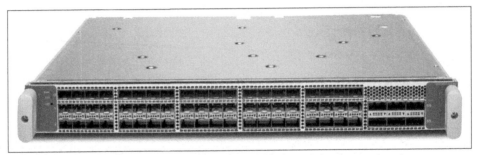

Figure 1-28. Juniper QFX10000-60S-6Q line card

A single Juniper Q5 chip is used to handle the first 48x10GbE ports; a second Juniper Q5 chip is used to handle the remaining 12x10GbE and 6x40GbE interfaces, as depicted in Figure 1-29. Each Juniper Q5 chip is connected to every SIB in a full mesh just like all of the other Juniper QFX10000 line cards.

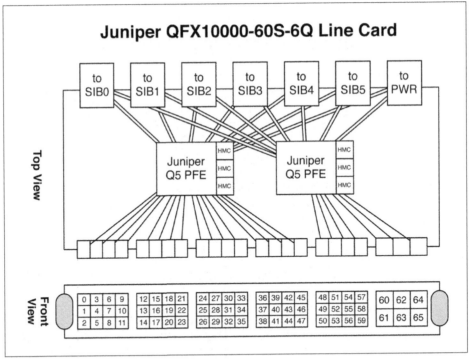

Figure 1-29. Juniper QFX10000-60S-6Q architecture

QFX10000 Control Board

The QFX10000 routing engine is basically a modern server. It has the latest Intel Ivy Bridge processor, SSD, and DDR3 memory. The routing engine provides the standard status LEDs, management interfaces, precision-timing interfaces, USB support, and built-in network cards, as shown in Figure 1-30.

Figure 1-30. Juniper QFX10000 routing engine

Here are the specifications of the Juniper QFX10000 routing engine:

- Intel Ivy Bridge 4-core 2.5 GHz Xeon Processor
- 32 GB DDR3 SDRAM—four 8 GB DIMMs
- 50 GB internal SSD storage
- One 2.5-inch external SSD slot
- Internal 10 GB NICs for connectivity to all line cards
- RS232 console port
- RJ-45 and SFP management Ethernet
- Precision-time protocol logic and SMB connectors
- 4x10GbE management ports

The routing engines also have hardware-based arbitration built in for controlling the line cards and SIBs. If the master routing engine fails over to the backup, the event is signaled in hardware so that all of the other chassis components have a fast and clean cutover to the new master routing engine.

SIBs

The SIBs are the glue that interconnect every single line card and PFE together in the chassis. Every PFE is only a single hop away from any other PE in the system. The Juniper QFX10008 and QFX10016 have a total six SIBs each; this provides 5 + 1 redundancy. If any single SIB were to fail, the other five SIBs can provide line-rate switching between all the PFEs. If additional SIBs were to fail, the system would gracefully fail and only reduce the overall bandwidth between line cards. Because of the physical height difference between the Juniper QFX10008 and QFX10016 chassis, they use different SIBs and cannot be shared between the chassis.

Request and grant

Every time a PFE wants to speak to another PFE, it must go through a request-and-grant system. This process lets the ingress PFE reserve a specific amount of bandwidth to an egress PFE, port, and forwarding class, as illustrated in Figure 1-31. The request and grant process is handled completely in hardware end-to-end to ensure full line-rate performance.

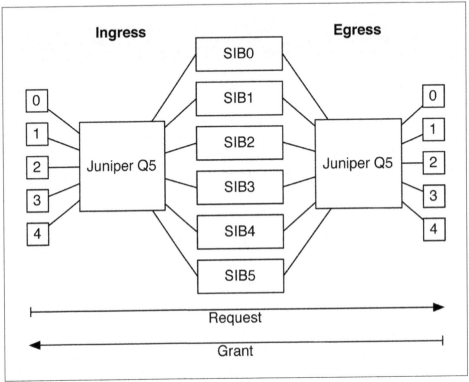

Figure 1-31. Juniper request-and-grant architecture

In the figure, the boxes labeled 0 through 4 represent ports connected to their respective Juniper Q5 chip. Each Juniper Q5 chip is connected to all six SIBs. The figure also shows an end-to-end traffic flow from ingress to egress. The request-and-grant system guarantees that traffic sent from the ingress PFE can be transmitted to the egress PFE. The request-and-grant process is very sophisticated and at a high level uses the following specifics to reserve bandwidth:

- Overall egress PFE bandwidth
- Destination egress PFE port's utilization
- Egress PFE's port forwarding class is in-profile

So for example, there might be enough bandwidth on the egress PFE itself, but if the specific destination port is currently over-utilized, the request-and-grant will reject the ingress PFE and prevent it from transmitting the data. If an ingress PFE receives a reject, it's forced to locally buffer the traffic in its VOQ until the request-and-grant system allows the traffic to be transmitted. The same is true for egress port forwarding classes as well; the request-and-grant system will ensure the destination forwarding class on a specific port is in-profile before allowing the ingress PFE to transmit the traffic.

Juniper Orthogonal Direct Connect

One common problem with chassis-based switches is the ability to upgrade it over time and take advantage of new line cards. Most chassis use a mid-plane that connects the line cards to the switching fabric; thus, depending on the technology used at the time of mid-plane creation, it will eventually limit the upgrade capacity in the future. For example, if the mid-plane had 100 connections, you would forever be limited to those 100 connections, even as line card bandwidth would continue to double every two years. So even though you have fast line cards and switching fabrics, eventually the older technology used in the mid-plane would limit the overall bandwidth between the components.

Juniper's solution to this problem is to completely remove the mid-plane in the Juniper QFX10000 chassis switches, as shown in Figure 1-32. This technology is called Juniper Orthogonal Direct Connect. If you imagine looking at the chassis from the side, you would see the SIBs running vertically in the back of the chassis. The line cards would run horizontally and be stacked on top of one another. Each of the line cards directly connect to each of the SIBs.

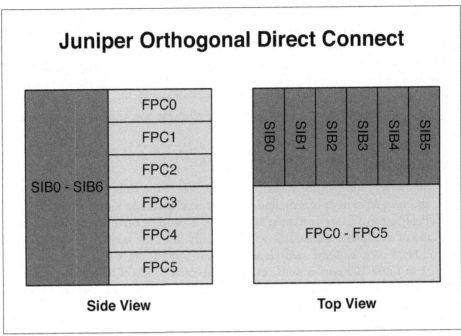

Figure 1-32. Side and top views of Juniper Orthogonal Direct Connect architecture

The top view shows exactly the same thing, but the SIBs in the back of the chassis are now stacked left-to-right. The line cards are stacked on top of one another, but run the entire length of the chassis so that they can directly attach to every single SIB in the system.

To get a full understanding of how the SIBs and FPCs are directly connected to one another, take a look at the front view in Figure 1-33. This assumes that there are four line cards installed into FPC0 through FPC3, whereas FPC4 through FPC7 are empty.

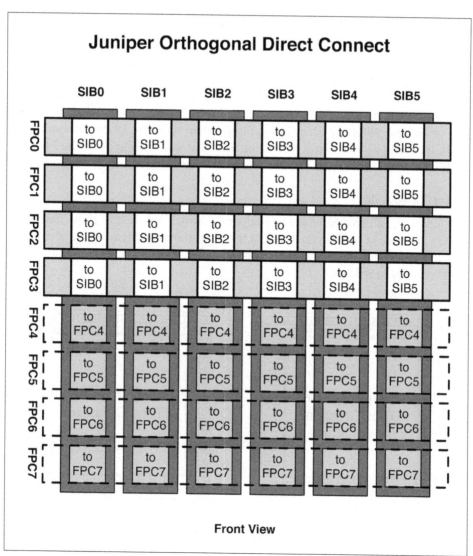

Figure 1-33. Front view of Juniper Orthogonal Direct Connect

The figure shows how the SIBs are installed vertically in the rear of the chassis and the line cards are installed horizontally in the front of the chassis. For example, FPC0 directly connects to SIB0 through SIB5. If you recall in Figure 1-25, there were six connectors in the back of the line card labeled SIB0 through SIB5; these are the connectors that directly plug into the SIBs in the rear of the chassis. In Figure 1-33, the dotted line in the bottom four slots indicates where FPC4 through FPC7 would have been installed. Without the FPCs installed, you can clearly see each SIB connector, and you can see that each SIB has a connector for each of the FPCs. For example, for SIB0, you can see the connectors for FPC4 through FPC7.

In summary, each SIB and FPC is directly connected to each other; there's no need for outdated mid-plane technology. The benefit is that as long as the SIBs and FPCs are of the same generation, you'll always get full non-blocking bandwidth within the chassis. For example, as of this writing, the Juniper QFX10000 chassis are running first generation FPCs and SIBs. In the future when there are fourth generation line cards, there will also be fourth generation SIBs that will accommodate the latest line cards operating at full speed. There's never a mid-plane to slow the system down.

Juniper QFX10008 SIB

The Juniper QFX10008 SIB has two Juniper Q5 Switch Fabric (SF) chips. Each Juniper Q5 SF crossbar can handle 8Tbps of traffic, as shown in Figure 1-34. Each SIB in the Juniper QFX10008 can handle 16Tbps of traffic, which brings the total switching fabric capacity to 96Tbps.

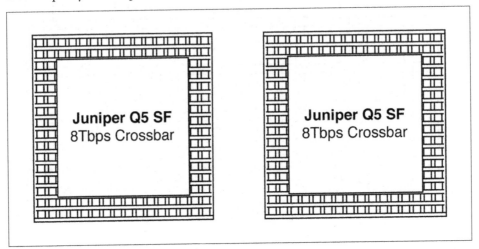

Figure 1-34. Juniper SF crossbar architecture

Each Juniper Q5 SF is attached directly to the line card connectors, so that every Juniper Q5 chip on a line card is directly connected into a full mesh to every single Juniper Q5 SF chip on the SIB, as demonstrated in Figure 1-35.

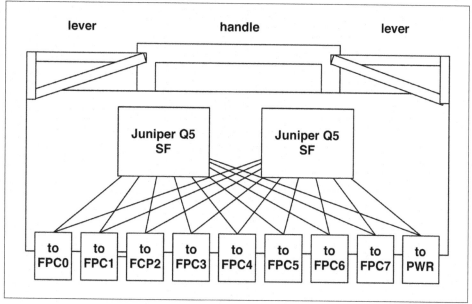

Figure 1-35. Juniper QFX1008 SIB architecture

We can use the Junos command line to verify this connectivity, as well. Let's take a look at a Juniper QFX10008 chassis and see what's in the first slot:

```
dhanks@st-u8-p1-01> show chassis hardware | match FPC0
FPC 0              REV 23   750-051354   ACAM9203        ULC-36Q-12Q28
```

In this example, we have a QFX1000-36Q line card installed into FPC0. If you recall, each QFX10000-36Q line card has three Juniper Q5 chips. Let's verify this by using the following command:

```
dhanks@st-u8-p1-01> show chassis fabric fpcs | no-more
Fabric management FPC state:
FPC #0
    PFE #0
        SIB0_FASIC0 (plane  0)   Plane Enabled, Links OK
        SIB0_FASIC1 (plane  1)   Plane Enabled, Links OK
        SIB1_FASIC0 (plane  2)   Plane Enabled, Links OK
        SIB1_FASIC1 (plane  3)   Plane Enabled, Links OK
        SIB2_FASIC0 (plane  4)   Plane Enabled, Links OK
        SIB2_FASIC1 (plane  5)   Plane Enabled, Links OK
        SIB3_FASIC0 (plane  6)   Plane Enabled, Links OK
        SIB3_FASIC1 (plane  7)   Plane Enabled, Links OK
        SIB4_FASIC0 (plane  8)   Plane Enabled, Links OK
        SIB4_FASIC1 (plane  9)   Plane Enabled, Links OK
        SIB5_FASIC0 (plane 10)   Plane Enabled, Links OK
        SIB5_FASIC1 (plane 11)   Plane Enabled, Links OK
    PFE #1
        SIB0_FASIC0 (plane  0)   Plane Enabled, Links OK
```

```
          SIB0_FASIC1 (plane  1)    Plane Enabled, Links OK
          SIB1_FASIC0 (plane  2)    Plane Enabled, Links OK
          SIB1_FASIC1 (plane  3)    Plane Enabled, Links OK
          SIB2_FASIC0 (plane  4)    Plane Enabled, Links OK
          SIB2_FASIC1 (plane  5)    Plane Enabled, Links OK
          SIB3_FASIC0 (plane  6)    Plane Enabled, Links OK
          SIB3_FASIC1 (plane  7)    Plane Enabled, Links OK
          SIB4_FASIC0 (plane  8)    Plane Enabled, Links OK
          SIB4_FASIC1 (plane  9)    Plane Enabled, Links OK
          SIB5_FASIC0 (plane 10)    Plane Enabled, Links OK
          SIB5_FASIC1 (plane 11)    Plane Enabled, Links OK
    PFE #2
          SIB0_FASIC0 (plane  0)    Plane Enabled, Links OK
          SIB0_FASIC1 (plane  1)    Plane Enabled, Links OK
          SIB1_FASIC0 (plane  2)    Plane Enabled, Links OK
          SIB1_FASIC1 (plane  3)    Plane Enabled, Links OK
          SIB2_FASIC0 (plane  4)    Plane Enabled, Links OK
          SIB2_FASIC1 (plane  5)    Plane Enabled, Links OK
          SIB3_FASIC0 (plane  6)    Plane Enabled, Links OK
          SIB3_FASIC1 (plane  7)    Plane Enabled, Links OK
          SIB4_FASIC0 (plane  8)    Plane Enabled, Links OK
          SIB4_FASIC1 (plane  9)    Plane Enabled, Links OK
          SIB5_FASIC0 (plane 10)    Plane Enabled, Links OK
          SIB5_FASIC1 (plane 11)    Plane Enabled, Links OK
```

We see that FPC0 has three PFEs labeled PFE0 through PFE2. In addition, we see that each PFE is connected to 12 planes across 6 SIBs. Each SIB has two fabric ASICs—the Juniper Q5 SF—which are referred to as a plane. Because there are 6 SIBs with 2 Juniper Q5 SFs each, that's a total of 12 Juniper Q5 SFs or 12 planes.

The show chassis fabric fpcs command is great if you need to quickly troubleshoot and see the overall switching fabric health of the chassis. If there are any FPC or SIB failures, you'll see the plane disabled and the links in an error state.

Let's dig a little bit deeper and see the individual connections between each PFE and fabric ASIC:

```
dhanks@st-u8-p1-01> show chassis fabric topology

 In-link  : FPC# FE# ASIC# (TX inst#, TX sub-chnl #) ->
            SIB# ASIC#_FCORE# (RX port#, RX sub-chn#, RX inst#)

 Out-link : SIB# ASIC#_FCORE# (TX port#, TX sub-chnl#, TX inst#) ->
            FPC# FE# ASIC# (RX inst#, RX sub-chnl #)
SIB 0 FCHIP 0 FCORE 0 :
-----------------------
         In-links            State          Out-links            State
------------------------------------------------------------------------
FPC00FE0(1,17)->S00F0_0(01,0,01) OK     S00F0_0(00,0,00)->FPC00FE0(1,09) OK
FPC00FE0(1,09)->S00F0_0(02,0,02) OK     S00F0_0(00,1,00)->FPC00FE0(1,17) OK
FPC00FE0(1,07)->S00F0_0(02,2,02) OK     S00F0_0(00,2,00)->FPC00FE0(1,07) OK
FPC00FE1(1,12)->S00F0_0(01,1,01) OK     S00F0_0(00,3,00)->FPC00FE1(1,06) OK
```

```
FPC00FE1(1,06)->S00F0_0(01,2,01) OK        S00F0_0(01,1,01)->FPC00FE1(1,12) OK
FPC00FE1(1,10)->S00F0_0(01,3,01) OK        S00F0_0(01,3,01)->FPC00FE1(1,10) OK
FPC00FE2(1,16)->S00F0_0(00,4,00) OK        S00F0_0(00,4,00)->FPC00FE2(1,08) OK
FPC00FE2(1,08)->S00F0_0(01,6,01) OK        S00F0_0(00,5,00)->FPC00FE2(1,16) OK
FPC00FE2(1,06)->S00F0_0(01,7,01) OK        S00F0_0(00,6,00)->FPC00FE2(1,06) OK
```

The output of the show chassis fabric topology command is very long, and I've truncated it to show only the connections between FPC0 and the first fabric ASIC on SIB0. What's really interesting is that there are three connections between each PFE on FPC0 and SIB0-F0. Why is that?

Each Juniper Q5 chip on the QFX10008 has three connections to every single fabric ASIC to provide enough bandwidth to run the line cards at line-rate. However, the Juniper QFX10016 has six fabric ASICs per SIB and only requires a single connection between each PFE and fabric ASIC.

Juniper QFX10016 SIB

The Juniper QFX10016 SIB is very similar to the QFX10008 SIB; the only difference is that it has six fabric ASICs instead of two. Each fabric ASIC is directly attached to an FPC connector, as shown in Figure 1-36. The Juniper QFX10016 SIB has 48Tbps of switching capacity because each of the fabric ASICs can handle 8Tbps.

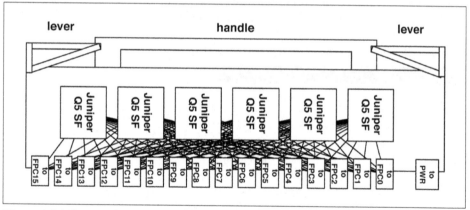

Figure 1-36. Juniper QFX10016 SIB architecture

The reason the Juniper QFX10016 SIB has six fabric ASICs is to handle the additional FPCs in such a large chassis. In the first generation line cards, there could be up to 96 Juniper Q5 chips in a single Juniper QFX10016 chassis. Each PFE has a single connection to every fabric ASIC across all the SIBs.

Optical Support

The Juniper QFX10000 Series supports a wide variety of optics ranging from 1GbE to 100GbE. Each of the optics varies in the distance, speed, and other options.

40GbE

The Juniper QFX10000 supports six different types of 40GbE optics: SR4, ESR4, LR4, LX4, 4x10BASE-IR, and 40G-BASE-IR4. Table 1-6 lists the attributes for each.

Table 1-8. 40GbE optic support on Juniper QFX10000

Attribute	SR4	ESR4	LR4	LX4	4x10BASE-IR	40G-BASE-IR4
Break-out cable	Yes (10GBASE-SR)	Yes (10GBASE-SR)	No	No	No	No
Distance	150M	OM3: 300M OM4: 400M	10K	OM3: 150M OM4: 150M	1.4K	2K
Fibers used	8 out of 12	8 out of 12	2	2	8 out of 12	2
Optic mode	MMF	MMF	SMF (1310nm)	MMR	SMF (1310nm)	SMF (1310nm)
Connector	MTP	MTP	LC	LC	MTP	LC
Form factor	QSFP+	QSFP+	QSFP+	QSFP+	QSFP+	QSFP+

100GbE

The Juniper QFX10000 supports four different types of 100GbE optics: PSM4, LR4, CWDM4, and SR4. Table 1-7 presents their attributes.

Table 1-9. 100GbE optic support on Juniper QFX10000

Attribute	PSM4	LR4	CWDM4	SR4
Break-out cable	No	No	No	No
Distance	500M	10K	2K	100M
Internal speeds	4x25GbE	4x25GbE	4x25GbE	4x25GbE
Fibers used	8 out of 12	2	2	8 out of 12
Optic mode	SMF	SMF	SMF	MMF (OM4)
Connector	MTP	LC	LC	MTP
Form factor	QSFP28	QSFP28	QSFP28	QSFP28

Summary

This chapter has covered a lot of topics, ranging from the QFX10002 to the large QFX10016 chassis switches. The Juniper QFX10000 Series was designed from the ground up to be the industry's most flexible spine switch. It offers incredibly high scale, tons of features, and deep buffer. The sizes range from small 2RU switches that can fit into tight spaces, all the way up to 21RU chassis that are designed for some of the largest data centers in the world. No matter what type of data center you're designing, the Juniper QFX10000 has a solution for you.

Chapter Review Questions

1. Which interface speed does the Juniper QFX10000 not support?

   a. 1GbE

   b. 10GbE

   c. 25GbE

   d. 40GbE

   e. 50GbE

   f. 100GbE

2. Is the QFX10000 a single or multichip switch?

   a. Switch-on-a-chip (SoC)

   b. Multichip architecture

3. How many MAC entries does the QFX10000 support?

   a. 192K

   b. 256K

   c. 512K

   d. 1M

4. How many points in the Juniper Q5 packet-processing pipeline support looping the packet?

   a. 2

   b. 3

   c. 4

   d. 5

5. Which interface within a port group must be configured for channelization?

   a. First

   b. Second

   c. Third

   d. Fourth

6. What's the internal code name for the Juniper Q5 chipset?

   a. Eagle

   b. Elit

   c. Paradise

   d. Ultimat

7. How many switching fabrics are in the QFX10008?

   a. 2

   b. 4

   c. 6

   d. 8

Chapter Review Answers

1. **Answer: C and E.** The Juniper QFX10000 Series is designed as a spine switch. 25/50GbE are designed as access ports for servers and storage. If you need 25/50GbE interfaces, the Juniper QFX5200 supports it. However, the Juniper QFX10000 focuses on 40/100GbE for leaf-to-spine connections.

2. **Answer: B.** Each of the Juniper QFX10000 switches use a multichip architecture to provide non-blocking bandwidth for high-scale, large buffers, and tons of features.

3. **Answer: B, C, and D.** Depending on the QFX10000 switch, the MAC scale is different. The QFX10002-36Q supports 256 K, QFX10002-72Q supports 512 K, and the QFX10008/QFX10016 supports 1 M*.

4. **Answer: D.** The Juniper Q5 PFE supports looping the packet in five different locations within the ingress to egress PFE pipeline.

5. **Answer: A.** You must configure the first interface within a port group for channelization. After it is configured, all remaining interfaces within the same port group are also channelized to 4x10GbE.

6. **Answer: D.** Trick question. The chapter never told you what the name was, but I slipped it into the chapter review questions for the astute reader.

7. **Answer: C.** The Juniper QFX10008 and QFX10016 support six switching fabric cards to provide non-blocking bandwidth to all of the line cards in a 5 + 1 redundant configuration.

CHAPTER 2

QFX10000 Software Architecture

The software architecture on the Juniper QFX10000 Series has significantly changed from what has been previously available from Juniper. The first big change is that Juniper has taken advantage of the power of the Linux operating system and has integrated it into the foundation of the Juniper QFX10000. Applications are now running directly on top of Linux as daemons or have been placed into either Linux containers or virtual machines (VMs) to provide additional abstraction and protection. The second big change is that the entire software architecture has been opened up. You can install your software, access any component of the switch, and even use common REST APIs to do so.

Software Architecture

The Juniper QFX10000 marks the journey of software disaggregation. Decoupling the network operating system from the underlying hardware has both technical and business benefits. Each layer in the networking stack has traditionally been vertically integrated and restricted access for customers. The new Juniper QFX10000 software architecture removes these previous restrictions and makes it possible for users to freely modify many aspects of the software and hardware, as illustrated in Figure 2-1.

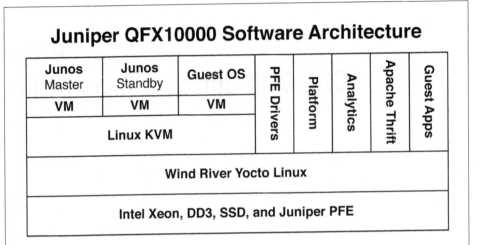

Figure 2-1. Juniper QFX10000 software architecture

The software side of the Juniper QFX10000 really looks more like a data center server than it does a traditional network switch. This was a conscious decision to remove all traditional restrictions and let you modify the software to your particular environment. You have all of the access to add software into the host operating system and Junos network operating system. In addition, you can create VMs or even use Linux containers.

Overview

The Juniper QFX10000 implements a new, secure boot loader that ensures that the network operating system and host operating system are verified as production software images from Juniper Networks. The Open Network Install Environment (ONIE) sits atop the boot loader and offers the user a quick and flexible way to install new host and network operating systems. The host operating system is Yocto Linux by Wind River (Figure 2-2). Yocto Linux is a carrier-class operating system that provides a stable foundation for all software on the Juniper QFX10000.

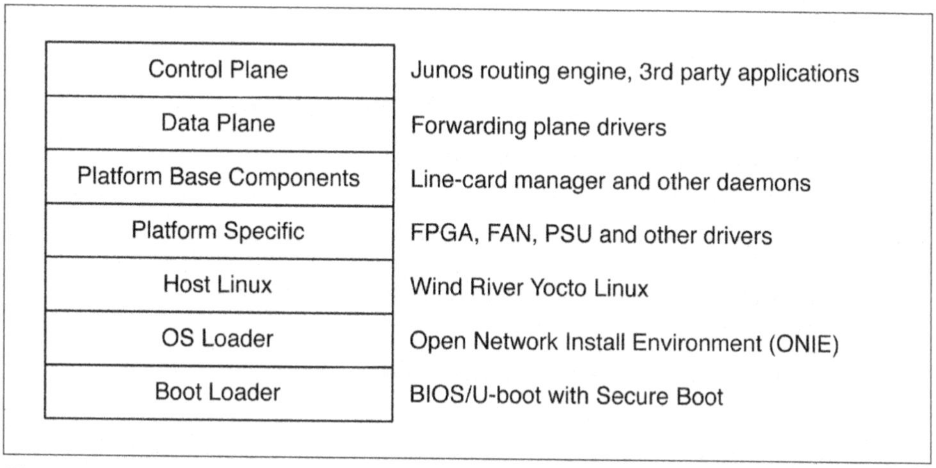

Control Plane	Junos routing engine, 3rd party applications
Data Plane	Forwarding plane drivers
Platform Base Components	Line-card manager and other daemons
Platform Specific	FPGA, FAN, PSU and other drivers
Host Linux	Wind River Yocto Linux
OS Loader	Open Network Install Environment (ONIE)
Boot Loader	BIOS/U-boot with Secure Boot

Figure 2-2. Juniper QFX10000 software architecture stack

Many non-network functions have traditionally been embedded into the Junos network operating system. Going forward, the Juniper QFX10000 has removed nonessential network functions from Junos and moved them directly into Yocto Linux. For example, the platform-specific drivers and configuration now operates as a simple daemon in Yocto Linux; previously these were embedded into Junos itself. The benefit is that Junos is back to its single network operating system roots; you can use the same code across multiple platforms without having to worry about the underlying firmware and drivers.

The platform-specific drivers include components such as the fans, power supplies, and other environmental functions. One of the biggest changes is that the Juniper QFX10000 has removed the ASIC drivers from Junos and now runs them directly on Yocto Linux. You can now independently upgrade the control plane from the data plane using different software images. Traditionally, these have been bundled together in large Junos updates that can be more than 700 MB in size. Now, the software has two options: bundled and unbundled. The bundled option is the traditional *jinstall* image, which includes all of the software: host operating system, platform drivers, base components, ASIC drivers, and, of course, Junos. With the second option, each function comes unbundled in a Linux Red Hat Package Manager (RPM) format. For example, if you needed to update only the ASIC drivers, you simply download the ASIC drivers and install them without having to worry about the rest of the drivers. The Linux RPM format automatically handles software dependencies, so if the latest ASIC driver requires a control plane or platform-specific version, it will automatically create the dependency tree and download the other software.

No more having to copy files. You can simply use Juniper's public RPM repository or your own private repository. Simply upgrade the switch with a single command. Note that Yocto Linux uses the `smart` command instead of `rpm`:

```
dhanks@QFX10002:~# smart update
Loading cache...
Updating cache...
########################################################### [100%]

Fetching information for 'junos smart channel'...
http://jnpr.net/repo/repomd.xml
repomd.xml
########################################################### [ 50%]
-> http://jnpr.net/repo/primary.xml.gz
primary.xml ############################################### [ 75%]
-> http://jnpr.net/repo/filelists.xml.gz
filelists.xml
########################################################### [100%]

Updating cache...
########################################################### [100%]

Channels have 1 new packages:
    qfx-10-f-data-plane-15.1X51-D12.1@x86_64

Saving cache...
```

The new RPM tool is in addition to the existing method of "request software add"; it doesn't replace it. You can still use the old method of installing software; however, the new RPM method is going to be much easier.

Host Operating System

When the Juniper QFX10000 starts, it does so directly into Linux. Specifically, it's Wind River Yocto Linux; this provides the operating system and virtualization foundation for Junos and all other network-related functionality.

Let's log in to the host operating system and explore about:

```
dhanks@qfx10000> request app-engine host-shell
Last login: Sat Mar 26 22:18:21 PDT 2016 from vjunos0 on pts/2
```

Now let's take a peek at the PCI bus and see what's installed on the host operating system:

```
root@localhost:~# lspci
00:00.0 Host bridge: Intel Corporation 3rd Gen Core processor DRAM Controller
(rev 09)
00:01.0 PCI bridge: Intel Corporation Xeon E3-1200 v2/3rd Gen Core processor PCI
Express Root Port (rev 09)
< ... truncated ... >
12:00.0 Unassigned class [ff00]: Juniper Networks Device 0076 (rev 01)
18:00.0 Unassigned class [ff00]: Juniper Networks Device 0077 (rev 01)
< ... truncated ... >
```

The two Juniper Networks devices are interesting. What are they? These are the Field-Programmable Gate Array (FPGA) controllers that are responsible for the chassis fan, sensors, and other environmental functions.

Let's take a closer look at the CPU:

```
root@localhost:~# cat /proc/cpuinfo
processor       : 0
vendor_id       : GenuineIntel
cpu family      : 6
model           : 58
model name      : Intel(R) Xeon(R) CPU  @ 2.50GHz
stepping        : 9
microcode       : 0x17
cpu MHz         : 2499.826
cache size      : 8192 KB
physical id     : 0
siblings        : 8
core id         : 0
cpu cores       : 4
apicid          : 0
initial apicid  : 0
fpu             : yes
fpu_exception   : yes
cpuid level     : 13
wp              : yes
flags           : fpu vme de pse tsc msr pae mce cx8 apic sep mtrr pge mca cmov
pat pse36 clflush dts acpi mmx fxsr sse sse2 ss ht tm pbe syscall nx rdtscp
lm constant_tsc arch_perfmon pebs bts rep_good nopl xtopology nonstop_tsc
aperfmperf eagerfpu pni pclmulqdq dtes64 monitor ds_cpl vmx smx est tm2 ssse3
cx16 xtpr pdcm pcid sse4_1 sse4_2 x2apic popcnt tsc_deadline_timer aes xsave
avx f16c rdrand lahf_lm arat epb xsaveopt pln pts dtherm tpr_shadow vnmi
flexpriority ept vpid fsgsbase smep erms
bogomips        : 4999.65
clflush size    : 64
cache_alignment : 64
address sizes   : 36 bits physical, 48 bits virtual
power management:
< ... truncated ... >
```

The CPU is a server-class Intel Xeon processor. This is a dual socket processor with four cores, which give it plenty of power to operate multiple VMs and the network operating system.

Let's take a look at the memory:

```
root@localhost:~# free
             total       used       free     shared    buffers     cached
Mem:      15899972    6224460    9675512          0     247596    1507096
-/+ buffers/cache:    4469768   11430204
Swap:      1114252          0    1114252
```

After other hardware and the kernel reserving some of the memory, we can see that we have about 9.6 GB left over.

Now let's take a look at how many disks there are and how they're partitioned:

```
root@localhost:~# fdisk -l

Disk /dev/sda: 25.0 GB, 25015689216 bytes, 48858768 sectors
Units = sectors of 1 * 512 = 512 bytes
Sector size (logical/physical): 512 bytes / 512 bytes
I/O size (minimum/optimal): 512 bytes / 512 bytes
Disk label type: dos
Disk identifier: 0x000d737d

   Device Boot      Start         End      Blocks   Id  System
/dev/sda1   *       15625     2000000      992188   83  Linux
/dev/sda2         2000001     6458984     2229492   83  Linux
/dev/sda3         6458985    28757812    11149414   83  Linux
/dev/sda4        28757813    46593750     8917969    f  W95 Ext'd (LBA)
/dev/sda5        28757814    44365234     7803710+  83  Linux
/dev/sda6        44365236    46593750     1114257+  83  Linux

Disk /dev/sdb: 25.0 GB, 25015689216 bytes, 48858768 sectors
Units = sectors of 1 * 512 = 512 bytes
Sector size (logical/physical): 512 bytes / 512 bytes
I/O size (minimum/optimal): 512 bytes / 512 bytes


Disk /dev/mapper/vg0_vjunos-lv_junos: 12.9 GB, 12884901888 bytes,
                            25165824 sectors
Units = sectors of 1 * 512 = 512 bytes
Sector size (logical/physical): 512 bytes / 512 bytes
I/O size (minimum/optimal): 512 bytes / 512 bytes


Disk /dev/mapper/vg0_vjunos-lv_junos_recovery: 12.1 GB, 12125732864 bytes,
                            23683072 sectors
Units = sectors of 1 * 512 = 512 bytes
Sector size (logical/physical): 512 bytes / 512 bytes
I/O size (minimum/optimal): 512 bytes / 512 bytes
```

The host system has two SSD storage devices that are 25 GB each. From the partition layout, we can see that we're running the Linux Volume Manager (LVM).

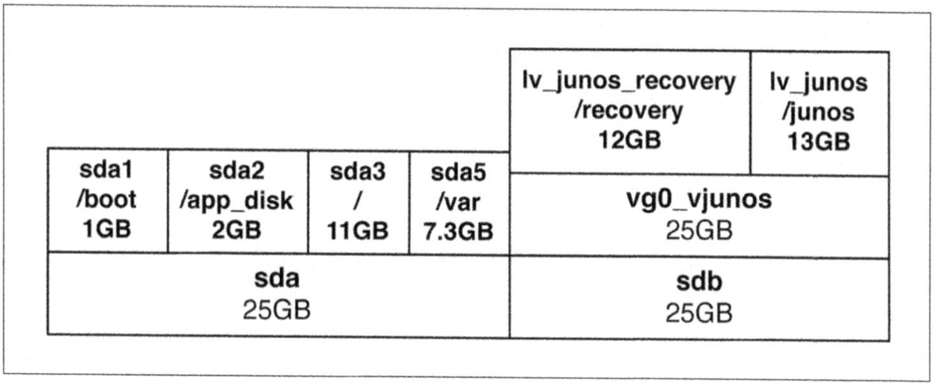

				lv_junos_recovery /recovery 12GB	lv_junos /junos 13GB
sda1 /boot 1GB	sda2 /app_disk 2GB	sda3 / 11GB	sda5 /var 7.3GB	vg0_vjunos 25GB	
sda 25GB				sdb 25GB	

Figure 2-3. Linux LVM and storage design

There are two 25 GB SSDs, which are part of the Linux LVM. The primary volume group is vg0_vjunos. This volume group has two volumes that Junos uses:

- lv_junos_recovery
- lv_junos

The first SSD uses standard Linux partitions to run the host operating system. The /boot, /app_disk, /, and /var file systems are partitioned out across /dev/sda, as shown in Figure 2-3.

Linux KVM

As mentioned in the previous section, when the Juniper QFX10000 starts, the host operating system is Linux. All of the control-plane operations happen inside of the network operating system called Junos. The Juniper QFX10000 takes advantage of compute virtualization in the host operating system using Linux KVM. A VM is created specifically for Junos. Given that KVM can create multiple VMs, the Juniper QFX10000 has the ability to perform In-Service Software Upgrades (ISSU) and support third-party VMs that can host additional services such as network management and monitoring.

virsh

The Juniper QFX10000 uses the *libvir* library as well as the libsh management user interface to interact with Linux KVM. If you're familiar with *libvir*, walking around the virtualization capabilities of the Juniper QFX10000 will come as second nature. If you're unfamiliar with *libvir*, let's use virsh to walk around and explore to see what's happening under the hood.

The first thing we need to do is drop into the host shell from the Junos CLI:

```
dhanks@qfx10000> request app-engine host-shell
Last login: Sat Mar 26 22:18:21 PDT 2016 from vjunos0 on pts/2
```

Now, let's take a look at the VMs installed in the Linux KVM:

```
-sh-4.1# virsh list --all
 Id    Name                           State
----------------------------------------------------
 2     vjunos0                        running
```

By default there's a single VM running the Junos networking operating system. The VM's name is vjunos0 with an ID of 1 and we can see that the state is running.

Hmm. Are you curious as to what version of the *libvir* library and QEMU the Juniper QFX10000 is using? Let's find out:

```
-sh-4.1# virsh version
Compiled against library: libvirt 1.1.2
Using library: libvirt 1.1.2
Using API: QEMU 1.1.2
Running hypervisor: QEMU 1.5.0
```

Now, let's take a look at the overall host memory and CPU statistics:

```
-sh-4.1# virsh nodememstats
total  :           15899972 KiB
free   :            9674312 KiB
buffers:             247612 KiB
cached :            1507296 KiB
```

```
-sh-4.1# virsh nodecpustats
user:                73301210000000
system:              26242560000000
idle:              2054414620000000
iowait:               1491080000000
```

Now that we're familiar with what the host system is capable of, the software versions, and, of course, how many VMs are configured, let's take a closer look at the Junos VM:

```
-sh-4.1# virsh dominfo vjunos0
Id:             2
Name:           vjunos0
UUID:           dc38e169-c1f4-0200-0000-564a554e4f53
OS Type:        hvm
State:          running
CPU(s):         1
CPU time:       48939.3s
Max memory:     3440640 KiB
Used memory:    3440640 KiB
Persistent:     no
Autostart:      disable
Managed save:   no
```

```
Security model: none
Security DOI:   0
```

Each VM has a unique identifier that can be used to refer to it. One of the more interesting attributes is the OS Type, which is set to hvm; this stands for Hardware Virtual Machine. Because Junos is based on FreeBSD and heavily modified to support network control-plane functions, it's difficult to say that it's pure FreeBSD. Instead, the alternative is to use a vendor-neutral OS Type of hvm, which basically means that it's an x86-based operating system.

Let's take a closer look at the memory and network settings for vjunos0:

```
-sh-4.1# virsh dommemstat vjunos0
rss 3458308

-sh-4.1# virsh domiflist vjunos0
Interface   Type      Source     Model    MAC
-------------------------------------------------------------
vnet0       bridge    eth0br     e1000    52:54:00:12:cc:1a
iri1        bridge    ctrlbr0    e1000    52:54:00:1c:95:51
vnet1       bridge    virbr0     e1000    52:54:00:c8:b6:62
vnet2       bridge    eth1br     e1000    52:54:00:7e:63:f7
```

Another interesting place to look for more information is in the */proc* file system. We can take a look at the PID of vjunos0 and get a peek at the task status:

```
-sh-4.1# cat /var/run/libvirt/qemu/vjunos0.pid
7257
-sh-4.1# cat /proc/7257/task/*/status
Name:       kvm
State:      S (sleeping)
Tgid:       7257
Pid:        16683
PPid:       1
TracerPid:      0
Uid:      0      0      0      0
Gid:      0      0      0      0
FDSize: 64
Groups: 0
VmPeak:   3876656 kB
VmSize:   3811380 kB
VmLck:          0 kB
VmPin:          0 kB
VmHWM:    3460332 kB
VmRSS:    3458308 kB
VmData:   3691596 kB
VmStk:        136 kB
VmExe:       4112 kB
VmLib:       7716 kB
VmPTE:       7052 kB
VmSwap:         0 kB
Threads:        3
```

```
SigQ:    1/123425
SigPnd: 0000000000000000
ShdPnd: 0000000000000000
SigBlk: fffffffe7ffbfeff
SigIgn: 0000000000001000
SigCgt: 0000000180006243
CapInh: 0000000000000000
CapPrm: 0000001ffffffff
CapEff: 0000001ffffffff
CapBnd: 0000001ffffffff
Seccomp:         0
Cpus_allowed:    0c
Cpus_allowed_list:      2-3
Mems_allowed:    1
Mems_allowed_list:      0
voluntary_ctxt_switches:        10
nonvoluntary_ctxt_switches:     14
Name:   kvm
State:  S (sleeping)
Tgid:   7257
Pid:    7257
PPid:   1
TracerPid:       0
Uid:    0        0        0        0
Gid:    0        0        0        0
FDSize: 64
Groups: 0
VmPeak:  3876656 kB
VmSize:  3811380 kB
VmLck:         0 kB
VmPin:         0 kB
VmHWM:   3460332 kB
VmRSS:   3458308 kB
VmData:  3691596 kB
VmStk:       136 kB
VmExe:      4112 kB
VmLib:      7716 kB
VmPTE:      7052 kB
VmSwap:        0 kB
Threads:         3
SigQ:    1/123425
SigPnd: 0000000000000000
ShdPnd: 0000000000000000
SigBlk: 0000000010002240
SigIgn: 0000000000001000
SigCgt: 0000000180006243
CapInh: 0000000000000000
CapPrm: 0000001ffffffff
CapEff: 0000001ffffffff
CapBnd: 0000001ffffffff
Seccomp:         0
Cpus_allowed:    0c
```

```
Cpus_allowed_list:        2-3
Mems_allowed:    1
Mems_allowed_list:        0
voluntary_ctxt_switches:        287894555
nonvoluntary_ctxt_switches:     582962
Name:   kvm
State:  R (running)
Tgid:   7257
Pid:    7259
PPid:   1
TracerPid:      0
Uid:    0       0       0       0
Gid:    0       0       0       0
FDSize: 64
Groups: 0
VmPeak:  3876656 kB
VmSize:  3811380 kB
VmLck:         0 kB
VmPin:         0 kB
VmHWM:   3460332 kB
VmRSS:   3458308 kB
VmData:  3691596 kB
VmStk:       136 kB
VmExe:      4112 kB
VmLib:      7716 kB
VmPTE:      7052 kB
VmSwap:        0 kB
Threads:        3
SigQ:   1/123425
SigPnd: 0000000000000000
ShdPnd: 0000000000000000
SigBlk: ffffffe7ffbfeff
SigIgn: 0000000000001000
SigCgt: 0000000180006243
CapInh: 0000000000000000
CapPrm: 0000001fffffffff
CapEff: 0000001fffffffff
CapBnd: 0000001fffffffff
Seccomp:        0
Cpus_allowed:   08
Cpus_allowed_list:        3
Mems_allowed:    1
Mems_allowed_list:        0
voluntary_ctxt_switches:        561779400
nonvoluntary_ctxt_switches:     116297
```

One of the more interesting things to notice is the `Cpus_allowed_list`, which is set to a value of 3. By default, Juniper assigns the fourth CPU directly to the `vjunos0` VM; this guarantees that other tasks outside of the scope of the control plane doesn't negatively affect Junos. The value is set to 3, because the first CPU has a value of 0. We can verify this again with another `virsh` command:

```
-sh-4.1# virsh vcpuinfo vjunos0
VCPU:           0
CPU:            3
State:          running
CPU time:       28896.4s
CPU Affinity:   ---y----
```

We can see that the CPU affinity is set to "y" on the fourth CPU, which verifies what we've seen in the /proc file system.

App Engine

If you're interested in getting more information about the VMs but don't feel like dropping to the host shell and using virsh commands, there is an alternative called the Junos App Engine which is accessible within the Junos CLI.

The command to view the app engine settings is show app-engine. There are several different views that are available, as listed in Table 2-1.

Table 2-1. Junos App Engine views

View	Description
ARP	View all of the ARP entries of the VMs connected into all the bridge domains
Bridge	View all of the configured Linux bridge tables
Information	Get information about the compute cluster, such as model, kernel version, and management IP addresses
Netstat	Just a simple wrapper around the Linux netstat -rn command
Resource usage	Show the CPU, memory, disk, and storage usage statistics in an easy-to-read format

Let's walk through some of the most common Junos App Engine commands and examine the output:

```
dhanks@QFX10000> show app-engine arp
Compute cluster: default-cluster

  Compute node: default-node

  Arp
  ===
  Address              HWtype  HWaddress           Flags Mask   Iface
  128.0.0.1            ether   02:00:00:00:00:0a   C            ctrlbr0
  vjunos0              ether   00:31:46:7b:f1:08   C            virbr0
  128.0.0.32           ether   02:00:00:00:00:0a   C            ctrlbr0
```

This is just a simple summary show command that aggregates the management IP, MAC, and to what bridge table it's bound.

Let's take a look at the bridge tables:

```
dhanks@QFX10000> show app-engine bridge
Compute cluster: default-cluster
```

```
Compute node: default-node

  Bridge Table
  ============
  bridge name  bridge id            STP enabled    interfaces
  ctrlbr0             8000.fe54001c9551     no               iri1
  eth0br              8000.0031467be118     no               eth0
                                                              vnet0
  eth1br              8000.0031467be119     no               eth1
                                                              vnet2
  gluebr0             8000.000000000000     no
  gluebr1             8000.000000000000     no
  virbr0              8000.0031467be11b     yes              virbr0-nic
                                                              vnet1
```

Just another nice wrapper for the Linux `brctl` command. Recall that `vnet0` is for the regular control plane side of Junos, whereas `vnet1` is reserved for interrouting engine traffic during an ISSU:

```
dhanks@QFX10000> show app-engine resource-usage
Compute cluster: default-cluster

 Compute node: default-node
  CPU Usage
  =========
  22:26:30   CPU  %usr  %nice  %sys %iowait  %irq  %soft  %steal  %guest  %gnice   %idle
  22:26:30   all  2.81  0.00   1.21  0.07    0.00  0.01   0.00    0.59    0.00    95.31
  22:26:30   0    6.00  0.00   0.86  0.15    0.00  0.00   0.00    0.00    0.00    92.99
  22:26:30   1    1.10  0.00   0.16  0.04    0.00  0.00   0.00    0.00    0.00    98.71
  22:26:30   2    3.33  0.00   3.66  0.25    0.00  0.04   0.00    0.00    0.00    92.71
  22:26:30   3    0.06  0.00   2.92  0.00    0.00  0.03   0.00    4.92    0.00    92.06
  22:26:30   4    0.00  0.00   0.00  0.00    0.00  0.00   0.00    0.00    0.00   100.00
  22:26:30   5    0.00  0.00   0.00  0.00    0.00  0.00   0.00    0.00    0.00   100.00
  22:26:30   6    8.65  0.00   1.26  0.05    0.00  0.00   0.00    0.00    0.00    90.04
  22:26:30   7    3.24  0.00   0.92  0.06    0.00  0.00   0.00    0.00    0.00    95.77

  Memory Us
  age
  ===========
            total     used     free    shared    buffers    cached
  Mem:      15527     6078     9448        0         241      1472
  Swap:      1088        0     1088

  Disk Usage
  ==========
  Filesystem                      Size  Used Avail Use% Mounted on
  rootfs                           11G  552M  9.3G   6% /
  udev                            7.6G   52K  7.6G   1% /dev
  none                            7.6G   52K  7.6G   1% /dev
  tmpfs                           7.6G  316K  7.6G   1% /run
  /dev/sda3                        11G  552M  9.3G   6% /
  /dev/sda5                       7.3G   94M  6.8G   2% /var
  tmpfs                           7.6G  316K  7.6G   1% /run
  tmpfs                           7.6G     0  7.6G   0% /var/volatile
  /dev/sda1                       969M  405M  564M  42% /boot
  /dev/sda2                       2.1G  3.2M  2.0G   1% /app_disk
  /dev/mapper/vg0_vjunos-lv_junos  12G  4.3G  6.8G  39% /junos
  tmpfs                             7
```

```
 .6G  316K  7.6G   1% /run/named-chroot/var/run/named
tmpfs                    7.6G  316K  7.6G   1% /run/named-chroot/var/run/bind
none                     7.6G   52K  7.6G   1% /run/named-chroot/dev/random
none                     7.6G   52K  7.6G   1% /run/named-chroot/dev/zero
none                     7.6G   52K  7.6G   1% /run/named-chroot/dev/null

Storage Information
===================
  VG         #PV #LV #SN Attr   VSize  VFree
  vg0_vjunos   1   2   0 wz--n- 23.29g     0
```

show app-engine resource-usage is a nice aggregated command showing the utilization of the CPU, memory, disk, and storage information; it's very easy to get a bird's-eye view of the health of the App Engine.

ISSU

One of the great Junos features since the original M Series routers is its ability to support ISSU. With ISSU, the network operating can upgrade the firmware of the router without having to shut it down and affect production traffic. One of the key requirements for ISSU is to have two routing engines. During an ISSU, the two routing engines need to synchronize kernel and control-plane state with each other. The idea is that one routing engine will be upgraded while the other routing engine is handling the control plane.

Although the Juniper QFX10002 doesn't physically have two routing engines, it's able to functionally arrive at the same requirement thanks to the power of virtualization. The Juniper QFX10002 is able to create a second VM running Junos during an ISSU to meet all of the synchronization requirements, as depicted in Figure 2-3.

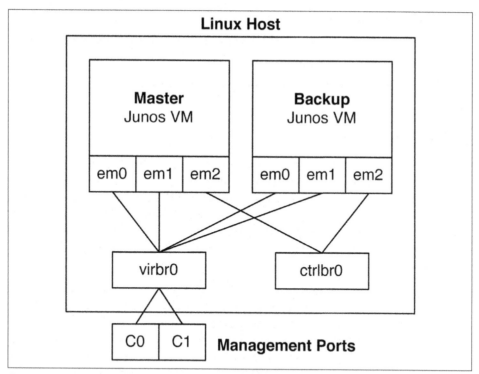

Figure 2-4. QFX10000 Linux KVM and management architecture

Each Junos VM has three management interfaces. Two of the management interfaces, em0 and em1, are used for management and map, respectively, to the external interfaces C0 and C1. The third management interface, em2, is used exclusively for communication between the two Junos VMs. For example, control-plane protocols such as NSR, NSB, and GRES is required for a successful ISSU completion; these protocols would communicate across the isolated em2 interface as well as an isolated ctrlbr0 bridge table in the Linux host.

The backup Junos VM is only created and running during an ISSU. At a high level, Junos goes through the following steps during an ISSU:

1. Backup Junos VM is created and started.
2. Backup Junos VM is upgraded to the software version specified in the ISSU command.
3. The Packet Forwarding Engine (PFE) goes into an ISSU-prepared state in which data is copied from the PFE into RAM.
4. The PFE connects to the recently upgraded backup Junos VM, which now becomes the master routing engine.

5. The PFE performs a warm reboot.

6. The new master Junos VM installs the PFE state from RAM back into the PFE.

7. The other Junos VM is shut down.

8. Junos has been upgraded and the PFE has performed a warm reboot.

Summary

This chapter covered the new software architecture in the Juniper QFX10000 series. Everything is about removing restrictions and opening up each layer in the networking stack. Users are now able to freely add software to the host operating system, in a VM, container, or even into Junos itself. The Juniper QFX10000 control plane is comparable to modern servers using modern Intel Xeon processors, DDR3 memory, and SSD storage. The beefy control plane lets you easily customize it with your own software without having to worry about degrading the network performance.

One of the largest changes in the Juniper QFX10000 Series is the unbundling of software. You can choose to continue using a single piece of firmware to upgrade the switch or avail yourself of the option to upgrade a specific piece of firmware or software based on Linux RPM. The files are ultimately smaller in size and makes the network software upgrade process look like a standard Linux server; this means that you can use existing tools such as Chef or Puppet to quickly upgrade all of the network switches.

CHAPTER 3

Next-Generation Internet Exchange Architecture Case Study

The Juniper QFX10000 Series has pushed new data center architectures that were previously not possible. The amount of features, scale, and port density brings a lot more possibilities to the table when it comes to designing a data center. Designing a data center network in 2016 looks radically different from designing a data center merely a year ago. For example, Virtual Extensible LAN (VXLAN) has brought a lot more to the table than just virtual machine–to–virtual machine traffic flows. Juniper has used VXLAN in combination with Ethernet VPN (EVPN) to create a new network fabric that's based on open protocols. Finally, Multiprotocol Label Switching (MPLS) has brought new architectures to the data center, as well, such as segment routing.

Introduction

The intent of this chapter isn't to go deep into any one specific technology or architecture. Instead, we will walk you through some new architectures and technologies that you can apply to an existing use case. There are many trade-offs when looking at different architectures, and sometimes it's difficult to capture all of the requirements and caveats.

This chapter focuses on building a next-generation Internet Exchange (IX) network. Until now, network operators generally built a very large broadcast domain and plugged a bunch of routers into it. Depending on when you implemented the network, the technology used would vary. Some of the first IX networks were based off some flavor of spanning tree. A generation after that came Multichassis Link Aggregation (MC-LAG) technologies; the benefit being in removing the need for spanning tree and having the ability to support all-active forwarding. As IX networks have grown over time, they require more port density and sometimes even sprawl over several small data centers in a geographic region. Some of the latest IX networks have been designed with MPLS and Virtual Private LAN Service (VPLS) to span a broadcast domain over many small data centers.

If you were to design an IX network today, what would it look like? There are many different options with many different technical trade-offs that need to be made. Do you know them all?

IX Requirements

Without going through the entire history of IX points (IXPs), we'll summarize the basic networking requirements here. If you want to know all the gory details, just do an Internet search for "Internet Exchange Design."

The most basic principle is called *bilateral peering*. There's a single connection between you and a peer, and only you and a peer exchange routing information. If the IX has a lot of members, this quickly becomes difficult. The route server (RS) provides multilateral peering. There's one Border Gateway Protocol (BGP) session between everyone and the RS, but you get everyone else's prefixes.

All of the traffic on the Internet is Layer 3 by nature, yet IX networks are based purely on Layer 2. Why is that? When you look at the peering arrangements of members within an IX, it isn't desirable to set up a BGP session with every other member in the IX. One creative way to avoid having to with every other member is to only peer once with a RS. Imagine an RS that functions very similar to a route reflector. Every member peers with the RS and advertises the prefixes that they want to exchange. In return, the RS will advertise everyone else's prefixes and next-hop to you. If every member was on the same Layer 2 network, external BGP (eBGP) doesn't change the next-hop. This makes it possible for you to peer with an RS and exchange routes, but all of the data-plane traffic can bypass the RS and go directly between members because they learn each other's next-hop through the RS. The big point is that members don't need to learn local IX routes to reach other members; they simply operate on the same Layer 2 network and avoid additional state in the Routing Information Base (RIB) and Forwarding Information Base (FIB).

RS Overview

The RS is very similar to a route reflector, but with some very important differences. Every member within an IX has its own AS number, so by its very nature everyone speaks eBGP. It's a difficult challenge to create an RS based on eBGP that appears to be transparent and advertises prefixes to everyone else. If you recall, eBGP doesn't advertise a prefix to a peer if it sees its own autonomous system (AS) in the AS_PATH.

In addition, attributes like MEDs aren't transitive. Figure 3-1 shows a typical IX network with an RS.

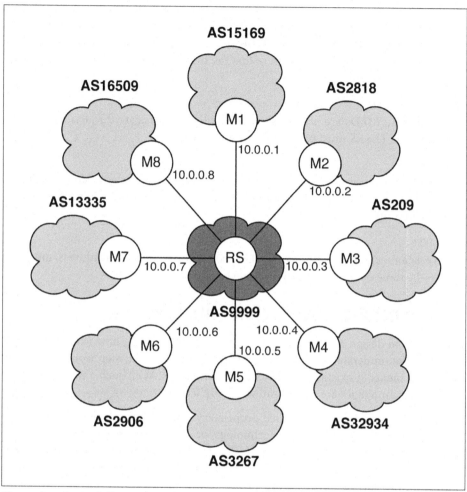

Figure 3-1. Logical illustration of an IX network showing how members connect with an RS

In the figure, the RS is in the middle of the IX. The RS connects via eBGP to each member to learn and exchange prefixes with every other member in the IX. All members and RS are part of the same Layer 2 network, so that eBGP doesn't change the next-hop; this precludes each member from having to learn the local network. The benefit is that each member has a single BGP session with the RS and doesn't need to pollute its route table with local IX addressing.

Let's review all of the functions an RS needs in order to allow multilateral peering:

AS_PATH
> The RS must never modify the AS_PATH as it exchanges routes between members. By default, a node using eBGP will insert its own AS into the AS_PATH; however, the RS cannot do this. The goal is to completely remove the RS from the forwarding path. The RS must also perform some sanity checks on the AS_PATH. Each prefix must be inspected to ensure that the first AS in the AS_PATH is the same AS of each member.

MULTI_EXIT_DISC
> By default, MEDs are nontransitive and will not propagate through multiple AS numbers. The RS must pass MEDs between members.

Communities
> The RS must not modify BGP communities between members. However, the IX network can set up special communities that the RS can process for different traffic handling.

NEXT_HOP
> By default, eBGP will modify the NEXT_HOP to the router's local address, unless it's on the same network. The RS must never modify the NEXT_HOP.

Next-Generation Architecture with EVPN

If you were to design a next-generation architecture for an IX, how would you do it? Now that you understand the basic IX requirements, the next step would be to map the requirements to existing and potential technologies. With such a map, you could see which technologies are strong and which are weak.

Traditionally, IX networks have used proprietary vendor technologies to create large Layer 2 Ethernet fabrics, MC-LAG technology, or simply used spanning tree. Some of the more recent IX networks have used VPLS-MPLS to take advantage of traffic engineering, traffic protection, and other technologies. Each option comes with its own trade-offs, as is shown in Table 3-1.

Table 3-1. Simple decision matrix of various technologies available to create an IX network architecture.

Attribute	Proprietary Fabric	MC-LAG	Spanning Tree	VPLS-MPLS	EVPN
Multivendor	No	PE-PE: No PE-CE: Yes	Yes	Yes	Yes
Minimize unknown unicast	Varies (generally yes)	No	No	No	Yes
Controlled learning with policy	Varies	No	No	No	Yes
MAC move friendly	Varies	No	No	No	Yes
All-active multihoming	Varies	Only two PEs	No	No	Yes

Attribute	Proprietary Fabric	MC-LAG	Spanning Tree	VPLS-MPLS	EVPN
Mass withdraw	Varies	No	No	No	Yes
Scale to 100K+ MACs	Varies	Slow	Slow	Yes	Yes
VPN	Varies	No	No	Yes	Yes
Autodiscovery	Varies	No	No	Yes	Yes
Layer 3 underlay	Varies	No	No	Yes	Yes

Given the large Layer 2 requirements by IX networks, EVPN is a logical choice. One of the biggest factors that separate proprietary Ethernet fabrics from EVPN is being able to operate in a multivendor environment. For example, Juniper QFabric was a predraft implementation of EPVN and enjoyed all of the same benefits, but it only worked on Juniper switches. Given the desire of IX networks to be transparent and manage risk, it's desirable to operate a multivendor network. In the end, EVPN just makes more sense in an IX network; it enjoys all of the benefits without being tied to a single vendor.

Before moving into the data-plane encapsulations, let's take a look at the IX network and understand how EVPN as a control plane will fit in. We'll need to basically create a very large bridge domain across a large number of member ports.

Topology

The topology of IX networks mainly depend on which region you are operating in. Generally, in the United States, you'll find more spine-and-leaf topologies that mimic data centers. In Europe, the predominant topologies are more spread out across major cities. In Japan, you'll find that IX topologies are vertical through multistory buildings with very small floors, as shown in Figure 3-2. Keep in mind this is a very broad generalization.

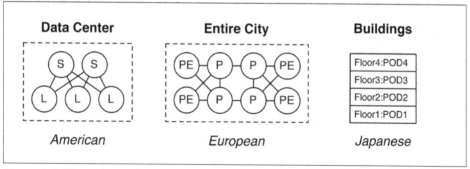

Figure 3-2. Network topologies vary around the world

In summary, there's no right answer. You need to work with the physical constraints placed on you. A good operator will choose an architecture that works the same and provides all services no matter what topology you choose. For example, Loop-Free

Alternate (LFA) requires triangle topologies and actually creates loops in a square topology. (More on this later.)

Recall that EVPN is agnostic to the data-plane encapsulation. The two popular data-plane encapsulations are MPLS and VXLAN. Both of these technologies are based on an IPv4 fabric, as demonstrated in Figure 3-3.

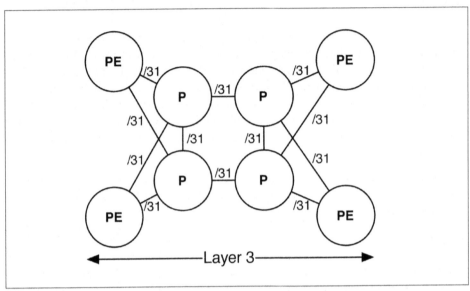

Figure 3-3. An IPv4 Layer 3 fabric

If you decide to use EVPN-MPLS, you still need to build an IPv4 fabric as the foundation. If you decide to use EVPN-VXLAN, you still require the IPv4 fabric.

The big advantage to an IPv4 fabric underlay is that it's inherently stable and loop-free. It's very easy to implement traffic engineering and traffic protection on such a stable foundation. Tunneling Layer 2 traffic across a stable, protected IPv4 fabric foundation has some important benefits:

- The overlay network can take advantage of the underlay traffic protection and traffic engineering.
- The underlay doesn't need to participate in the overlay network address learning.
- The overlay can use the underlay for loop prevention.

Layer 2 Services

At the heart of an IX network is a single, large Layer 2 service that interconnects every single member router (CE), as illustrated in Figure 3-4. The Layer 2 service lets every single member be on the same network.

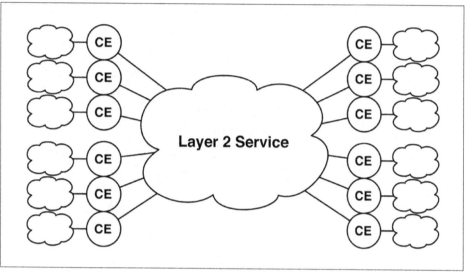

Figure 3-4. IXP Layer 2 service for multilateral peering

When each member peers with the RS, they get all of the prefixes and next-hop from every other member router. Because everyone is on the same network, eBGP doesn't modify the next-hop. Therefore, every member router is reachable across the Layer 2 service without the need for the IX or other members to participate in learning the underlying network.

Customer Peering Models

There are two common peering models when it comes to peering at an IX, as shown in Figure 3-5.

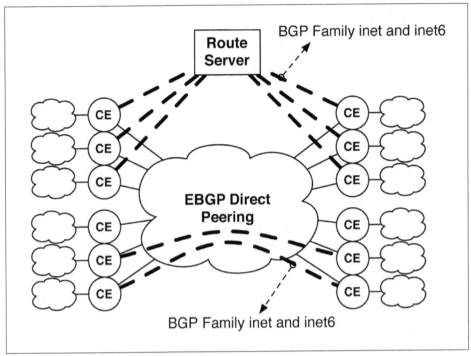

Figure 3-5. Customer peering models with an RS and direct peering

There are two primary types of peering available: public and private. Let's review each in more detail:

Public Peering Interconnection (PPI)
> PPI is available to every member within an IX through the RS. Each IX has different rules when it comes to multilateral peering agreements (MLPA). For example, some IXs require mandatory MLPA, whereas the majority do not. Regardless of IX policy, the PPI/MLPA is implemented through the common Layer 2 service and the IX RS.

Private Network Interconnection (PNI)
> PNI is exactly the opposite of PPI. Each member can choose who they want to peer with, custom prefixes, custom AS numbers, and other technical and business agreements outside of the purview of the IX. PNI can be accomplished over the same Layer 2 service or with dedicated point-to-point circuits between the two members.

Single EVPN Instance

The IX only has a requirement for a single Layer 2 service for PPI. This can be accomplished with a single EVPN instance (EVI) per Provider Edge (PE) router, as illustrated in Figure 3-6. PNI can be interested, because the IX can provide PNI as a service with dedicated bandwidth allocations for an additional fee. This model would require an EVI per PNI agreement.

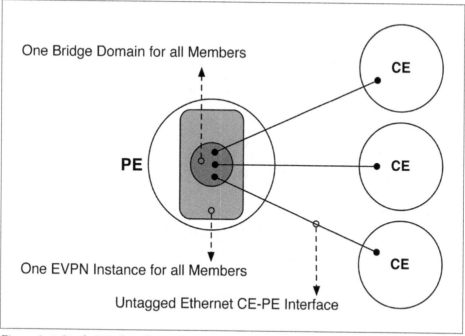

Figure 3-6. Single EVI for all members in IX

Bridge domains, or VLANs, are created within an EVI. Each EVI is capable of multiple bridge domains, but in the context of PPI, only a single bridge domain is needed for the global Layer 2 service. Each member CE connects into the PPI Layer 2 service.

Multihoming

The IX can provide link-level and node-level protection through EVPN Ethernet segments (ES) to enable multihoming, as depicted in Figure 3-7. Each member has its own EVPN Segment ID (ESI) which is used for EVPN mass withdraw and loop prevention. Each ESI can operate in all-active or active-standby node.

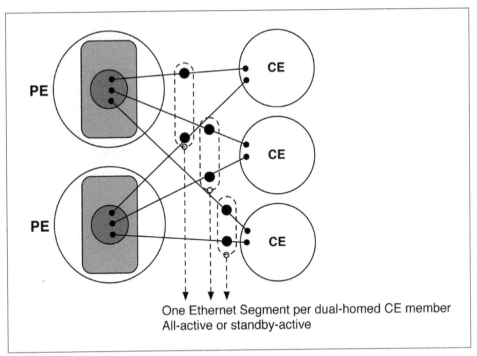

One Ethernet Segment per dual-homed CE member
All-active or standby-active

Figure 3-7. All-active multihoming for IX members

Each ESI supports either a static LAG or IEEE 803.2AX Link Aggregation Control Protocol (LACP). The same EVI and bridge domain exists on each pair of PE routers.

EVPN Control Plane

EVPN requires a full mesh BGP session between all PE routers in the IX network. There are two common options: use a route reflector or create a manual full mesh. The generally accepted method is to use route reflectors, but there is no right or wrong answer. Manually configuring a full-mesh actually provides faster convergence; however, it's at the expense of additional BGP state and having to touch every PE router when expanding the network.

Route Reflectors

The most common method to interconnect PE routers is through a route reflector, as shown in Figure 3-8. The benefit is that each PE has a single BGP session to a route reflector but receives every other PE prefix and next-hop, because the route reflector makes a copy of each PE prefix for each client.

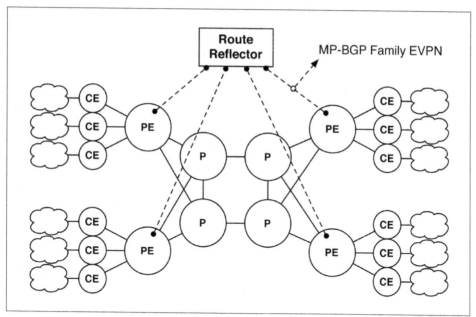

Figure 3-8. Single route reflector for EVPN PE routers

When you add additional PE routers in the topology, you need to set up only a single BGP connection between the new PE and route reflector. The only drawback is that the route reflector is a single point of failure. A more common option is to deploy a pair or set of route reflectors, as demonstrated in Figure 3-9.

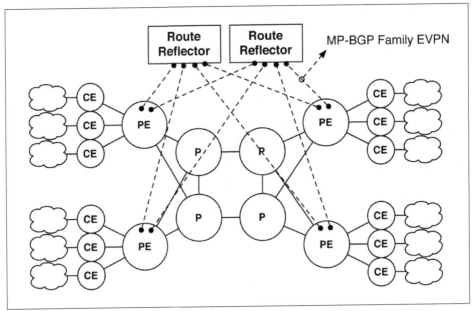

Figure 3-9. Redundant route reflectors for EVPN PE routers

Now each PE has two BGP connections. If a route reflector has issues, the other route reflector is there for protection. Due to the nature of BGP, the two route reflectors operate in an active-active mode.

Full mesh

Generally, the least desirable option is to manually create a full mesh of BGP sessions between each PE router, as depicted in Figure 3-10.

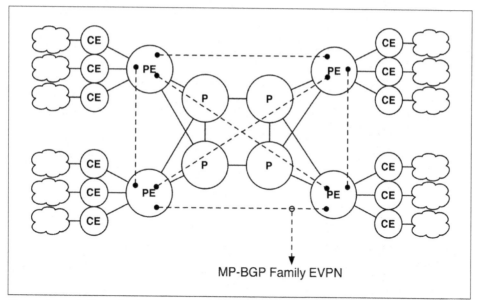

Figure 3-10. Full mesh of EVPN PE routers with no route reflector

Funny enough, it actually provides the fastest convergence. However, it's very difficult to operate without full automation. There's also generally an upper limit to how many BGP sessions you want per PE, so the route reflector helps logical scale in larger network topologies.

EVPN and RS

Now that we understand the general EVPN and RS requirements from a control-plane point of view, what does it look like? Let's roll the two designs together into a single view, as shown in Figure 3-11.

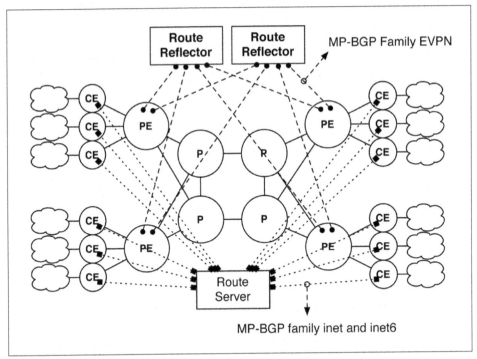

Figure 3-11. Bringing EVPN and RS into the architecture

Each CE-RS session uses Multiprotocol BGP (MP-BGP) for both IPv4 and IPv6 peering for PPI. Each PE-RR session uses MP-BGP family EVPN for MAC address learning. Let's break down what each member is learning and why:

CE-PE

There is no active control-plane protocol on the CE-PE link. However, the CE will use Address Resolution Protocol (ARP) for MAC address learning, and the PE will assist in the unknown unicast flooding.

PE-P

This generally depends on the underlay being used. For EVPN-MPLS, it's very common to use an interior gateway protocol (IGP) such as Open Shortest Path First (OSPF) or Intermediate System to Intermediate System (IS-IS); this allows RSVP to use traffic engineering. For EVPN-VXLAN, it's common to use either an IGP or BGP; just as long as each PE router has IPv4 connectivity to every other PE router.

CE-CE

Pure Layer 2. It doesn't matter if it's IPv4 or IPv6. Each CE cares only about MAC address learning.

CE-RS

Each CE peers with the RS via MP-BGP with family inet and inet6. The RS reflects all of the other member prefixes and next-hop to every other member in the IX network.

PE-RR

Each PE peers with the route reflector via MP-BGP with family evpn. The route reflector copies all of the other PE prefixes and next-hop to every other PE in the network. MAC addresses are learned on each PE and flooded throughout the topology.

In summary, EVPN is an excellent control-plane protocol for an IX use case. It is agnostic to the underlying data-plane encapsulation, provides all-active forwarding, efficient unknown unicast flooding, and is based on open standards.

EVPN-VXLAN

One of the biggest choices in an EVPN architecture is which data-plane encapsulation to use. We'll walk through each function and look at the trade-offs. Some encapsulations lend themselves better to traffic protection and engineering, whereas other encapsulations take better advantage of low-cost hardware at the sacrifice of traffic protection.

The first requirement for EVPN-VXLAN is an IPv4 fabric. Generally, this is accomplished with OSPF, IS-IS, or even BGP. The only requirement is that each PE has loopback reachability with every other PE in the topology.

EVPN-VXLAN assumes that each PE in the topology acts as a VXLAN Layer 2 gateway. The PE would take Ethernet frames from the PE and encapsulate them into a VXLAN header and then transmit them to the remote PE via the IPv4 fabric. Each PE would also have a Virtual Tunnel End-Point (VTEP) used for MAC address learning. Generally, the PE loopback is used for the VTEP address. As each PE learns local MAC addresses, it will advertise each MAC address to every other VTEP in the network, using its loopback address as the next-hop.

Traffic Protection

The only traffic protection available on standard IPv4 fabrics would be offered through the native IGP. In the case of OSPF and IS-IS, you can use LFAs, as depicted in Figure 3-12.

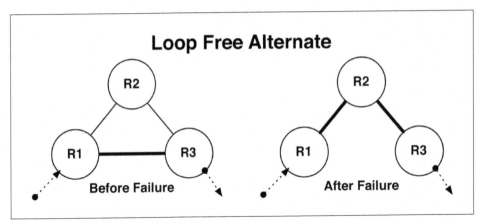

Figure 3-12. LFA architecture

The idea in Figure 3-12 is that traffic is entering the topology in R1 and needs to exit on R3. During normal operation, R1 has a direct route to R3 and takes the southern path. Now, assume that the southern path R1–R3 has failed. LFA allows R1 to quickly forward traffic to the next best path, which is R1–R2, while the IGP is reconverging. After the IGP is converged, the LFA repair is removed and recalculated. LFA works really great in very specific triangle topologies such as that shown in Figure 3-12. The problem is that in the real world no one builds triangle topologies.

Now take a look at Figure 3-13, which shows a square topology with LFA enabled. Assume that traffic is entering at R1 and exiting at R3. During normal operations, R1 has a direct link to R3 and everything is good.

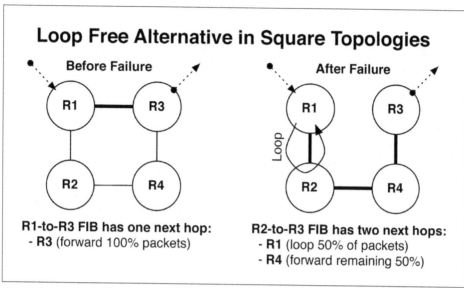

Figure 3-13. LFAs in square topologies

Now consider if the R1–R3 link fails. What happens while the IGP tries to converge? LFA kicks in with the next best path, which is R1–R2. So R1 forwards all traffic destined to R3 through R2. The problem is that R2 hasn't reconverged yet and still has an old forwarding and routing table. From the perspective of R2, traffic can reach R2 via R2–R1–R3 or R2–R4–R3. So, it will perform Equal-Cost Multipath (ECMP) and send half the traffic to R1 and the other half to R4. Because half of the traffic is sent back to R1, where the LFA repair happened, it's looped back to R2, because it's the repair route. In summary, half the packets are looped back to R1, whereas the other half manage to get through via R4. Therefore, EVPN-VXLAN with a standard IPv4 fabric is subject to microloops, regardless of whether you use LFA. There's no traffic protection with EVPN-VXLAN and standard IPv4 fabrics.

Traffic Engineering

With the lack of MPLS and RSVP, we have to resort to crude traffic engineering using BGP attributes as AS_PATH padding, as illustrated in Figure 3-14. The topology on the left shows an ingress flow on PE1 and egressing on PE4, with no traffic engineering applied. The flow simply follows the shortest path according to the BGP best-path selection algorithm.

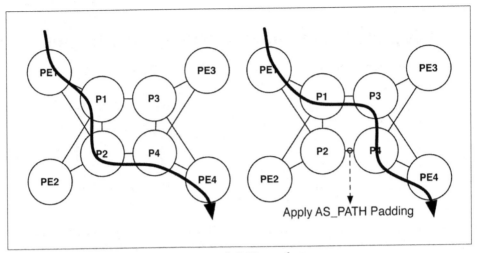

Figure 3-14. Crude traffic engineering with BGP attributes

If you wanted to influence the traffic from PE1 to PE4 to always take the northern route between P1–P3, you can apply AS_PATH padding between P2–P4, as shown on the right in Figure 3-14. Now the traffic will change from PE1–P1–P2–P4–PE4 to PE1–P1–P3–P4–PE4 due to the AS_PATH being longer between P2–P4.

In summary, there really isn't much you can do with traffic engineering on EVPN-VXLAN besides playing with BGP attributes.

Load Balancing

To better understand how load balancing will work with EVPN-VXLAN, let's break down the overall data going across the wire as seen in Figure 3-15. VXLAN is basically a MAC-over-UDP encapsulation. The original Ethernet payload is buried behind a new Ethernet frame, IP packet, and UDP segment.

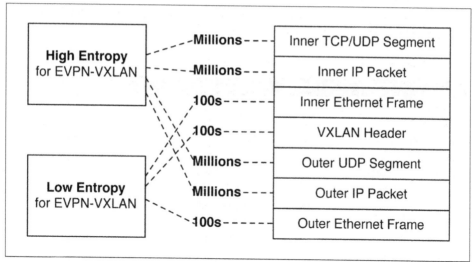

	Inner TCP/UDP Segment
High Entropy for EVPN-VXLAN	Inner IP Packet
	Inner Ethernet Frame
	VXLAN Header
	Outer UDP Segment
Low Entropy for EVPN-VXLAN	Outer IP Packet
	Outer Ethernet Frame

Millions — Inner TCP/UDP Segment
Millions — Inner IP Packet
100s — Inner Ethernet Frame
100s — VXLAN Header
Millions — Outer UDP Segment
Millions — Outer IP Packet
100s — Outer Ethernet Frame

Figure 3-15. EVPN-VXLAN load-balancing entropy

One thing to note is that VXLAN always uses a UDP destination port of 4,789, so we'll lose 16-bits of entropy on the destination port alone. However, the PE router can still use 16-bits of entropy on the UDP source port. The VXLAN header has 24-bits of entropy for the VXLAN network identifier (VNID), but in an IX environment we'll only be using a single Virtual Network Instance (VNI) for the PPI, and perhaps a few hundred VNIs for PNI. The outer IP source and destination address has the potential to have millions of combinations, but in an IX use case, it's only as large as the number of PE devices in the topology, which will probably be less than 100.

However, EVPN-VXLAN will still have really good load balancing throughout the entire topology, thanks to the UDP source port in combination with the other entropy data plane. Each P router has to look at only the outer IP and UDP segment to get enough entropy to hash efficiently.

Platform Options

Now that we understand how EVPN-VXLAN works in an IX and the limitations when it comes to traffic engineering and traffic protection, the next step is to determine what platform works the best. Just like before, the best method is to map the requirements and attributes to a set of options and see which one makes the most sense.

Core

Let's take a look at the core device for the EVPN-VXLAN topology. In this context, the only real requirement is to be able to route IP packets. All of the other attributes are dependent on the business policies, risk, and access options to member equipment. Table 3-2 reviews some of the options.

Table 3-2. Platform comparison for EVPN-VXLAN core devices

Attribute	PTX5000	MX2020	QFX10016	QFX5200
OSPF/IS-IS/BGP	Yes	Yes	Yes	Yes
BFD interval	10 ms	10 ms	10 ms	300 ms
100GbE density	240	320	480	32
40GbE density	384	480	576	64
Packet buffer	100 ms	100 ms	100 ms	40 µs
Silicon	Juniper ExpressPlus	Juniper Trio	Juniper Q5	Broadcom Tomahawk
IPv4 FIB	2M	10M	256K/2M	128K
IPv6 FIB	2M	10M	256K/2M	98K
PACL	384K	16M	64K	1K
Integrated Optical	Yes	Yes	Yes	No

Also keep in mind the inherent lack of traffic engineering and traffic protection in EVPN-VXLAN, because it's based on a simple IPv4 fabric and standard IGP. In my opinion, unless you require advanced optical integration, the Juniper QFX might be a better fit in the context of a core device for EVPN-VXLAN. The reason being is that the PTX and MX devices are geared toward high-end features, high scale, and optical integration. Given the limitations of EVPN-VXLAN and the requirements of an IX network with a single EVI and bridge domain, the extra features and logical scale just isn't needed.

The better option at this point is the Juniper QFX10000 for the following reasons:

- You can easily upgrade to EVPN-MPLS in the future.
- Higher port density.
- Larger packet buffer.
- Optical integration.

In summary, the Juniper QFX10000 would probably make the best EVPN-VXLAN core switch, given the humble requirements. The Juniper QFX5200 would functionally work just fine, but at the expense of no buffer, no scale, and no upgrade path to EVPN-MPLS.

Edge

Let's take a look at the edge requirements for EVPN-VXLAN. The biggest difference is that we now have to only look at platforms that support VXLAN Layer 2 gateway. I

---

have removed the PTX and added the Juniper QFX5100 for completeness, as shown in Table 3-3.

Table 3-3. Platform comparison for EVPN-VXLAN edge devices

Attribute	MX2020	QFX10016	QFX5200	QFX5100
OSPF/IS-IS/BGP	Yes	Yes	Yes	Yes
BFD Interval	10 ms	10 ms	300 ms	300 ms
25/50GbE density	N/A	N/A	128/64	N/A
100GbE density	320	480	32	0
40GbE density	480	576	64	32
10GbE density	1,920	2,304	128	102
Packet buffer	100 ms	50 ms	40 µs	50 µs
Silicon	Juniper Trio	Juniper Q5	Broadcom Tomahawk	Broadcom Trident-2
MAC FIB	1M	1M*	136K	288K
IPv4 FIB	10M	256K/2M	128K	128K
IPv6 FIB	10M	256K/2M	98K	64K
PACL	16M	60K	1K	1K
Integrated optical	Yes	Yes	No	No

One interesting thing to note is that if you require 25/50GbE access ports, the only option would be the Juniper QFX5200. One big question to ask yourself is do you need packet buffer? If so, the only viable options are the Juniper MX and Juniper QFX10000. If this was a green-field installation, the Juniper QFX10000 would make more sense than the Juniper MX, simply because you do not need the additional logical scale. However, in a migration, reallocating an existing Juniper MX would make a lot of sense.

The two best options for a green-field installation would be the Juniper QFX10000 or the Juniper QFX5000 Series. The biggest decision you need to make is how much port density do you need and how much packet buffer.

Summary

EVPN-VXLAN is a really great way to build a simple, functional IX network. However, it comes at the expense of no traffic protection and no traffic engineering. Many large IX networks take pride in a very high uptime and always being able to quickly repair traffic during failures. If yours is a prestigious IX network such as this, you might want to consider EVPN-MPLS instead, as EVPN-VXLAN isn't able to provide the extra level of traffic protection and traffic engineering.

However, if you're a startup or small IX that needs to build a cost-effective network, EVPN-VXLAN is very attractive. You can use cost optimized hardware in the core and edge and still get the basic EVPN functionality at the expense of additional resiliency in the network.

EVPN-MPLS

The other data-plane encapsulation for EVPN is MPLS. Obviously, MPLS comes with an entire suite of traffic protection and traffic engineering tools at your fingertips. EVPN-MPLS is a very robust and feature-rich architecture when it comes to building the next-generation IX network. For more information about Juniper's MPLS implementation, check out *MPLS in the SDN Era* (O'Reilly, 2016) by Antonio Sanchez Monge and Krzysztof Grzegorz Szarkowicz.

Traffic Protection

Traffic protection in MPLS comes in two common forms: facility protection and path protection, as illustrated in Figure 3-16. The path protection Layered Service Provider (LSP) can be an active or standby LSP that is used if the primary LSP were to fail. Facility protection or "Bypass" LSPs are used when a protected link or node fails. While the control plane is still reconverging, the bypass LSPs provide a local repair service for any affected LSPs to allow continued forwarding via an alternative path. After the control-plane convergences and the affected LSPs are rerouted, the bypass LSPs become inactive. This is referred to as *make-before-break*.

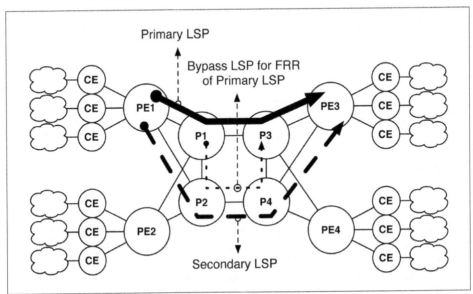

Figure 3-16. Extensive traffic protection with MPLS and RSVP

There are many variations and options when it comes to traffic protection with MPLS. You can use either link or node protection and create many path protection services.

Traffic Engineering

When using RSVP-MPLS, you can also explicitly route an LSP, thereby defining the exact path an LSP should take through a topology, regardless of IGP metrics, as shown in Figure 3-17. There are many reasons to use explicit routing, such as avoiding hotspots or simply geographic redundancy.

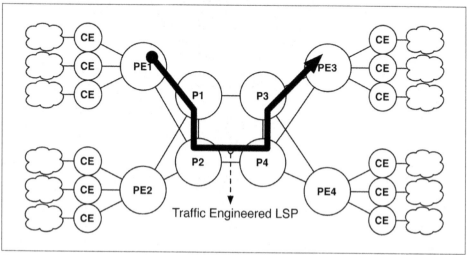

Figure 3-17. Basic MPLS RSVP traffic engineering with EVPN

Explicit Route Objects (EROs) are generally calculated with offline traffic engineering tools that try to analyze the traffic and optimize the path of each LSP. A great alternative to offline calculation is performing online or real-time calculations. Juniper Northstar performs LSP optimization in real time by using Path Computation Element Protocol (PCEP) to dynamically signal the EROs. In addition, Juniper Northstar can handle multilayer packet optical integration with abstract topologies.

Another helpful RSVP option feature is to use Shared-Risk Link Groups (SRLGs). SRLGs let MPLS be aware of links that have some common fate-sharing attribute. For example, all links that are routed via the same fiber conduit would share the same SRLG value and you can ensure that protection LSPs (path or facility) aren't subject to a common fate if the fiber conduit were to be cut.

One new concept is a container LSP with which you can create a set of sub-LSPs, as shown in Figure 3-18. The idea is that the head and tail of the container LSP is pinned to the ingress and egress PE, but the sub-LSPs that make up the container can be routed along other paths in the topology independent of one another.

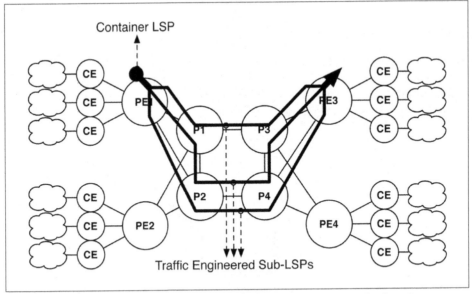

Figure 3-18. Advanced container LSP with multiple traffic engineered sub-LSPs

Although PE1 has a single LSP to PE3, it effectively has three sub-LSPs that each follow different paths in the topology for better load balancing and failure recovery characteristics. Each sub-LSP is subject to the same traffic protection and traffic engineering schemes as a regular LSP.

Load Balancing

Load balancing with MPLS is a little different than VXLAN or IP. Figure 3-19 shows the various fields on the data plane. Notice that the dotted boxes indicate an optional field in the data plane.

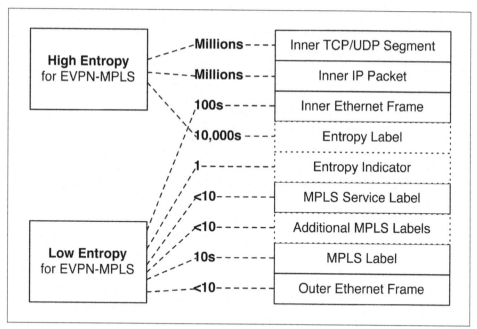

Figure 3-19. High entropy versus low entropy for EVPN-MPLS

The best way EVPN-MPLS can get very good load balancing is looking deep into the payload or using an entropy label. In the IX use case, some fields only render tens or hundreds of possible values and do not offer very good load balancing alone.

Load balancing with EVPN-MPLS can also happen at several different points in the topology, as demonstrated in Figure 3-20. The first point of load balancing is on the CE–PE links if the CE is deployed with all-active load balancing within the ESI. The next point of load balancing is across multiple LSPs on the ingress PE router.

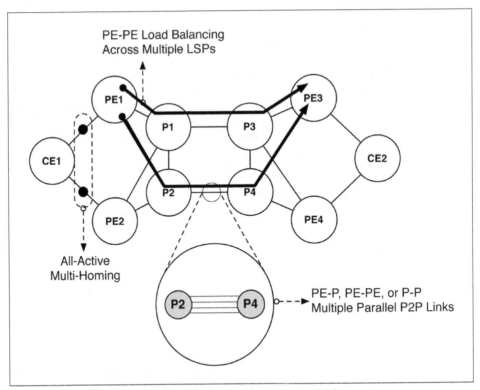

Figure 3-20. Multiple levels of load balancing for EVPN-MPLS

The final point of load balancing happens between the PE-P, PE-PE, or P-PE nodes; some routers can have multiple parallel point-to-point links. This can be either multiple Layer 3 links or a Link Aggregation (LAG).

Multiple parallel Layer 3 links

The first option is standard multiple parallel Layer 3 links, as shown in Figure 3-21. In this case, P1 has three links to P2. There are six incoming flows on P1 that need to be load balanced equally across each of the parallel links.

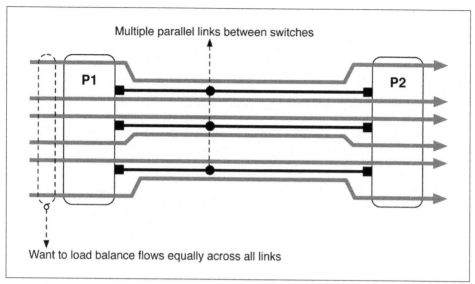

Figure 3-21. Load balancing across multiple parallel Layer 3 links

Obviously, each individual Layer 3 link would need its own IP address and subnetwork. One thing to consider is that different nodes in the network might contain a different number of point-to-point links between them. For example, A–B might have three links, whereas B–C might have five. You can use offline tools such as Juniper's NorthStar TE Controller to determine how to balance the A–C traffic.

Using LAGs

The next alternative is to simply create a single LSP from PE to PE, as depicted in Figure 3-22. P1 and P2 have three links in a single LAG. The LSP simply forwards over the LAG. Load balancing is dependent on the existence of entropy within the packet.

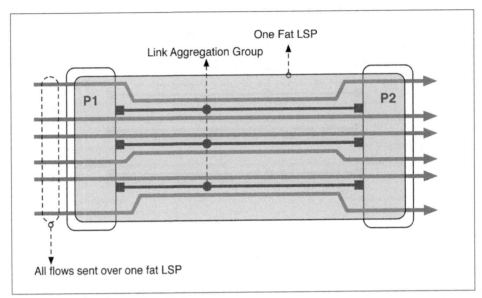

Figure 3-22. One fat LSP load balancing

If the PE router supports entropy labels, it will use the original payload to derive the load balancing for the entropy label. If there's no entropy label present, the load-balancing hash is performed by inspecting the payload of the packet by looking beyond the MPLS label stack.

Using parallel Layer 3 links

The next option is to use multiple LSPs, as shown in Figure 3-23, as opposed to a single LSP. Flows are load balanced over the multiple LSPs on the ingress PE instead of at each hop while traversing the network.

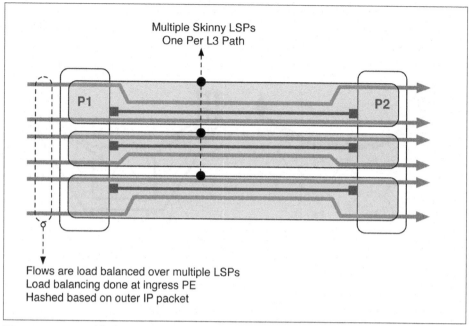

Figure 3-23. *Load balancing across multiple skinny LSPs*

One advantage of multiple LSPs is that load balancing becomes deterministic because it only happens on the ingress router and not hop by hop. Another advantage is that many LSPs exhibit better recovery behaviors because LSPs can be spread across all the available resources, much like the container-LSP/sub-LSP example described earlier.

MPLS Options Summary

There are many ways to accomplish load balancing in an MPLS topology. Each option has its own advantages and disadvantages. There's no right or wrong way to design load balancing, as each option has been designed for a particular use case. Table 3-4 describes three of the most LSP architectures.

Table 3-4. *Fat versus skinny LSPs with RSVP*

Attributes	One fat LSP with entropy	One fat LSP without entropy	Multiple skinny LSPs
Links between adjacent switches	LAG	LAG	LAG or parallel Layer 3 links
Load balancing over network paths	No	No	Yes
Where traffic is distributed	Each hop	Each hop	Ingress PE
Load balancing a function of	Entropy label	Hash on MPLS headers	Hash of payload at ingress PE

In an IX use case, the multiple skinny LSP method seems to be more fitting because we can load balance over more network paths, get better traffic protection, and better load balancing, as shown in Figure 3-24.

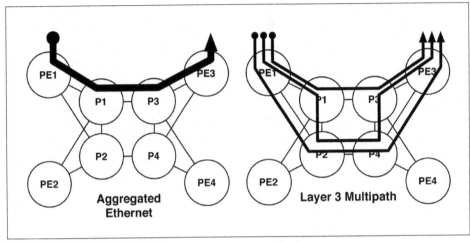

Figure 3-24. Aggregated Ethernet versus Layer 3 multipath

For example, the figure shows that a single LSP is capped for capacity between P1–P3. To add more capacity to the network, you need to physically add more links between P1–P3. However, with Layer 3 multipath, you can simply break up the single LSP into multiple LSPs and use traffic engineering and traffic protection to increase the capacity without the need to physically install new links.

Platform Options

Now that we understand how EVPN-MPLS works in an IX and the advanced feature when it comes to traffic engineering and traffic protection, the next step is to determine what platform works the best. Just like before, the best method is to map the requirements and attributes to a set of options and see which one makes the most sense.

Core

Let's take a look at the core device for the EVPN-MPLS topology. In this context, the key requirements are to support traffic protection and traffic engineering. All of the other attributes are dependent on the business policies, risk, and access options to member equipment. Let's review some of the options in Table 3-5.

Table 3-5. Platform comparison for EVPN-MPLS core devices

Attribute	PTX	MX	QFX10000	QFX5200
OSPF/IS-IS/BGP	Yes	Yes	Yes	Yes
BFD interval	10 ms	10 ms	10 ms	300 ms
100GbE density	240	320	480	32
40GbE density	384	480	576	64
Packet buffer	100 ms	100 ms	50 ms	40 µs
Silicon	Juniper ExpressPlus	Juniper Trio	Juniper Q5	Broadcom Tomahawk
IPv4 FIB	2M	10M	512K	128K
IPv6 FIB	2M	10M	512K	98K
PACL	384K	16M	30K	1K
Integrated optical	Yes	Yes	Yes	No
TE	Yes	Yes	Yes	Yes
TE+/PCEP	Yes	Yes	Yes	No

The lack of packet buffer and integrated optical rules out the Juniper QFX5200 as an EVPN-MPLS core device. The decision becomes a little bit more difficult when looking at the PTX, MX, and Juniper QFX10000. We can probably rule out the Juniper MX as a core device, because we simply do not need the additional logical scale in the core. This leaves the Juniper PTX and Juniper QFX10000 as potential candidates for EVPN-MPLS core devices. If you need additional optical integration, the Juniper PTX makes more sense. The PTX also has more packet buffer and scale, although you could argue we don't need the additional logical scale. However, the Juniper QFX10000 offers more port density. There's really no right or wrong answer here. It all boils down to what you consider more important for your environment.

Edge

Let's take a look at the edge requirements for EVPN-MPLS. The biggest difference is that we now have to look only at platforms that support EVPN-MPLS and split-horizon labels for loop protection. I have removed the Juniper QFX5200 because it doesn't support split-horizon labels and EVPN-MPLS; this is because the Broadcom chipset in the Juniper QFX5200 can't handle more than three labels. The two viable platforms are the Juniper MX and Juniper QFX10000, as shown in Table 3-6.

Table 3-6. Platform comparison for EVPN-MPLS edge devices

Attribute	MX2020	QFX10016
OSPF/IS-IS/BGP	Yes	Yes
BFD interval	10 ms	10 ms
25/50GbE density	N/A	N/A
40GbE density	480	576
10GbE density	1,920	2,304

Attribute	MX2020	QFX10016
Packet buffer	100 ms	100 ms
Silicon	Juniper Trio	Juniper Q5
MAC FIB	1M	1M
IPv4 FIB	10M	256K/2M
IPv6 FIB	10M	256K/2M
PACL	16M	30K
Integrated optical	Yes	Yes

Thankfully, this decision is a little bit easier on two fronts: there's only two options, and it's only a matter of logical scale. In an IX use case, we're only learning a single MAC address from each CE router. If we had 2,000 IX members, that's only 2,000 MAC addresses. Because we use an RS and do not participate in learning network addresses, the only thing we need to worry about is the number of MAC addresses. The Juniper QFX10000 makes more sense here just because you don't need the additional logical scale. However, if you need additional packet buffer or better integrated optics, it could push you back to the Juniper MX, instead.

Summary

This chapter has taken apart the IX use case and inspected every basic element. We took our time and reviewed the technical requirement of each element and the different connection, access, and peering models. After we had a full understanding of the use case, we compared the requirements against existing technology and the new EVPN technology. EVPN was the clear winner and provided the best in class features required for an IX network.

We took a close look at how to design EVPN to support an IX network: a single EVI and bridge domain to create the Layer 2 service; ESI for redundant member connections; and how to combine route reflectors and RSs in the overall EVPN and IX architecture.

Next, we examined the data-plane options between EVPN-VXLAN and EVPAN-MPLS. Each option is optimized for different vectors such as cost, traffic protection, and traffic engineering. Depending on the size, scale, and environment of the IX, you have an option to use either EVPN-VXLAN or EVPN-MPLS to get the job done. Finally, we took a look at the platform options for both EVPN-VXLAN and EVPN-MPLS.

EVPN is the future of IX networks and will become commonplace in the years to come. It's simply the next natural progression of technology.

Chapter Review Questions

1. What's the difference between an RS and route reflector?

   a. Route reflector is for iBGP, and RS is for eBGP

   b. Both route reflector and RS do not change the next-hop for clients on the same network

   c. RS will modify the MED

   d. RS will modify the community

2. How many VLANs does an IX need for PPI?

   a. 1

   b. 2

   c. 3

   d. 4

3. How does EVPN support multihoming?

   a. Communities

   b. ES

   c. ESI

   d. LACP

4. What's the big disadvantage of EVPN-VXLAN?

   a. No traffic engineering

   b. No traffic protection

   c. No multihoming

   d. Microloops

5. What's the advantage of EVPN-VXLAN?

   a. Cost

   b. Speed

   c. Works with existing equipment

   d. None

6. What's the advantage of EVPN-MPLS?

   a. Traffic engineering

   b. Traffic protection

   c. Cost

d. Performance

Chapter Review Answers

1. **Answer: A and B.** Both the RS and reflector will never modify the next-hop for clients on the same network. Route reflector is only for iBGP, and the RS is primarily for eBGP.

2. **Answer: A.** An IX just needs a single VLAN for the Layer 2 service for PPI.

3. **Answer: A, B, C, and D.** EVPN supports all-active multihoming with ES that are identified by an ESI. The ESI is advertised to other PEs through BGP communities. LACP is used between the PE and CE.

4. **Answer: A, B, and D.** EVPN-VXLAN lacks traffic engineering and traffic protection because it's a standard IPv4 fabric. LFA doesn't work in Clos or square topologies and can result in microloops while the IGP reconverges.

5. **Answer: A and C.** EVPN-VXLAN can operate on cost-optimized hardware. In terms of the core, any existing equipment that can speak standard IPv4 could be used.

6. **Answer: A and B.** EVPN-MPLS can use RSVP, PCEP, and Juniper NorthStar to provide excellent traffic protection and traffic engineering. Performance is debatable because it depends on the hardware platform. Both EVPN-VXLAN and EVPN-MPLS are processed in hardware, so the overall speed would be similar.

CHAPTER 4

Performance and Scale

One of the more challenging tasks of a network architect is ensuring that a design put forth meets the end-to-end solution requirements. The first step is identifying all of the roles in an architecture. This could be as simple as defining the edge, core, aggregation, and access tiers in the network. Each role has a specific set of responsibilities in terms of functionality and requirements. To map a product to a role in an architecture, the product must meet or exceed the requirements and functionality required by each role for which it's being considered. Thus, building an end-to-end solution is a bit like a long chain: it's only as strong as the weakest link.

The most common method of trying to identify the product capabilities, performance, and scale are through datasheets or the vendor's account team. However, the best method is actually testing going through a proof of concept or certification cycle. Build out all of the roles and products in the architecture and measure the end-to-end results; this method quickly flushes out any issues before moving into procurement and production.

This chapter walks through all of the performance and scaling considerations required to successfully map a product into a specific role in an end-to-end architecture. Attributes such as MAC address, host entries, and IPv4 prefixes will be clearly spelled out. Armed with this data, you will be able to easily map the Juniper QFX10000 Series into many different roles in your existing network.

Design Considerations

Before any good network architect jumps head first into performance and scaling requirements, he will need to make a list of design considerations. Each design consideration places an additional tax on the network that is beyond the scope of traditional performance and scaling requirements.

Juniper Architectures Versus Open Architectures

The other common design option is to weight the benefits of Juniper architectures with open architectures. The benefits of a Juniper architecture is that it has been designed specifically to enable turn-key functionality, but the downside is that it requires a certain set of products to operate. The other option is open architecture. The benefit to an open architecture is that it can be supported across a set of multiple vendors, but the downside is that you might lose some capabilities that are only available in the Juniper architectures.

Generally, it boils down to the size of the network. If you know that your network will never grow past a certain size and you're procuring all of the hardware upfront, using a Juniper architecture might simply outweigh all of the benefits of an open architecture, because there isn't a need to support multiple vendors.

Another scenario is that your network is large enough that you can't build it all at once and want a pay-as-you-grow option over the next five years. A logical option would be to implement open architectures so that as you build out your network, you aren't limited in the number of options going forward. Another option would be to take a hybrid approach and build out the network in points of delivery (POD). Each POD could have the option to take advantage of proprietary architectures or not.

Each business and network are going to have any number of external forces that weigh on the decision to go with Juniper architectures or open architectures; more often than not, these decisions change over time. Unless you know 100 percent of these nuances up front, it's important to select a networking platform that offers both Juniper architectures and open architectures.

The Juniper QFX10000 Series offers the best of both worlds. It equally supports Juniper architectures as well as open architectures:

Juniper architectures
> The Juniper QFX10000 supports a plug-and-play Ethernet and fabric called Junos Fusion for Data Center (JFDC), which offers a single point of management for a topology of up to 64 top-of-rack (ToR) switches. JFDC allows for simple software upgrades one switch at a time, because it's based on simple protocols such as IEEE 802.1BR and JSON.

Open architectures
> The Juniper QFX10000 supports Ethernet VPN (EVPN)-Virtual Extensible LAN (VXLAN), which is quickly gaining traction as the de facto "open Ethernet fabric." It also supports Multichassis Link Aggregation (MC-LAG) so that downstream devices can simply use IEEE 802.1AX Link Aggregation Control Protocol (LACP) to connect and transport data. The Juniper QFX10000 also supports a wide range of open protocols such as Border Gateway Protocol (BGP), Open

Shortest Path First (OSPF), Intermediate System to Intermediate System (IS-IS), and a suite of Multiprotocol Label Switching (MPLS) technologies.

The Juniper QFX10000 makes a great choice no matter where you place it in your network. You could choose to deploy an open architecture today and then change to a Juniper architecture in the future. One of the best tools in creating a winning strategy is to keep the number of options high.

Performance

With the critical design considerations out of the way, now it's time to focus on the performance characteristics of the Juniper QFX10000 series. Previously, in Chapter 1, we explored the Juniper Q5 chipset and how the Packet Forwarding Engine (PFE) and Switch Interface Board (SIB) work together in a balancing act of port density versus performance. Performance can be portrayed through two major measurements: throughput and latency. Let's take a closer look at each.

Throughput

RFC 2544 was used as a foundation for the throughput testing. The test packet sizes ranged from 64 to 9,216 bytes, as shown in Figure 4-1. Both IPv4 and IPv6 traffic was used during the testing, and the results are nearly identical, so I displayed them as a single line. L2, L3, and VXLAN traffic was used during these tests.

The Juniper QFX10000 supports line-rate processing for packets above 144 bytes. 64 byte packets are roughly processed at 50 percent; as you work your way up to 100 bytes, they're processed around 80 percent. At 144 bytes, the Juniper QFX10000 supports line-rate.

When it comes to designing an application-specific integrated circuit (ASIC), there are three main trade-offs: packet processing, power, and data path (buffering and scheduling). To create the Juniper Q5 chip with large buffers, high logical scale, and lots of features, a design trade-off had to be made. It was either increase the power, decrease the logical scale, reduce the buffer, or reduce the packet processing. Given the use cases for the data center, it's common to not operate at full line-rate for packets under 200 bytes. You can see this design decision across all vendors and chipsets. Reducing packet processing for packets under 144 bytes was an easy decision, given that the majority of use cases do not require it; thus, the Juniper Q5 chip gets to take full advantage of low power, high scale, lots of features, and large buffer.

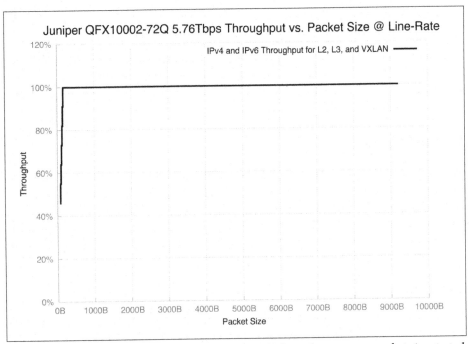

Figure 4-1. Graph showing Juniper QFX10002-72Q throughput versus packet size, tested at 5,760Gbps

> To learn more detailed test reports regarding EVPN-VXLAN, check out NetworkTest's results (*http://www.networktest.com/ jnprqfx10k/jnprqfx10k.pdf*). Big thanks to Michael Pergament for organizing the EVPN-VXLAN test results.

The data-plane encapsulation is also important to consider when measuring throughput. The following scenarios are very common in the data center:

- Switching Ethernet frames
- Routing IP packets
- Encapsulating VXLAN headers
- Switching MPLS labels
- IPv4 versus IPv6

Each data-plane encapsulation requires different packet processing and lookups. The throughput graph in Figure 4-1 is an aggregate of IPv4, IPv6, switching, routing, MPLS, and VXLAN. The results were identical and so I combined them into a single throughput line. The Juniper Q5 chip has enough packet processing to handle a wide variety of data-plane encapsulations and actions (logging, policers, and filters) that it can handle five actions per packet without a drop in performance.

Latency

Latency is defined as the amount of time the network device takes to process a packet between ingress and egress port. The Juniper QFX10000 series has two ways to measure latency: within the same PFE, and between PFEs. If it's within the same PFE, the latency is roughly 2.5 μs. If it's between PFEs, it's roughly 5.5 μs. There's also a lot of variance between packet size and port speed. Check out Figure 4-2 for more detail.

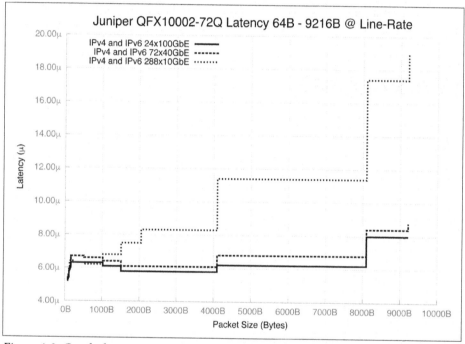

Figure 4-2. Graph showing Juniper QFX10002-72Q latency versus packet size for 100/40/10GbE, tested at line-rate

The tests performed for Figure 4-2 were done between PFEs, which is the worst-case scenario. For example, it would be between port et-0/0/0 and et-0/0/71 which are located on different PFEs.

Logical Scale

Knowing the logical scale for a particular platform is crucial for understanding how well it can perform in a specific role in an overall network architecture. Most often, it requires you invest a lot of time testing the platform to really understand the details of the platform.

One caveat to logical scale is that it's always a moving target between software releases. Although the underlying hardware might be capable of more scale, the software must fully support and utilize it. Some logical scale is limited by physical constraints such as the number of ports. For example, the Juniper QFX10002-72Q supports only 144 aggregated interfaces. This seems like a very low number until you realize that the maximum number of 10GbE interfaces is 288; and if you bundle all of the interfaces with two members each, it's a total of 144 aggregated interfaces.

Table 4-1 takes a closer look at the logical scale as of the Juniper QFX10002-72Q running Junos 15.1X53D10.

Table 4-1. Juniper QFX10002-72Q logical scale based on Junos 15.1X53-D10

Attribute	Result
VLAN	4,093
RVI	4,093
Aggregated interfaces	144
Subinterfaces	16,000
vMembers	32,000 per PFE
MSTP instances	64
VSTP instances	510
PACL ingress terms	64,000
PACL egress filters	64,000
VACL ingress filters	4,093
VACL egress terms	4,093
VACL ingress filters	64,000
VACL egress filters	64,000
RACL ingress filters	10,000
RACL egress filters	10,000
RACL ingress terms	64,000
RACL egress terms	64,000
PACL policers	8,192
VACL policers	8,192
RACL policers	8,192
Firewall counters	64,000
BGP neighbors	4,000
OSPF adjacencies	1,000
OSPF areas	500
VRRP instances	2,000
BFD clients	1,000
VRFs	4,000

Attribute	Result
RSVP ingress LSPs	16,000
RSVP egress LSPs	16,000
RSVP transit LSPs	32,000
LDP sessions	1,000
LDP labels	115,000
GRE tunnels	4,000
ECMP	64-way
ARP—per PFE	64,000
MAC—per PFE	96,000
IPv4 FIB	256,000/2,000,000
IPv6 FIB	256,000/2,000,000
IPv4 hosts	2,000,000
IPv6 hosts	2,000,000
IPv4 RIB	10,000,000
IPv6 RIB	4,000,000

Some attributes are global maximums, whereas others are listed as per PFE. There are features such as MAC address learning and Access Control Lists (ACLs) that can be locally significant and applied per PFE. For example, if you install MAC address 00:00:00:00:00:AA on PFE-1, there's no need to install it on PFE-2, unless it's part of an aggregated interface. For attributes that are per PFE, you can just multiply that value by the number of PFEs in a system to calculate the global maximum. For example, the Juniper QFX10002-72Q has six PFEs, so you can multiply 6 for the number of MAC addresses, which is 576,000 globally.

Be aware that Table 4-1 shows the logical scale for the Juniper QFX10002-72Q based on Junos 15.1X53D10. Keep in mind that these scale numbers will change between software releases and improve over time.

Firewall Filter Usage

One of the more interesting scaling attributes are firewall filters, which you can apply anywhere within the system. Such filters could be per port, which would limit the network state to a particular ASIC within the system. You could apply other firewall filters to a VLAN, which would spread the firewall filter state across every single ASIC within the system. Over time, firewall filters will grow in size and scope; ultimately, there will exist state fragmentation on the switch, by the nature and scope of the firewall filters.

One common question is "How do you gauge how many system resources are being used by the firewall filters?" There's no easy way to do this directly in the Junos command line; it requires that you drop to the microkernel and perform some low-level commands to get hardware summaries.

Dropping to the microkernel is different depending on what platform you're using. For the Juniper QFX100002, it's fairly straightforward because there's a single FPC: FPC0. However, if you're using a Juniper QFX10008 or QFX10016, you'll need to log in to each line card separately to look at the hardware state.

In our example, we'll use a Juniper QFX10002-72Q. Let's drop into the shell:

```
{master:0}
root@st-v44-pdt-elite-01> start shell
root@st-v44-pdt-elite-01:~ # vty fpc0


TOR platform (2499 Mhz Pentium processor, 2047MB memory, 0KB flash)

TFXPC0(vty)#
```

The next step is to use the show filter hw summary command:

```
TFXPC0(vty)# show filter hw sum

  Chip Instance: 0

  HW Resource    Capacity        Used          Available
  - - - - - - - - - - - - - - - - - - - - - - - - - - - - - - - - - - -

  Filters        8191            2             8189
  Terms          65536           69            65467

  Chip Instance: 1

  HW Resource    Capacity        Used          Available
  - - - - - - - - - - - - - - - - - - - - - - - - - - - - - - - - - - -

  Filters        8191            2             8189
  Terms          65536           69            65467

  Chip Instance: 2

  HW Resource    Capacity        Used          Available
  - - - - - - - - - - - - - - - - - - - - - - - - - - - - - - - - - - -

  Filters        8191            2             8189
  Terms          65536           69            65467

  Chip Instance: 3

  HW Resource    Capacity        Used          Available
  - - - - - - - - - - - - - - - - - - - - - - - - - - - - - - - - - - -

  Filters        8191            2             8189
  Terms          65536           69            65467
```

```
Chip Instance: 4

HW Resource    Capacity         Used            Available
-----------------------------------------------------------
Filters        8191             2               8189
Terms          65536            69              65467

Chip Instance: 5

HW Resource    Capacity         Used            Available
-----------------------------------------------------------
Filters        8191             2               8189
Terms          65536            69              65467
```

The hardware resources are summarized by each PFE. In the case of the Juniper QFX10002-72Q, there are six ASICs. Firewall filters are broken down by the number of actual filters and the number of terms within. Each PFE on the Juniper QFX10000 can support 8,192 filters and 65,536 terms. These available allocations are global and must be shared for both ingress and egress filters.

I have created a simple firewall filter and applied it across an entire VLAN that has port memberships across every ASIC in the switch. Let's run the command and see how the allocations have changed:

```
TFXPC0(vty)# show filter hw sum

Chip Instance: 0

HW Resource    Capacity         Used            Available
-----------------------------------------------------------
Filters        8191             3               8188
Terms          65536            71              65465

Chip Instance: 1

HW Resource    Capacity         Used            Available
-----------------------------------------------------------
Filters        8191             3               8188
Terms          65536            71              65465

Chip Instance: 2

HW Resource    Capacity         Used            Available
-----------------------------------------------------------
Filters        8191             3               8188
Terms          65536            71              65465

Chip Instance: 3

HW Resource    Capacity         Used            Available
-----------------------------------------------------------
```

HW Resource	Capacity	Used	Available
Filters	8191	3	8188
Terms	65536	71	65465

Chip Instance: 4

HW Resource	Capacity	Used	Available
Filters	8191	3	8188
Terms	65536	71	65465

Chip Instance: 5

HW Resource	Capacity	Used	Available
Filters	8191	3	8188
Terms	65536	71	65465

The new VLAN filter has used a single filter and two term allocations on each ASIC within the system. However, if you created a simple firewall filter and applied it to only an interface, you would see allocations being used on a single ASIC.

Hashing

There are two types of hashing on the Juniper QFX10000 Series: static and adaptive. *Static hashing* is basically the type of hashing you are already familiar with: the switch looks at various fields in the packet header and makes a decision as to which interface to forward it. *Adaptive hashing* is a little bit different; it incorporates the packets per second (pps) or bits per second (bps) to ensure that new flows are not hashed to over-utilized links. The goal of adaptive hashing is to have all links in an aggregated Ethernet (AE) bundle being used equally over time.

Static

Every time you create an AE bundle in Junos, it internally allocates 256 buckets per AE. The buckets are equally divided across the number of member links. For example, if ae0 has 4 links, each member would be assigned 64 buckets each, as shown in Figure 4-3.

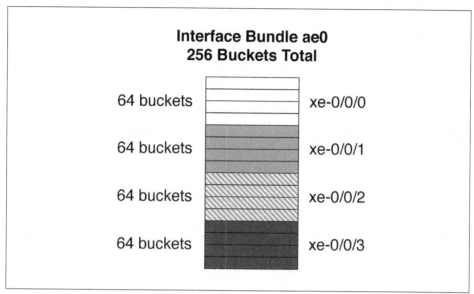

Figure 4-3. Static hashing on an interface bundle with four members

The number of buckets has no special meaning; it's just an arbitrary number that aligns well with Juniper's hashing algorithm. What matters is the distribution of buckets across the member interfaces. When all member interfaces are up and forwarding traffic, the number of buckets is equally distributed across each member interface. However, if there is a link failure, the number of buckets is redistributed to the remaining number of member interfaces. For example, if there were a single link failure in Figure 4-3, the three remaining links would receive 85, 85, and 86 buckets, respectively. When the failed link comes back up, the number of buckets assigned to each member interface would revert back to 64.

At a high level, ingress packets are inspected for interesting bits, which are passed on to the hash function, as depicted in Figure 4-4. The hash function takes the interesting bits as an input and outputs a number between 0 and 255, which corresponds to a bucket number. Also in the figure, the hash function decided to use bucket 224, which is currently owned by member interface xe-0/0/3. As soon as the ingress packet is mapped to a specific bucket, the traffic is forwarded to the corresponding interface.

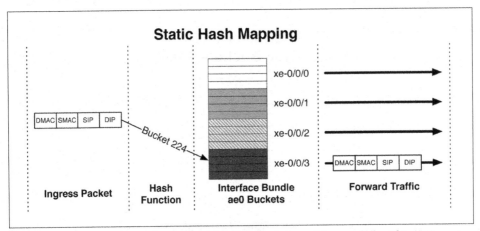

Figure 4-4. How ingress packets are mapped to buckets and forwarded within AE bundles

Adaptive

Adaptive load balancing uses the same bucket architecture as static hashing; however, the big difference is that adaptive can change bucket allocations on the fly. There are two stages with adaptive load balancing: calculation and adjustment. You can think of the calculation phase as a scan interval. Every so often the AE bundle will look at all of the member links and evaluate the amount of traffic flowing through each. The adjustment phase changes the bucket allocations so that member links with a lot of traffic can back off, and under-utilized member links can take additional load. The intent is for each member of the AE bundle to have an equal amount of traffic.

The traffic can be measured at each scan interval in two different ways: pps or bps. Depending on the use case of the AE bundle, pps and bps play a large role. For example, if you're a company that processes a lot of small web queries that are fairly static in nature, using pps might make more sense because it's transaction oriented. On the other hand, if you're handling transit traffic and have no control of the flows, bps will make more sense.

Take, for example, an AE bundle with four links, as illustrated in Figure 4-5. During the calculation phase, the AE bundle inspects the pps of each member link. If the pps isn't within a specific threshold, the AE bundle will adjust the bucket allocation so that under-utilized links will attract more hash functions and over-utilized links will attract less hash functions.

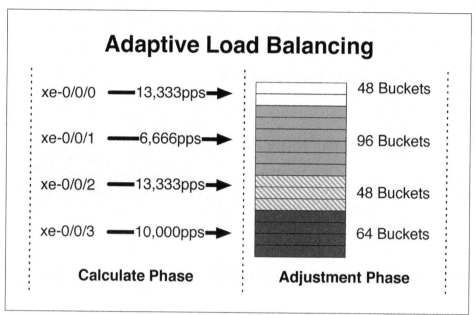

Figure 4-5. Adaptive load balancing

For example, in the figure, interface xe-0/0/0 and xe-0/0/2 are handling 13,333 pps, whereas xe-0/0/1 is only at 6,666 pps. The AE bundle reduces the number of bucket allocations for both xe-0/0/0 and xe-0/0/2 and increases the bucket allocations for xe-0/0/1. The intent is to even out the pps across all four interfaces. A single calculation phase isn't enough to correct the entire AE bundle, and multiple scans are required over time to even things out.

Adaptive load balancing can be enabled on a per AE basis (Figure 4-6). In other words, you can have a set of AE interfaces that are a normal static LAG and another set of AE interfaces that are enabled for adaptive load balancing.

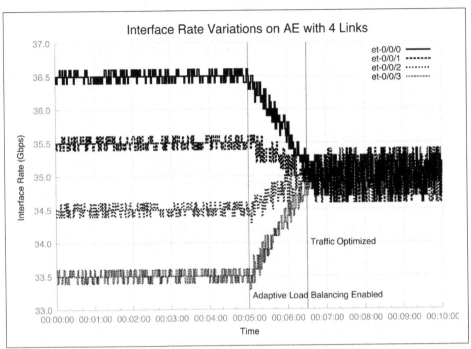

Figure 4-6. Adaptive load balancing enabled on an AE bundle

Configuration

Now that you understand more about adaptive load balancing, let's take a look at how to configure it. You'll find the new knob under `aggregated-ether-options`:

```
dhanks@QFX10002# set interfaces ae0 aggregated-ether-options load-balance adaptive ?
Possible completions:
  enable              Enable
  tolerance           Tolerance in percentage (1..100, default 20percent)
  scan-interval       Scan interval in seconds (10..600, default 30sec)
  criterion            pps or bps (default bps)
```

There are four new options: `enable`, `tolerance`, `scan-interval`, and `criterion`. You must set the `enable` knob for it to work. The `tolerance` sets the percentage of variance between flows; by default, it's set to 20 percent. The smaller the tolerance, the better it balances better bandwidth, but it takes longer.

The `scan-interval` sets the frequency at which the AE interface performs the calculation phase and recalculates the bucket allocations. By default, it's set to 30 seconds. The final option is the `criterion`, with which you can select pps or bps; by default, it's bps.

```
dhanks@QFX10002> show interfaces ae0 extensive
Physical interface: ae0, Enabled, Physical link is Up
```

```
<truncated>
  Logical interface ae0.0
<truncated>
    Adaptive Statistics:
        Adaptive Adjusts    :        264
        Adaptive Scans      :     172340
        Adaptive Tolerance:          20%
        Adaptive Updates    :         20
```

You can use the show interfaces command with the extensive knob to get all the gory details about adaptive load balancing. You can see how many adjustments it made to the buckets, how many times it has scanned the particular interface, and how many times it has been updated.

Forwarding Options

When it comes to hashing, the Juniper QFX10000 Series has a lot of different options for various types of data-plane encapsulations. Table 4-2 lists these options.

Table 4-2. Static hash and ECMP support on Juniper QFX10002-72Q on Junos 15.1X53D10

Attributes	Field Bits	L2	IPv4	IPv6	MPLS
Source MAC	0–47	0	0	0	0
Destination MAC	0–47	0	0	0	0
EtherType	0–15	D	D	D	D
VLAN ID	0–11	D	D	D	D
GRE/VXLAN	Varies	0	0	0	0
Source IP	0–31		D	D	D
Destination IP	0–31		D	D	D
Ingress interface		D	D	D	D
Source port	0–15		D	D	D
Destination port	0–15		D	D	D
IPv6 flow label	0–19			D	D
MPLS					D

In Table 4-2, "O" stands for optional, and "D" for default. So, whenever you see a default setting, that's just how the Juniper QFX10000 works out of the box. If you want to add additional bits into the hash function, you can selectively enable them per data-plane encapsulation if it's listed as "O."

Summary

This chapter has covered the major design decisions between Juniper architectures and open architectures. Juniper architectures allow for ease of use at the expense of only working with Juniper switches. The open architectures make it possible for any other vendor to participate with open protocols, but sometimes at the expense of features. We also reviewed the performance in terms of throughput and latency. The Juniper QFX10000 operates at line rate above 144 byte packets while performing any data-plane encapsulation, deep buffering, and high logical scale. Next, we took a look at the logical scale of the QFX10002-72Q with Junos 15.1X53D10. We wrapped up the chapter with a review on how the Juniper QFX10000 handles static and adaptive hashing.

Chapter Review Questions

1. Which is a Juniper architecture?

    a. MC-LAG

    b. Junos Fusion

    c. MP-BGP

    d. EVPN-VXLAN

2. The Juniper QFX10002-72Q is line-rate after what packet size?

    a. 64B

    b. 128B

    c. 144B

    d. 200B

3. Juniper QFX10002-72Q supports 1 M IPv4 entries in the FIB. What about IPv6?

    a. Only half the amount of IPv4

    b. Only a quarter amount of IPv4

    c. The same as IPv4

4. Why does the Juniper QFX10002-72Q support only 144 AE interfaces?

    a. Kernel limitations

    b. Not enough CPU

    c. Physical port limitations

    d. Not enough memory

5. How do you set the threshold between flows for adaptive load balancing?

    a. `scan-interval`

    b. `enable`

    c. `tolerance`

    d. `buckets`

Chapter Review Answers

1. **Answer: A and B.** MC-LAG is a little tricky; it depends how you view it. From the perspective of the CE, it works with any other device in the network. However, between PE switches, it must be a Juniper device for ICCP to work. Junos Fusion for Data Center requires the Juniper QFX10000 as the aggregation device and Juniper top-of-rack switches for the satellite devices.

2. **Answer: C.** The Juniper QFX10002-72Q is line-rate for packets over 144 bytes.

3. **Answer: C.** The Juniper QFX10002-72Q supports 1M entries in the FIB for both IPv4 and IPv6 *at the same time*.

4. **Answer: C.** The Juniper QFX10002-72Q had a maximum of 288x10GbE interfaces. If you pair of every single 10GbE interface, that is a total of 144 AE interfaces. It's purely a physical port limitation.

5. **Answer: C.** Adaptive load balancing can adjust the variance between flows with the `tolerance` knob.

CHAPTER 5

Junos Fusion

Enterprises need to build simple, flexible networks within their data centers to handle any type of business function. The first challenge is that network operators are expected to manage an ever-increasing number of devices; the operator-to-device ratio keeps incrementing. The second challenge is that network operators often find a lack of logical scale and features when deploying top-of-rack (ToR) switches that are based on merchant silicon hardware.

How do you solve these challenges? Do you try to develop your own solution? What does the life cycle look like? Do you use a vendor solution? What are its limitations? What does the failure domain look like? These are some of the many questions network operators ask themselves when evaluating options for creating a new enterprise data center architecture.

Overview

Junos Fusion solves these two challenges and many more. Juniper's next generation fabric is based on Junos Fusion and has three key pillars: *provider edge*, *campus*, and *data center*. Each of the pillars is a different flavor of Junos Fusion that's custom tailored to solve specific use case requirements.

Junos Fusion Provider Edge (JFPE)
> JFPE is optimized to maximize edge router slot utilization. In other words, take the advanced features and scale of Juniper MX line cards and extend it to Juniper ToR switches.

Junos Fusion for Enterprise (JFE)
> JFE is optimized for aggregating wiring closets, simplified management, and Power-over-Ethernet (PoE). JFE is built using the Juniper EX9200 and ToR switches.

Junos Fusion for Data Center (JFDC)

JFDC is optimized for active-active topologies, all-active multihoming, and high-port density that is required in the data center. JFDC is built using the Juniper QFX10000 series and ToR switches.

Junos Fusion is a technology with which you can build an entire network fabric using multiple devices, but logically it appears and operates as a single device. For example, if you built a data center with 64 racks, it would appear as a single network chassis with 64 line cards, as opposed to 64 individual devices.

Being able to quickly add capacity to Junos Fusion is a core design principle. As you add new ToR switches into Junos Fusion, it operates in a plug-and-play fashion; all software and configuration is automatically provisioned to the new ToR switch.

Network operators know the challenge of having to manage software upgrades in a data center. Traditionally network fabrics have required a large software upgrade process. For example, if you upgrade to a new version of software, every single network device in the fabric needs to be upgraded. Junos Fusion removes this limitation, making it possible for a network operator to upgrade one switch at a time in the network fabric. You can have multiple switches in the fabric running various versions of software, and Junos Fusion continues to operate normally.

The scope of this chapter focuses on JFDC and excludes the other platforms. JFPE is built using the Juniper MX series, JFE is built using the Juniper EX9200, and JFDC is built using the Juniper QFX10000 series.

Architecture

JFDC is built using a spine-and-leaf architecture. However, the spine is called an Aggregation Device (AD) and the leaf is called a Satellite Device (SD). The AD uses a cascade port to connect to a SD. The SD uses an upstream port to connect to an AD. Finally, the SD uses extended ports to connect to servers, storage, and other devices in the data center, as demonstrated in Figure 5-1.

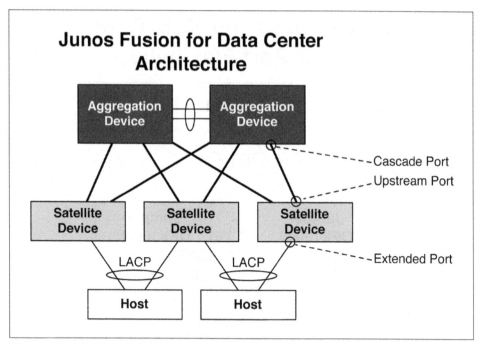

Figure 5-1. JFDC architecture

Previous fabric technologies such as Juniper Virtual Chassis Fabric and QFabric required that the entire system operate as a single fabric. One big difference with JFDC is that *Junos Fusion is enabled on a per-port basis,* as shown in Figure 5-2.

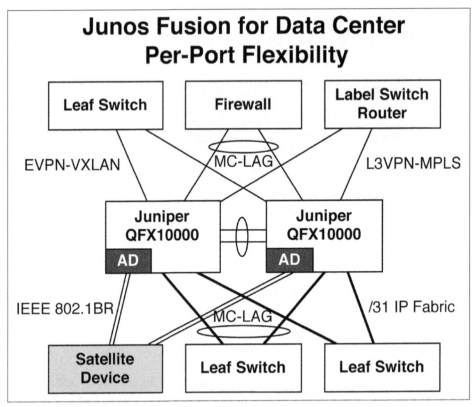

Figure 5-2. JFDC per-port flexibility

Being able to operate in different modes, depending on what is connecting into the network, is extremely powerful. Figure 5-2 illustrates how two Juniper QFX10000 spine switches are able to independently operate different protocols to various devices in the network. In summary, you can enable JFDC on a per-port or per-device basis. From the perspective of the two Juniper QFX10000 switches, they have a remote line card running in JFDC mode. Otherwise, the Ethernet VPN (EVPN)-Virtual Extensible LAN (VXLAN), Firewall, L3VPN-MPLS, Multichassis Link Aggregation (MC-LAG), and IP Fabric are running completely separate from JFDC.

Roles

JFDC has two primary roles in the topology: AD and SD. To fully extend the scale and features through port extension, you need two clear roles in the topology: one role for centralized processing and control, and the other role for aggregating and transporting traffic. Let's walk through the AD and SD in detail.

AD

The AD is the brains of JFDC. All routing protocols and processing of traffic is handled in the AD. The architecture is that the AD is a full-featured device with high logical scale, lots of features, and deep buffers. With JFDC, you can extend the same high logical scale and features into smaller ToR switches.

The AD will handle the majority of traffic processing and forwarding. Traffic sent to the SD will be encapsulated with the IEEE 802.1BR format. The SD will look at the IEEE 802.1BR header and forward the traffic to the correct destination port with minimal processing.

Each AD acts as an individual control plane. In JFDC there are two ADs, so you'll have two separate control planes in an all-active configuration. If an AD were to fail, the other AD will continue to operate as normal. Configuration changes are synchronized by using MC-LAG. For example, if you make a change on the first AD, it will automatically be synchronized to the second AD.

The aggregation device is always running the full-featured Junos network operating system. For example, the Juniper QFX10000 will be running the latest version of Junos with all features available. One of the major advantages of Junos Fusion is that you can extend aggregation device features to a remote satellite device.

You can use the following devices as an AD for JFDC:

- Juniper QFX10002-36Q
- Juniper QFX10002-72Q
- Juniper QFX10008
- Juniper QFX10016

SD

The primary function of the SD is to aggregate all server-facing ports, provide minimal traffic processing, and forward the remaining traffic to the AD for further processing. By the nature of the JFDC design, the SD is very lightweight because of the limited number of functions it is required to perform. The idea is that if a SD doesn't natively support an advanced feature, it can simply forward the traffic to the AD for advanced processing instead. The end result is that all advanced features on the AD are extended to all SDs, even if the SDs do not natively support the advanced features; this is because the AD treats the SDs as a simple port extender using the IEEE 802.1BR header.

The SD is running a very small version of Linux instead of the full version of the Junos network operating system. This is because it only needs to forward traffic based on IEEE 802.1BR metadata as opposed to running a bunch of routing protocols.

There is a special software package that you must install on each SD. This software package includes a small version of Linux with a minimal networking stack that lets it speak IEEE 802.1BR, NETCONF, and LLDP.

You can use the following devices as an SD for JFDC:

- Juniper QFX5100-32Q
- Juniper QFX5100-48S
- Juniper QFX5100-48T
- Juniper QFX5100-96S
- Juniper QFX5200-32C
- Juniper QFX5200-64Q
- Juniper EX4300-32F
- Juniper EX4300-24T
- Juniper EX4300-48S

Features

Junos Fusion is the next-generation of Ethernet fabrics. By taking advantage of open protocols and encapsulations, Junos Fusion creates some very interesting features. Let's walk through them one by one.

Any feature, anywhere

One of the great things about Junos Fusion is that any feature that's supported on the AD is automatically supported on the remote SDs, even if they don't support that feature natively. This is because the traffic is simply encapsulated between the SD and AD; all the SD needs to do is simply forward the traffic based on the metadata in the encapsulation; it doesn't need to worry about processing the traffic. For example, let's assume that the Juniper QFX10000 was the AD and the Juniper EX4300 was the SD. Although the EX4300 doesn't natively support VXLAN, Junos Fusion can push VXLAN functionality to the SDs by simply encapsulating the traffic in IEEE 802.1BR. Imagine a bare-metal server plugged into the Juniper EX4300 on a 1GbE interface that needs to be encapsulated with VXLAN and sent across the WAN to a remote VTEP. Junos Fusion will use the VXLAN functionality of the Juniper QFX10000 acting as the AD to perform the VXLAN features, whereas the Juniper EX4300 acting as the SD simply forwards traffic based on the IEEE 802.1BR tag.

In summary, you can extend any feature that's natively supported on the Juniper QFX10000 to any SD. This makes it possible for you to create a very flexible architecture that's able to quickly adapt to new networking and business requirements.

Any version, anywhere

One major drawback in most Ethernet fabrics is the requirement for all of the physical devices to operate using the same software image. This creates operational challenges when it comes to upgrading the Ethernet fabric. After you upgrade the software, it's a major event that must be planned because all physical devices must be upgraded before the Ethernet fabric is functional again.

Junos Fusion uses standard IEEE 802.1BR for the data-plane encapsulation and control-plane protocols such as LLDP and JSON. The result is that each physical device can operate a different software image, including the ADs, as depicted in Figure 5-3.

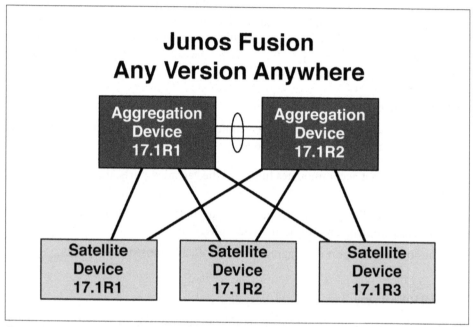

Figure 5-3. Junos Fusion supports any version, anywhere

With Junos Fusion, software upgrades are a non-event. You simply upgrade each switch one at a time without affecting the functionality of the Ethernet fabric. You have full control over whether you want to upgrade a single switch, rack, or even the entire points of delivery (POD) at once. Because Junos Fusion uses standard control-plane protocols, it's just like upgrading a set of routers and switches running BGP. It doesn't matter what version of Junos you're using, BGP just works. In this case, Junos Fusion just works—any version, anywhere.

Single point of management

The very nature of IEEE 802.1BR makes it so the AD can see all of the SDs as an extended port or line card. You can log in to Junos Fusion through either of the two ADs. Each of the ADs is a separate control plane. Any changes made on one AD will be propagated automatically to the other. Although there are two separate control planes, the entire system looks and feels like a single chassis. Each of the SDs appears as a line card; and each port on a particular SD appears as a port on that particular line card.

Plug and play

Common tasks in a large topology include adding and removing overall capacity through ToR switches. As SDs are added or removed from Junos Fusion, it automatically takes care of all discovery, configuration synchronization, and other network state. Junos Fusion behaves just like a large chassis; you simply add capacity by adding line cards, but in this case you add SDs.

Juniper extensions

Juniper has taken advantage of the extensibility of IEEE 802.1BR to make several performance and functionality enhancements:

- Better QoS that accommodates tuning of the cascaded ports, upstream ports, and access ports.
- Edge Control Protocol (ECP) that is based on TCP/IP, which supports multiple links, flow control, and traffic analytics collection.
- The ability to support two aggregation devices, as opposed to only one.

Universal SDN gateway

As network operators build networks in a data center, there are scenarios for which you need to encapsulate traffic. One example could be for a Software-Defined Networking (SDN) controller using VXLAN. Another example could be routing across a backbone with Multiprotocol Label Switching (MPLS). Because all advanced traffic forwarding happens in the AD, we can apply all of the advanced traffic processing of the Juniper QFX10000. In summary, JFDC is able to handle any encapsulation, thanks to the Juniper QFX10000 acting as the AD.

Modes

There are two modes for JFDC: extended and local switching. The extended mode is designed so that all features on the AD are extended to the SD. However, if you want to optimize for traffic forwarding, you can operate in local switching mode at the cost

---

of limited Layer 2 switching functions on the SD. Each SD must operate in only one mode; however, the AD can support multiple modes. For example, the first SD can operate in extended mode, whereas the second SD can operate in local switching mode. In other words, the operating mode is a local operation for each SD.

Extended mode

The default mode for JFDC is extended mode. All features in the AD are extended to the SD. In other words, all traffic processing and forwarding happens in the AD, as shown in Figure 5-4.

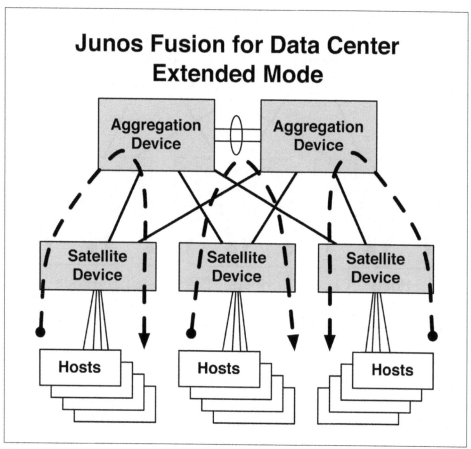

Figure 5-4. Junos Fusion for data center extended mode

There's an engineering trade-off: to get all advanced traffic processing in the AD, all traffic must flow through the AD, even when simple traffic forwarding could have happened locally at the SD. The benefit is that any and all advanced traffic processing is available to the SD in extended mode.

Local switching mode

If you do not have advanced traffic forwarding and processing requirements and you want to optimize for traffic forwarding, local switching mode makes more sense, as is illustrated in Figure 5-5.

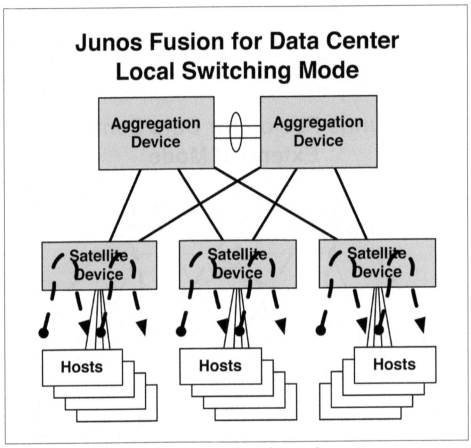

Figure 5-5. Junos Fusion for data center local switching mode

All local switching can happen locally at each SD when it operates in local switching mode. The drawback is that advanced traffic processing isn't available. The benefit is that traffic doesn't need to go up to the AD and back, which lowers the overall latency and increases the speed.

Summary

Let's take a look at extended and local switching mode in more detail in Table 5-1.

Table 5-1. Summary of JFDC extended mode versus local switching Mode

Attribute	Extended mode	Local switching mode
VLAN Auto-Sense	Yes	Yes
QoS	Yes	Yes
Multicast local replication	Yes	Yes
IGMP snooping	Yes	Yes
STP	Edge + block	Edge + block
LACP/LLDP	Distributed	Distributed
Local mirroring	Yes	Yes
Storm control	Centralized/on AD	Centralized/on AD
Firewall filters	Local/on SD[a]	Centralized/on AD
Sflow	Local/on SD[b]	Centralized/on AD

[a] An implicit roadmap item.
[b] An implicit roadmap item.

Topologies

JFDC supports dual ADs, as depicted in Figure 5-6. Each topology has two ADs and multiple SDs. Recall that each SD can either be in extended mode (SD-E) or local switching mode (SD-L).

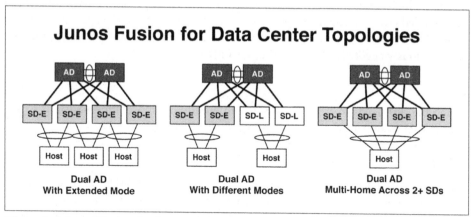

Figure 5-6. Junos Fusion for data center topology choices

The most common topology is the first option shown in Figure 5-6: dual AD with all SDs in extended mode. However, it is also common to have some SDs in local switching mode, as shown in the middle option. JFDC also supports multihoming beyond two SDs, as shown on the right.

There are a few rules when it comes to multihoming servers with JFDC. The first rule is that servers must be multihomed to a set of SDs that connect to the same ADs. The second rule is that the set of SDs must be operating in the same mode.

Servers cannot be multihomed between an AD and SD. Servers cannot be multihomed between a set of SDs that are not operating in the same mode.

Protocols

Junos Fusion is based on open standards such as IEEE 802.1BR for the data plane; Link Layer Discovery Protocol (LLDP) for neighbor discovery; JSON-RPC and NET-CONF for configuration; and Interchassis Control Protocol (ICCP) for LAG synchronization between ADs. Let's take at each protocol in more detail.

IEEE 802.1BR

The forwarding plane between the AD and SD relies on IEEE 802.1BR. The AD will assign a 12-bit extended port ID (EPID) to each port on each SD. The EPID is local to each SD. The forwarding behavior on each SD is very simple and doesn't require any L2 or L3 processing. Instead, it simply forwards traffic based on the EPID value. Each AD has a logical interface for each extended port for every SD. To forward traffic to an extended port, the AD inserts the IEEE 802.1BR header with the appropriate EPID value. The SD forwards the traffic based on an EPID to extended port mapping that was previously negotiated between the AD and SD.

LLDP

When the AD needs to detect new SDs and additional information—such as which port the SD is connected to and its firmware—it uses LLDP.

NETCONF

There is a need to synchronize configuration between the ADs to ensure they're always up to date and in an active-active deployment. There's also a requirement for the ADs to push configuration changes to SDs. For such configuration changes, NET-CONF is used between all ADs.

ICCP

There is additional network state that needs to be synchronized between the two AD controlling bridges to maintain an active-active architecture: port priorities, aggregator IDs, port ID offsets, MAC addresses, and interface operational status. To keep the two ADs synchronized, Junos Fusion uses MC-LAG and ICCP. From the perspective of an SD, the two separate ADs appear as a single, logical device thanks to MC-LAG. Traffic can flow to any of the two ADs and will be handled seamlessly.

No L3 on SD Ports

Junos Fusion only supports configuring SD access ports in switching mode. You cannot directly configure a routed interface on an SD access port. For example, you can only configure an SD access port as `family ethernet-switching` with `interface-mode access` or `interface-mode trunk`. You cannot configure `family inet` with an IP address on a remote SD port.

If you want to provide L3 access for remote servers, simply set up an Integrated Routing and Bridging (IRB) interface and configure the server's VLAN to have a `l3-interface`. If you need to configure a real routed interface, because you're connecting another networking device into the topology, simply configure a routed interface *outside the scope of Junos Fusion*. Recall that Junos Fusion is a *per-port* architecture from the perspective of the AD. Simply plug the device requiring routed support into another port on the AD, and then you can configure it as `family inet` with an IP address and routing protocols. If you don't want to plug the routed device directly into the AD, use a dedicated leaf switch that's used for routing. Between the AD and the dedicated leaf switch, just configure a standard routed IP network. Then, you can plug your routed device into the leaf switch that's configured for IP routing. Refer to Figure 5-2 to see how each leaf switch can operate in different modes. There's no requirement to operate every leaf switch as Junos Fusion.

 If you have a topology with a single AD, you can configure a native L3 port on a SD. However, in a data center environment it's recommended to use two ADs. If you are looking at provider edge use cases, a single AD makes more sense and is able to offer native L3 functionality. Junos Fusion for Provider Edge (*http://juni.pr/29vwAmr*) has more information.

Packet Walk-Through

One of the best ways to fully understand how a new architecture works is to perform a packet walk. Where do packets start? How are they encapsulated? How are they processed each step of the way? Let's take a look at the four most common scenarios: single AD with unicast; dual AD with unicast; single AD with multicast; and, finally, dual AD with multicast.

The following topologies are drawn logically without the use of physical links. We can assume a full-mesh topology between the ADs and SDs. We can also assume a set of interchassis links (ICLs) between both ADs for ICCP traffic and a backup path in the event of link failures.

Single AD—Unicast—Extended Mode

Although a single AD isn't recommended due to lack of high availability, we'll still cover the packet walk so that you have a full understanding of the differences between single and dual AD topologies. Figure 5-7 shows a very simple single AD topology.

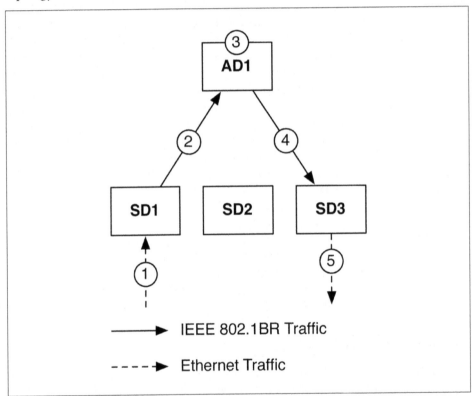

Figure 5-7. Single AD—unicas—extended mode

Let's walk through a day in the life of a packet, step by step:

1. Server sends L2 traffic to SD1 on port 22.

2. Frame is encapsulated in IEEE 802.1BR with the corresponding metadata to represent port 22.

3. AD1 receives the frame and performs a destination MAC address lookup. If destination MAC address is unknown, it will be flooded to all SDs participating in the same ingress bridge domain. Otherwise, the frame will be forwarded to the corresponding SD. In this example, let's assume that AD1 knows the destination for this frame and forwarded it to SD3.

4. AD1 pops the old IEEE 802.1BR tag from SD1 and pushes a new tag with corresponding metadata for SD3. AD1 forwards the newly encapsulated frame to SD3.

5. SD3 removes the IEEE 802.1BR tag and forwards out the corresponding egress port.

Dual AD—Unicast—Extended Mode

Now, let's add a second AD to the mix, as shown in Figure 5-9.

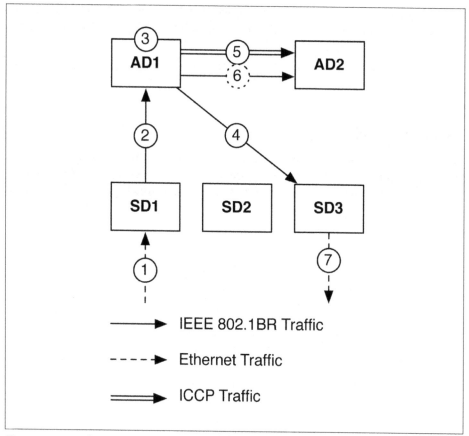

Figure 5-8. Dual AD—unicast—extended mode

Again, let's walk through a day in the life of a packet, step by step:

1. Server sends L2 traffic to SD1 on port 22.

2. Frame is encapsulated in IEEE 802.1BR with the corresponding metadata to represent port 22.

3. AD1 receives the frame and performs a destination MAC address lookup. If destination MAC address is unknown, it will be flooded to all SDs participating in the same ingress bridge domain. Otherwise, the frame will be forwarded to the corresponding SD. In this example, let's assume that AD1 knows the destination for this frame and forwarded it to SD3.

4. AD1 pops the old IEEE 802.1BR tag from SD1 and pushes a new tag with corresponding metadata for SD3. AD1 forwards the newly encapsulated frame to SD3.

5. AD1 will inform AD2 of this new destination MAC address over ICCP.

6. This step is optional. For a situation in which a destination SD might not be dual-homed by both AD1 and AD2, AD1 can use the ICL to forward the frame to AD2, so that it can reach its final AD.

7. SD3 removes the IEEE 802.1BR tag and forwards out the corresponding egress port.

Single AD—Multicast

Now, let's take a look at how multicast traffic is handled in Junos Fusion. By default, the supported multicast algorithm is assisted replication. Figure 5-9 shows an example of a single AD with three leaf switches. Let's walk through the multicast replication.

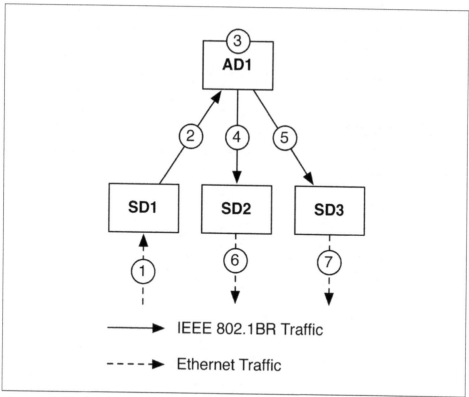

Figure 5-9. Single AD—multicast

Let's walk through this step by step:

1. Server sends L2 multicast traffic to SD1 on port 22.

2. Frame is encapsulated in IEEE 802.1BR with the corresponding metadata to represent port 22.

3. AD1 receives the frame and determines which other SDs and access ports must receive a copy of the multicast frame. AD1 creates a copy of the original frame for each remote port that requires a copy, even if they're on the same SD. For example, if SD2 had 20 ports that wanted a copy of the multicast packet, AD1 would make and forward 20 copies. Each copy is encapsulated with a new IEEE 802.1BR tag with the corresponding egress access port on the SD.

4. AD1 pops the old IEEE 802.1BR tag from SD1 and pushes a new tag with corresponding metadata for SD3. AD1 forwards the newly encapsulated frame to SD3.

5. SD3 removes the IEEE 802.1BR tag and forwards out the corresponding egress port.

As of this writing, JFDC supports only ingress replication for multicast. Expect to see a future release that supports egress replication, so that the AD only sends a single copy of a multicast packet to a remote SD. If a remote SD has multiple ports interested in the multicast traffic, it can make a copy locally and forward it to the access ports.

Dual AD—Multicast

Now let's take a look at how multicast works in a topology with two ADs, as illustrated in Figure 5-10.

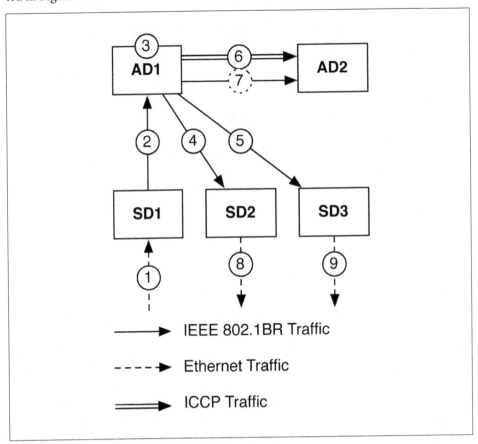

Figure 5-10. Dual AD—Multicast

Here's a step-by-step explanation of this process:

1. Server sends L2 multicast traffic to SD1 on port 22.

2. Frame is encapsulated in IEEE 802.1BR with the corresponding metadata to represent port 22.

3. AD1 receives the frame and determines which other SDs and access ports must receive a copy of the multicast frame. AD1 creates a copy of the original frame for each remote port that requires a copy, even if they're on the same SD. For example, if SD2 had 20 ports that wanted a copy of the multicast packet, AD1 would make and forward 20 copies. Each copy is encapsulated with a new IEEE 802.1BR tag with the corresponding egress access port on the SD.

4. AD1 pops the old IEEE 802.1BR tag from SD1 and pushes a new tag with corresponding metadata for SD2. AD1 forwards the newly encapsulated frame to SD2.

5. AD1 pops the old IEEE 802.1BR tag from SD1 and pushes a new tag with corresponding metadata for SD3. AD1 forwards the newly encapsulated frame to SD3.

6. AD1 will inform AD2 of this new destination MAC address over ICCP.

7. This step is optional. For a situation in which a destination SD might not be dual-homed by both AD1 and AD2, AD1 can use the ICL to forward the frame to AD2, so that it can reach its final AD.

8. SD2 removes the IEEE 802.1BR tag and forwards out the corresponding egress port.

9. SD3 removes the IEEE 802.1BR tag and forwards out the corresponding egress port.

As you can see, the life of the packet varies depending on the topology and type of traffic Junos Fusion is processing. Traffic enters the system as standard Ethernet and then is encapsulated and forwarded using the IEEE 802.1BR format. The ADs receive the encapsulated traffic and process the frame or packet as required. The AD then encapsulates the traffic again to reach the final remote SD. Finally, the remote SDs will strip the encapsulation and simply forward the traffic to the corresponding port.

Laboratory and Configuration

To further understand Junos Fusion, you need to get your hands dirty. There's nothing better than creating a detailed laboratory diagram and going through the command line to break down a new architecture. In this section, we'll build a very simple Junos Fusion topology, look at the new configuration statements, and run through all of the new command-line options.

Topology

We'll keep things very simple and use a single AD topology, as presented in Figure 5-11. Although the recommendation for a data center use case is to have two

ADs, we want to keep this laboratory basic so that we can just focus on the new functionality and command line.

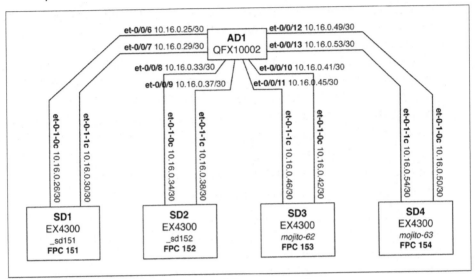

Figure 5-11. Junos Fusion for data center laboratory topology

The figure depicts a single AD called AD1; the AD is a Juniper QFX100002 switch running the standard full-featured version of Junos. There are four SDs: SD1, SD2, SD3, and SD3. Each of the SDs are a Juniper EX4300 running the special, lightweight satellite software, which is a small version of Linux and networking stack that supports IEEE 802.1BR.

Configuration

Let's begin by checking out the AD. We can see that it's a Juniper QFX10002-72Q from the following output:

```
dhanks@fusion> show chassis hardware | no-more
Hardware inventory:
Item              Version  Part number  Serial number  Description
Chassis                                 DB590          QFX10002-72Q
Pseudo CB 0
Routing Engine 0           BUILTIN      BUILTIN        RE-QFX10002-72Q
FPC 0             REV 20   750-055415   ACMS8250       QFX10002-72Q
  CPU                      BUILTIN      BUILTIN        FPC CPU
  PIC 0                    BUILTIN      BUILTIN        72X40G
    Xcvr 0        REV 01   740-032986   QB070272       QSFP+-40G-SR4
    Xcvr 1        REV 01   740-032986   QB170917       QSFP+-40G-SR4
< ... snip ... >
  Mezz            REV 10   711-053333   ACMS9512       Mezzanine Board
Power Supply 0    REV 03   740-054405   1EDN5190021    AC AFO 1600W PSU
```

```
Power Supply 1    REV 03   740-054405   1EDN5190023    AC AFO 1600W PSU
Power Supply 2    REV 03   740-054405   1EDN5190084    AC AFO 1600W PSU
Power Supply 3    REV 03   740-054405   1EDN5190144    AC AFO 1600W PSU
Fan Tray 0                                             QFX10002 Fan Tray 0
Fan Tray 1                                             QFX10002 Fan Tray 1
Fan Tray 2                                             QFX10002 Fan Tray 2
```

All SDs will be directly connected to the Juniper QFX10002-72Q. We currently have four active SDs. Let's add the new `satellite` option to check out the hardware details:

```
{master:0}
dhanks@fusion> show chassis hardware satellite | no-more
Hardware inventory:
Item            Version  Part number  Serial number    Description
FPC 151         REV 10   650-044931   PE3714100759     EX4300-48T
  PIC 0         REV 10   BUILTIN      BUILTIN          48x 10/100/1000 Base-T
  PIC 1         REV 10   BUILTIN      BUILTIN          4x 40GE
    Xcvr 1      REV 01   740-032986   QB170006         QSFP+-40G-SR4
    Xcvr 2      REV01    740-061001   LE015280024      QSFP+-40G-CU3M
    Xcvr 3      REV 01   740-038624   MOC13016240120   QSFP+-40G-CU3M
  PIC 2         REV 05   611-044925   MY3714320100     4x 1G/10G SFP/SFP+
    Xcvr 0      REV 01   740-021308   T09L19553        SFP+-10G-SR
    Xcvr 1      REV 01   740-030658   AD0950A01KT      SFP+-10G-USR
    Xcvr 2      REV 01   740-030658   AD0951A025M      SFP+-10G-USR
  Power Supply 0 REV 01  740-046873   1EDE4080823      JPSU-350-AC-AFO
  Fan Tray 0                                           EX4300 Fan Tray 0
  Fan Tray 1                                           EX4300 Fan Tray 1
< ... snip ... >
FPC 154         REV 10   650-044931   PE3714100300     EX4300-48T
  PIC 0         REV 10   BUILTIN      BUILTIN          48x 10/100/1000 Base-T
  PIC 1         REV 10   BUILTIN      BUILTIN          4x 40GE
    Xcvr 0      REV 01   740-032986   QB070421         QSFP+-40G-SR4
    Xcvr 1      REV 01   740-032986   QB070286         QSFP+-40G-SR4
    Xcvr 2      REV 01   740-032986   QB441673         QSFP+-40G-SR4
    Xcvr 3      REV 01   740-032986   QB441661         QSFP+-40G-SR4
  PIC 2         REV 05   611-044925   MY3714390734     4x 1G/10G SFP/SFP+
    Xcvr 0      REV 01   740-030658   AD0946A02M9      SFP+-10G-USR
    Xcvr 1      REV 01   740-030658   AD0928A00MN      SFP+-10G-USR
    Xcvr 2      REV 01   740-021308   88D709A00143     SFP+-10G-SR
  Power Supply 0 REV 01  740-046873   1EDE4080939      JPSU-350-AC-AFO
  Fan Tray 0                                           EX4300 Fan Tray 0
  Fan Tray 1                                           EX4300 Fan Tray 1
```

That's a lot of output. Let's step through it a piece at a time. We see that we have a few new FPCs: 151, 152, 153, and 154. However, FPC 152 and 153 were truncated to save space. The remote SDs simply appear as a line card on the Juniper QFX10002-72Q. Each FPC is broken down into the standard Junos PICs and ports, as well. We can see that SD4/FPC 154 has 4x40GbE optics for the uplinks. The 40GbE interfaces on SD4 appear as interface names et-154/1/0 through et-154/1/3.

Satellite management

The next step is to create a hierarchy of line cards and cascade ports. Each line card/FPC needs a set of cascade ports. For example, FPC 151 contains cascade ports et-0/0/6 and et-0/0/7, as shown here:

```
chassis {
    satellite-management {
        fpc 151 {
            cascade-ports [ et-0/0/6 et-0/0/7 ];
        }
        fpc 152 {
            cascade-ports [ et-0/0/8 et-0/0/9 ];
        }
        fpc 153 {
            alias st-v44-mojito-62;
            cascade-ports [ et-0/0/10 et-0/0/11 ];
        }
        fpc 154 {
            alias st-v44-mojito-63;
            cascade-ports [ et-0/0/12 et-0/0/13 ];
        }
        redundancy-groups {
            chassis-id 1;
            rg1 {
                redundancy-group-id 1;
                peer-chassis-id 2 {
                    inter-chassis-link ae999;
                }
                satellite [ 151 152 153 154 ];
            }
        }
        upgrade-groups {
            mojito_sd {
                satellite [ 151 152 153 154 ];
            }
        }
    }
}
```

If we were configuring a dual-AD topology, we also would need to configure the redundancy groups. This is exactly like configuring redundancy groups in MC-LAG, except we add the new option called `satellite` which contains a set of FPC values of the remote SDs.

The last piece of configuration is establishing upgrade groups. Suppose that you want to update the software on the SDs. You can do so individually, or you can create a logical group and upgrade them all at once with upgrade groups. You simply give the upgrade group a name by using the new `upgrade-groups` option and then a set of satellite FPC IDs. In our example, we have an upgrade group name of `mojito_sd` with satellites 151 through 154.

Interfaces

Now that we have created a list of FPCs and their respective cascade ports, we need to actually change the interface mode into a real cascade port by using the new cascade-port option:

```
interfaces {
    et-0/0/6 {
        cascade-port;
    }
    et-0/0/7 {
        cascade-port;
    }
    et-0/0/8 {
        cascade-port;
    }
    et-0/0/9 {
        cascade-port;
    }
    et-0/0/10 {
        cascade-port;
    }
    et-0/0/11 {
        cascade-port;
    }
    et-0/0/12 {
        cascade-port;
    }
    et-0/0/13 {
        cascade-port;
    }
    ae999 {
        aggregated-ether-options {
            lacp {
                active;
                periodic fast;
            }
        }
        unit 0 {
            family ethernet-switching {
                interface-mode trunk;
                vlan {
                    members all;
                }
            }
        }
    }
}
```

If we were configuring a dual-AD topology, we also would need to configure an ICL link between the two ADs to avoid packet loss during link failures. To do so, simply configure an aggregated Ethernet bundle with access to all VLANs. Again, this is identical to a traditional MC-LAG architecture.

ICCP and LLDP

Although our topology has only a single AD, we are going to review how to configure ICCP in for a dual AD topology. It's just like MC-LAG; there are no new options here:

```
protocols {
    iccp {
        local-ip-addr 20.20.20.1;
        peer 20.20.20.2 {
            redundancy-group-id-list 1;
            liveness-detection {
                minimum-interval 2000;
                multiplier 3;
                transmit-interval {
                    minimum-interval 60;
                }
            }
        }
    }
    lldp {
        interface all;
    }
}
```

Don't forget to configure LLDP on all of the cascade ports. I was lazy and just enabled LLDP on all ports. Be careful doing this in production because you might not want to enable LLDP on management and loopback interfaces. We need LLDP enabled because we want to automatically discover and provision SDs after they're plugged into the AD.

Verification

Junos Fusion is very easy to configure. Now let's walk through the new commands and verify that our satellites are up and running.

FPC slots

Let's take a look at SD1, which is FPC 151:

```
{master:0}
dhanks@fusion> show chassis satellite fpc-slot 151
                Device          Cascade   Port     Extended Ports
Alias           Slot   State    Ports     State    Total/Up
_sd151          151    Online    et-0/0/6  down     54/25
                                 et-0/0/7  online

Summary
```

We can see that Junos has automatically defined an alias called _sd151 because we never specified one in the configuration. The line card is online with the correct cascade ports et-0/0/6 and et-0/0/7. However, we see that cascade port et-0/0/6 is down. (More on this later.) We also see that FPC 151 has a total of 54 remote ports and 25 of them are connected to servers.

Let's take a look at SD3, which is FPC 154:

```
{master:0}
dhanks@fusion> show chassis satellite fpc-slot 154
                 Device      Cascade     Port       Extended Ports
Alias            Slot   State    Ports       State     Total/Up
mojito-63 154           Online    et-0/0/12   online    55/26
                                  et-0/0/13   online
```

Now we see our alias called mojito-63 instead of an automatically generated alias. Both cascade ports are online.

Neighbors

Let's take a look at the neighbor relationship between the AD and each SD. The new neighbor option shows us this output. Let's focus on SD1 on cascade ports et-0/0/6 and et-0/0/7:

```
{master:0}
dhanks@fusion> show chassis satellite neighbor terse et-0/0/6
Interface   State      Port Info   System Name  Model          SW Version
et-0/0/6    Dn
```

Interesting. Not much output here. I disconnected the cable intentionally to show you what the system looks like during a failure. Let's check the other cascade port et-0/0/7:

```
{master:0}
dhanks@fusion> show chassis satellite neighbor terse et-0/0/7
Interface   State      Port Info   System Name  Model       SW Version
et-0/0/7    Two-Way    et-0/1/1    sd151        EX4300-48T  15.1-20160515_s3_linux_v44.0
```

That's much better. We can see that cascade port et-0/0/7 on SD1 detected the state, port information, system name, model, and software version.

Now let's switch our attention to SD2 on cascade port et-0/0/8, but this time let's get a little bit more information by using the brief option:

```
{master:0}
dhanks@fusion> show chassis satellite neighbor brief et-0/0/8
Interface   State      Port Info   System Name  Model       SW Version
et-0/0/8    Two-Way    et-0/1/0    sd152        EX4300-48T  15.1-20160515_s3_linux_v44.0
  Adjacency up-down transition count: 1 Last transition: 04:13:24
  Device Serial Number: PE3714100218 Chassis ID: f4:b5:2f:4c:c1:fa
  Device Family Name: ppc Version Sequence Number: 1
  System Description: Juniper Networks, Inc. EX4300-48T , version 15.1-20160515_s3_linux_v44.0
  Build date: Mon May 16 20:48:52 2016
  Hello interval (msec): 10000
  Satellite hello interval (msec): 10000
```

```
Local assigned primary address:
    Local-end: 10.16.0.33/30 Remote-end: 10.16.0.34/30
```

With the new `brief` option, you can see the last adjacency transitions, serial numbers, chassis ID, and much more information. What's interesting here is an automatically assigned IP address of 10.16.0.33/30. What is this? This is a closed in-band network that the AD and SD use to communicate. It's used to detect new devices with LLDP, bring up the control plane, and for configuration provisioning. However, keep in mind that this is an internal-only network that isn't accessible directly from the AD or global routing table.

Satellite login

If you want to further investigate this new in-band network, you can log in to the satellite device directly. Use the new `request chassis satellite` command to log in to SD2:

```
{master:0}
dhanks@fusion> request chassis satellite login fpc-slot 152
Warning: Permanently added '172.16.0.152' (ECDSA) to the list of known hosts.
Last login: Sat May 28 16:45:03 2016 from 172.16.1.1
```

Recall that the SD is running a lightweight version of Linux that's stripped down to only support the base functionality of IEEE 802.1BR. You can see this by using the following command:

```
root@sd152:~# uname -a
Linux sd152 3.10.62-ltsi-WR6.0.0.21_standard #1 SMP PREEMPT Thu Mar 3 23:09:19 PST 2016 ppc ppc ppc
GNU/Linux
```

You can use standard Linux commands such as `ifconfig` to check out the networking stack:

```
root@sd152:~# ifconfig et-0-1-0c
et-0-1-0c Link encap:Ethernet  HWaddr f4:b5:2f:4c:c1:fa
          inet addr:10.16.0.34  Bcast:0.0.0.0  Mask:255.255.255.252
          UP BROADCAST RUNNING MULTICAST  MTU:9178  Metric:1
          RX packets:1658622 errors:0 dropped:0 overruns:0 frame:0
          TX packets:1185036 errors:0 dropped:31 overruns:0 carrier:0
          collisions:0 txqueuelen:500
          RX bytes:348264824 (332.1 MiB)  TX bytes:624025699 (595.1 MiB)
```

Just as suspected, we can see that Linux controls the 40GbE uplink from the SD and we can see the internal network of 10.16.0.32/30. Let's see if the SD can ping the AD:

```
root@sd152:~# ping 10.16.0.33
PING 10.16.0.33 (10.16.0.33) 56(84) bytes of data.
64 bytes from 10.16.0.33: icmp_seq=1 ttl=64 time=5.22 ms
64 bytes from 10.16.0.33: icmp_seq=2 ttl=64 time=14.1 ms
64 bytes from 10.16.0.33: icmp_seq=3 ttl=64 time=3.24 ms
64 bytes from 10.16.0.33: icmp_seq=4 ttl=64 time=3.16 ms
^C
```

```
--- 10.16.0.33 ping statistics ---
4 packets transmitted, 4 received, 0% packet loss, time 3000ms
rtt min/avg/max/mdev = 3.164/6.447/14.150/4.523 ms
```

Yes. No big surprise there. However, the AD cannot ping the SD from the standard Junos command line.

Satellite VTY

You can access the command line of the Junos microkernel from the Linux prompt by using the following command:

```
root@sd152:~# vty
connect to 127.0.0.1:33000
```

Use the ? attribute to see a list of available commands:

```
spfe# ?
    bcmshell              BCM-SDK shell
    clear                 clear system information
    debug                 enable system debugging features
    eth                   eth commands
    quit                  quit from this cli
    set                   set system parameters
    show                  show system information
    test                  run test command
    undebug               disable system debugging features
    unset                 unset command
```

Let's check out the version of the microkernel:

```
spfe# show version

Build info
  @(#)Junos Fusion SNOS SVN-Revision: 9853 spfe built by dc-builder on 2016-05-15 14:12:20 UTC
  @(#)/volume/fsg-builds/dc-builder/v44-daily/DEV_S3_LINUX_BRANCH/1463317281/sb-linux/v44/obj-ppc
```

Now let's take a look at some more detailed information about the SD:

```
spfe# show chassis

Product model:         145
Product name:          EX4300-48T
Product family:        EX4300
Chassis assembly ID:   0xF08F
Board assembly ID:     0x0B5C
Board revision:        6
Base MAC Addr:         f4:b5:2f:4c:c1:c0
Serial Number:         PE3714100218
Satellite Device ID:   152
System started (UTC):  Tue May 17 03:48:55 2016
PFE Up time:           up 1 week, 4 days, 20 hours, 2 minutes, 17 seconds, 501 milliseconds
                       (1022537501 msec)
Current time (UTC):    Sat May 28 23:51:13 2016

Build info
  @(#)Junos Fusion SNOS SVN-Revision: 9853 spfe built by dc-builder on 2016-05-15 14:12:20 UTC
  @(#)/volume/fsg-builds/dc-builder/v44-daily/DEV_S3_LINUX_BRANCH/1463317281/sb-linux/v44/obj-ppc
```

If you needed to troubleshoot the SD and see if it has connectivity to the AD, you can use the following command:

```
spfe# show sd connectivty

Dual ADs: Yes
Number of active ADs: 2
Global AD-ID-Bitmap: 0x0006

AD-1    : Loopback Address 0xac100101
AD-2    : Loopback Address 0xac100201
SD-ID:  152,   AD-ID-Bitmap 0x0002
```

Although we're focusing on a single AD in this chapter, the actual laboratory has two ADs, as you can see in the preceding output.

Upgrade groups

Now let's go back to the command line on the AD. That's the entire point of Junos Fusion, a single point of management. Let's check out the upgrade group that we created for FPC 151 through 154:

```
dhanks@fusion> show chassis satellite upgrade-group
            Group       Device
Group       Sw-Version                      State     Slot State
mojito_sd   15.1-20160525_s3_linux_v44.0    in-sync   151 version-in-sync
                                                      152 version-in-sync
                                                      153 version-in-sync
                                                      154 version-in-sync
```

Everything looks great. We can now use the `mojito_sd` upgrade group in the `request software add` command when we upgrade the system software, and only upgrade the SDs in that particular upgrade group.

Adding a New SD

Now that we have seen how to configure and verify our existing SDs, let's see how you can add a new one. The first step is to install the satellite software on the SD. To do this, simply download the satellite package from the Juniper website (*http://www.juniper.net*) and then use the `request software add` command. Now you can simply plug the new SD into the AD.

Unprovisioned

Satellites that have yet to be configured are kept in the unprovisioned list. Use the new `unprovision` command to see a list of satellites waiting to be deployed:

```
dhanks@fusion> show chassis satellite unprovision
        Device       Cascade Port
System-Id            Serial-Number     State         Ports       State
```

```
5c:45:27:28:c0:00    TA3715140102      Present          xe-0/0/31:0present
                                                         xe-0/0/31:1present
88:e0:f3:1a:32:e0    MX3113200002      Present          et-0/0/36  present
cc:e1:7f:c8:cd:40    TR0214400030      Present
f4:b5:2f:4e:c0:80    PE3714100847      Present
```

Let's grab the new SD plugged into the et-0/0/36 port on the AD. All you need to do is configure et-0/0/36 as a cascade port and assign it to an FPC.

Configuration

We'll use FPC 196 for the new cascade port et-0/0/36. The configuration is simple:

```
{master:0}
dhanks@fusion> configure
Entering configuration mode

{master:0}[edit]
root@st-v44-pdt-elite-01# set chassis satellite-management fpc 196 alias dhanks cascade-ports et-0/0/36

{master:0}[edit]
root@st-v44-pdt-elite-01# set interfaces et-0/0/36 cascade-port

{master:0}[edit]
root@st-v44-pdt-elite-01# commit and-quit
configuration check succeeds
commit complete
Exiting configuration mode
```

That's it. Go ahead and check the unprovisioned list again:

```
dhanks@fusion> show chassis satellite unprovision
      Device          Cascade Port
System-Id             Serial-Number     State            Ports     State
5c:45:27:28:c0:00     TA3715140102      Present          xe-0/0/31:0present
                                                         xe-0/0/31:1present
cc:e1:7f:c8:cd:40     TR0214400030      Present
f4:b5:2f:4e:c0:80     PE3714100847      Present
```

Just as suspected: the new satellite plugged into et-0/0/36 has been provisioned and removed from the unprovisioned list. You can verify this by using the following command:

```
dhanks@fusion> show chassis hardware satellite slot-id 196
Hardware inventory:
Item          Version  Part number   Serial number   Description
FPC 196       REV 01   611-050030    MX3113200002    EX4300-32F
  PIC 0       REV 01   BUILTIN       BUILTIN         32x 1G SFP, 4x 1G/10G SFP/SFP+
    Xcvr 0    REV 01   740-037249    MOL10412490035  SFP+-10G-ACU1M
    Xcvr 1    REV 01   740-030076    APF12270016H83  SFP+-10G-CU1M
    Xcvr 2    REV 01   740-030076    APF14450013T92  SFP+-10G-CU1M
    Xcvr 3    REV 01   740-030076    APF14450013T7J  SFP+-10G-CU1M
    Xcvr 4    REV 01   740-030076    APF14480016LAK  SFP+-10G-CU1M
    Xcvr 5    REV 01   740-030076    APF14450013TBW  SFP+-10G-CU1M
    Xcvr 6    REV 01   740-030076    APF14450013T46  SFP+-10G-CU1M
    Xcvr 8    REV 01   740-030076    APF14480016L7P  SFP+-10G-CU1M
    Xcvr 9    REV 01   740-030076    APF14450013T8W  SFP+-10G-CU1M
    Xcvr 10   REV 01   740-030076    APF14450013T80  SFP+-10G-CU1M
  PIC 1       REV 01   BUILTIN       BUILTIN         2x 40GE
```

```
   Xcvr 0        REV 01   740-032986   QB170912        QSFP+-40G-SR4
   PIC 2         REV 01   611-051310   RX3113210018    8x 1G/10G SFP/SFP+
Power Supply 1   REV 01   740-046873   1EDE3220042     JPSU-350-AC-AFO
```

Very cool. You can now see the new satellite acting as FPC 196 on the AD. You can see that it's another Juniper EX4300. Let's take a look at the neighbor relationship with the SD on port et-0/0/36:

```
{master:0}
dhanks@fusion> show chassis satellite neighbor et-0/0/36
Interface   State      Port Info   System Name  Model      SW Version
et-0/0/36   Two-Way    et-0/1/0    sd196        EX4300-32F  15.1-20160525_s3_linux_v44.0
```

The SD is up in the correct two-way state. Next, check the status of the line card itself on FPC 196:

```
{master:0}
dhanks@fusion> show chassis satellite fpc-slot 196
                  Device              Cascade     Port      Extended Ports
Alias             Slot   State        Ports       State     Total/Up
dhanks            196    Online       et-0/0/36   online    11/1
```

You can see the new dhanks alias, slot ID, the state, and the number of ports that are on the satellite device. Take a look at the first port on the EX4300. Recall, this is a Juniper EX4300-32F which has 32x10GbE interfaces, so we'll use the xe-196/0/0 interface name instead of ge-196/0/0:

```
{master:0}
dhanks@fusion> show interfaces terse xe-196/0/0
Interface            Admin Link Proto    Local                Remote
xe-196/0/0           up    down
```

You can see that the AD recognizes the interface and is installed correctly into the Junos kernel. Let's put some basic VLAN configuration on xe-196/0/0:

```
dhanks@fusion> show configuration interfaces xe-196/0/0
unit 0 {
    family ethernet-switching {
        interface-mode access;
        vlan {
            members dhanks;
        }
    }
}
```

You simply make xe-196/0/0 an untagged interface on VLAN dhanks. Let's find out more about the VLAN:

```
dhanks@fusion> show vlans dhanks detail

Routing instance: default-switch
  VLAN Name: dhanks                              State: Active
Tag: 69
Internal index: 77, Generation Index: 77, Origin: Static
MAC aging time: 300 seconds
```

```
Layer 3 interface: irb.69
VXLAN Enabled : No
Interfaces:
    ae999.0*,tagged,trunk
    xe-196/0/0.0,untagged,access
Number of interfaces: Tagged 1     , Untagged 1
Total MAC count: 0
```

You can see that the VLAN ID is 69 with the untagged interface xe-196/0/0. The VLAN has a routed IRB that the attached servers can use for a default gateway.

Summary

This chapter covered the fundamental concepts for Junos Fusion. This new architecture is very powerful, and with it you can easily extend advanced features from the Juniper QFX10000 Series to more cost-optimized leaf switches such as the Juniper QFX5100 Series and EX4300. Junos Fusion provides you with the ability to have any feature and any version of software, anywhere in the network. All of the operational aspects have been consolidated into the aggregation devices to provide a single point of control. Simply log in to any AD, and Junos Fusion appears as a large, single device.

Also in this chapter, we walked through the various traffic patterns and experienced a day in the life of a packet in Junos Fusion. We looked at both single-AD and dual-AD topologies for unicast and multicast traffic.

To test our knowledge of Junos Fusion, we set up a laboratory and spent a lot of time on the command line learning the new commands and options. We looked at how satellites are simply line cards on Junos Fusion. Deploying a new satellite is as easy as plugging it in and configuring a cascading port. We also went behind the scenes and looked at the satellite operating system.

Chapter Review Questions

1. How many ADs does Junos Fusion support?

   a. 1

   b. 2

   c. 3

   d. 4

2. Which are valid modes for JFDC?

   a. Extended

   b. MPLS

c. Local Switching

d. VXLAN

3. Does JFDC support L3 interfaces on SD ports?

   a. Yes

   b. No

4. What's the default multicast replication for JFDC?

   a. Ingress replication

   b. Egress replication

   c. Assisted replication

   d. Modulated replication

5. Are you able to see the satellites by using the show chassis hardware command?

   a. Yes

   b. No

6. What operating system runs on the aggregated device?

   a. Regular Junos

   b. Linux

   c. FreeBSD

   d. SNOS

7. What operating system runs on the satellite?

   a. Linux

   b. LFE

   c. SNOS

Chapter Review Answers

1. **Answer: A and B.** As of this writing, Junos Fusion supports either one or two ADs.

2. **Answer: A and C.** As of this writing, JFDC supports two modes: extended mode and local switching mode.

3. **Answer: B.** JFDC doesn't support L3 interfaces on SD ports. If you need L3, use an IRB. The other option is to simply configure another port on the AD as a routed interface. Remember that JFDC is enabled per port.

4. **Answer: C.** As of this writing, the AD makes a copy for each port on remote SDs.

5. **Answer: B.** You must use the new satellite option to see the `satellite` devices. The command is `show chassis hardware satellite`.

6. **Answer: A, B, and C.** Depends on which layer you're looking at. The QFX10000 boots into Linux by default and uses KVM to virtualize Junos into a VM. Recall that Junos is based on FreeBSD.

7. **Answer: A, B, and C.** Trick question. There are various names for the satellite operating system. They are all correct: Linux, Linux Forwarding Engine (LFE), and Satellite Network Operating System (SNOS).

CHAPTER 6

Ethernet VPN

Ethernet VPN (EVPN) has solved three interesting challenges in networking. The first is providing better L2VPN connectivity in the WAN. The second is providing an agnostic control plane to handle various data-plane encapsulations for overlay networks. The third is creating a standards-based multitenant network for hosting providers.

EVPN is powerful because it combines both Layer 2 and Layer 3 advertisements into a single Border Gateway Protocol (BGP) family. People are constantly coming up with ideas on how to use EVPN to make their networks more efficient and easier to use.

The Need for EVPN

Do we really need yet another VPN? Are existing VPNs not sufficient? These are the questions that many network engineers ask when discovering and evaluating new technology. Let's walk through each of the problem statements in more detail.

Data Center Interconnect

Traditionally L3VPN and VPLS have been used in the WAN to provide Data Center Interconnect (DCI). However, when it came to L2VPNs, Virtual Private LAN Service (VPLS) provided the core functionality, but with a lot of drawbacks:

- No active-active multihoming
- No control plane or ability to create routing policies
- Inefficient flooding for MAC discovery and advertisements
- No intersubnet forwarding

- Limited MAC mobility and asymmetric traffic flows
- No advanced Ethernet Services
- No choice in data-plane encapsulation

Limitations aside, VPLS is still a widely used technology in the WAN because it offers a functional point-to-multipoint (P2MP) L2VPN. If all of the weaknesses of VPLS were to be corrected, what would it look like? Are there existing technologies that already address the problems? It turns out that vanilla L3VPN has solved all of the aforementioned problems, but in context of L3 instead of L2. The advent of EVPN has kept this in mind and has molded a lot of its design based on L3VPN principles.

Overlay Networking

As Software-Defined Networking (SDN) was growing and different solutions hit the market, one thing was absolutely clear: there was no standard way of signaling the creation of virtual networks and exchanging MAC addresses. VMware NSX for vSphere used a proprietary method using TCP; other implementations require multicast for Broadcast, Unknown unicast, and Multicast (BUM) traffic replication; later versions of VMware NSX moved to Open vSwitch Database (OVSDB); and Juniper Contrail uses EVPN.

The other issue with overlay networking is that there are many different data plane encapsulations:

- Virtual Extensible LAN (VXLAN)
- Network Virtualization using Generic Routing Encapsulation (NVGRE)
- Stateless Transport Tunneling (STT)
- Multiprotocol Label Switching (MPLS)-over-MPLS
- MPLS-over-User Datagram Protocol (UDP)

One of the design goals with EVPN is that it should be agnostic to the underlying data-plane encapsulation, because it has nothing to do with the actual function and design of the control plane protocol. Binding EVPN to a particular data-plane encapsulation would severely limit EVPN's use cases and deployment. Currently Juniper supports the following EVPN encapsulations: VXLAN, MPLS-over-MPLS, and MPLS-over-UDP.

Standards-Based Multitenancy

Infrastructure as a Service (IaaS) and cloud companies have been building multitenant networks for a long time. Many of the methods are proprietary or based on older technology such as basic Single-Tenant Properties (STP), Multichassis Link Aggregation (MC-LAG), or Virtual Router Redundancy Protocol (VRRP). Of course, such technologies have their own drawbacks:

- No active-active forwarding (STP and VRRP)
- Proprietary (MC-LAG)
- Consumes a lot of address space (VRRP)

EVPN was designed from the ground up to solve all of these issues. It provides native active-active forwarding, it's based on open standards in the IETF, and uses Anycast gateways that only require a single IP address across a set of network devices.

Juniper EVPN Architecture

The first thing to know about EVPN is that's it's implemented with Multiprotocol BGP (MP-BGP). It's just another BGP family. A big benefit is that you can now implement MP-BGP across your entire network, from data center to WAN using the same control-plane protocol. The architecture of EVPN is very similar to a traditional MPLS L3VPN; however, recall that EVPN is agnostic to the data-plane encapsulation. In our first introduction to EVPN, I'll use common MPLS terms such as Label Edge Router (LER), Label Switch Router (LSR), and Customer Edge (CE), as shown in Figure 6-1.

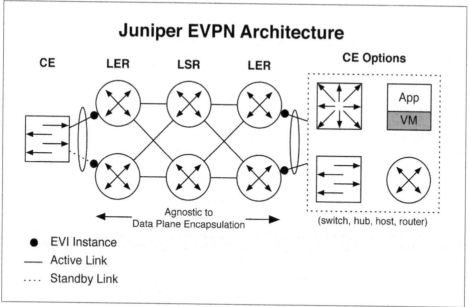

Figure 6-1. Juniper EVPN architecture

The figure shows a very traditional and simple architecture that's very similar to L3VPN. A CE device connects to a pair of LER/Provider Edge (PE) nodes, which in turn are connected into a full mesh to a pair of LSRs. It's the same thing again on the righthand side connecting to a pair of LERs. The righthand CE shows a list of options that's possible with EVPN. You can connect any type of device that speaks L2 or L3; the most common are switches, hubs, hosts, and routers.

The lefthand CE is connected to a pair of LERs, but notice that the north-bound link is active, whereas the south-bound link is standby. This is how VPLS works today, and EVPN is backward-compatible and supports both active-standby and active-active links. The righthand CE has a pair of active-active links.

Every LER has a routing instance that's associated to a particular CE. These routing instances are referred to as an EVPN Instance (EVI). In the example in Figure 6-1, we assume that both CEs are part of the same VPN instance, so the EVI is the same, although there are a total of four EVIs across the four LERs. If an LER had to host multiple CEs in different VPNs, there would be an EVI per VPN.

There are a set of links whenever EVPN operates in active-active or active-standby mode with a CE. In this case, each CE has links going to each LERs. Each of these links is referred to as an Ethernet Segment (ES). For example, the CE on the lefthand side has two ESs because it has two links going to the LERs; if it had four links, it would then have four ESs. All of the ESs work together to form a static Link-Aggregation Group (LAG) or support IEEE 802.3ax (Link Aggregation Control Protocol [LACP]) for a given CE. Each set of ESs has a unique identifier called an Ethernet Segment ID (ESI). For example, the lefthand CE has a single ESI to identify both links or ESs going to the LERs. The same is true for the righthand CE. The ESI is used to identify LAG groups and loop prevention.

NLRI Types

There are many Network Layer Reachability Information (NLRI) types for EVPN. I'll let you read the RFC for the complete list; however, I'll point out the most important NLRIs and how they're used in the design of EVPN architectures. Table 6-1 shows a summary of the EVPN NLRI types and their intended usage.

Table 6-1. EVPN NLRI types and summary

Route type	Description	Function	Standard
1	Ethernet auto-discovery	PE discovery and mass Withdraw	RFC 7432
2	MAC advertisement	Exchange MACs and host IPs	RFC 7432
3	Multicast route	BUM flooding	RFC 7432
4	Ethernet segment route	ES discovery and DF election	RFC 7432
5	IP prefix route	Exchange Prefix/Mask	draft-ietf-bess-evpn-prefix-advertisement

Type-1

The first EVPN NLRI handles discovery just like with a typical L3VPN. No need to define every LER in the network on each LER; EVPN handles that for you automatically. The type-1 NLRI is also used for mass withdraw; this is when all MAC advertisements are withdrawn from an LER in one fell swoop. Type-1 is also used for per-ES auto-discovery (A-D) route to advertise EPVN multihome mode. Finally, it's also used to advertise split-horizon labels for the ES.

Type-2

The next NLRI is type-2, which is the most commonly used; it's used to advertise MAC addresses between LERs.

Type-3

This NLRI handles the advertisement of multicast labels and inclusive multicast routes.

Type-4

This NLRI is mainly used for designated forwarder (DF) election between LERs.

Type-5

One of the recent additions to EVPN is the ability to exchange L3 information with the type-5 NLRI. Instead of exchanging MAC addresses, you can now exchange prefix/mask information, just like an L3VPN.

Data-Plane Metadata

Although EVPN is agnostic to the data plane, there needs to exist certain metadata in order for EVPN to function correctly. Following is a list of that metadata:

Forwarding

How does each network device forward the traffic to the next network device? There needs to be some sort of forwarding mechanism to find the next-hop and send it across the wire.

Service separation

How do we ensure that traffic is separated per tenant or virtual network? What if we have overlapping namespaces? There needs to be a method for partitioning this type of traffic.

Split horizon

EVPN offers active-active forwarding across links. How do we ensure that there are no loops? Split horizon is a method required in the data plane to know when to forward traffic and when to drop traffic to create a loop-free topology.

Hashing

We want to fully utilize all links in our network topology; the data-plane format affects how we handle Equal-Cost Multipathing (ECMP) to ensure all the traffic is equally distributed across all links.

The most common data-plane encapsulations are VXLAN and MPLS; we'll take a closer look at these encapsulations and how each option satisfies all of the just-described requirements.

VXLAN

At a high level, VXLAN encapsulation is simply MAC-over-UDP with a globally unique identifier. Feel free to look at RFC 7348 for all the details about the VXLAN packet format. We'll focus on how VXLAN is used with EVPN to meet the forwarding, service separation, split horizon, and hashing requirements, instead, as depicted in Figure 6-2.

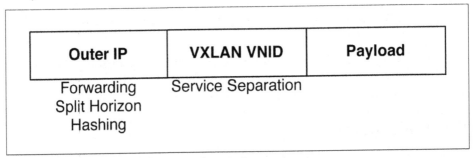

Figure 6-2. VXLAN data-plane metadata assignments

The outer IP handles the forwarding, split horizon, and hashing requirements of EVPN. The forwarding requirement is obviously met by using IPv4 to forward traffic between network nodes; this is often referred to as the *underlay*. You simply need to build an IP fabric that's based purely on L3 addressing across a network topology. Every node in the network should be reachable by every other node via L3.

Hashing is also handled by a combination of the outer IP and UDP metadata. Most network equipment is smart enough to look at L4 information and hash traffic equally based on the flows.

Service separation is handled by the VXLAN VNID, which is a globally unique identifier. Each tenant or virtual network has a unique VXLAN VNID. Each network device must know about this VXLAN VNID in order to forward the traffic into the correct bridge domain or routing instance; so it's critical that the VXLAN VNID be synchronized across all network devices.

At a high level, split horizon works with a combination of the outer IP and VXLAN VNID. A pair of LERs are able to detect if the traffic is destined to a particular ESI.

Each LER can do some sanity checks and determine whether its peer LER has already forwarded the traffic. We'll get much deeper into split-horizon algorithms later in this chapter.

MPLS

MPLS is fundamentally the same architecture, regardless of the VPN types used. Instead of using IP, MPLS uses a transport label. Instead of a globally unique VXLAN VNID, MPLS uses a locally significant service label, as demonstrated in Figure 6-3.

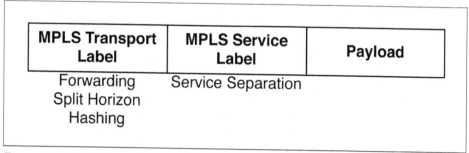

Figure 6-3. MPLS data-plane metadata assignments

The biggest difference between VXLAN and MPLS metadata is that VXLAN has globally significant namespace, whereas MPLS is locally significant. For example, a virtual network in MPLS could use the same service label on every single node in a topology, or it could use a different service label, as long as each node agreed what the service label was mapped to. However, with VXLAN, every single node in the network must use the same VNID for a virtual network.

EVPN Services

Now that EVPN uses MP-BGP, we can bring a host of control-plane policies into the design of the network. At a high level, there are three different types of Ethernet Services: VLAN-Based, VLAN Bundle, and VLAN-Aware. Let's walk through each option.

The first option is the EVPN VLAN-Based Service (Figure 6-4). Each VLAN is mapped directly to its own EVI. In summary, there's a direct 1:1 mapping between VLAN IDs and EVIs.

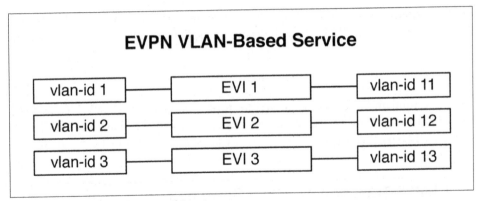

Figure 6-4. EVPN VLAN-Based Service

Because each VLAN ID has its own EVI, that means there's a route target per VLAN ID. So, when LERs advertise which route targets they're interested in, they're basically saying which specific VLAN IDs they're interested in. EVPN also assigns a label to each VLAN ID. In the case of VXLAN, the label is the VNID, and MPLS is the service label. Because each VLAN ID has its own label, we can support VLAN normalization on each side, as shown in Figure 6-4. For example, VLAN ID 1 can be changed to VLAN ID 11, because the labels map directly to a single VLAN ID. Thus, the LERs don't care what VLAN ID is used, because all of the forwarding and flooding happens with a label that's mapped to a VLAN.

One of the downsides to this service is that it will require a lot of label scale, because each VLAN is assigned its own label. Imagine if your network had 16,000 VLANs; this would mean that you would also need 16,000 labels and route targets per network node. The benefit is that it supports VLAN normalization and it has very efficient flooding.

The next type of EVPN service is VLAN Bundle. The biggest difference is that all of the VLAN IDs share the same EVI, as shown in Figure 6-5. This means that there is an n:1 ratio of VLAN IDs to an EVI. From a control plane point of view, there's a single route target, because there's a single routing instance. From an assignment point of view, it's also a single label. An entire set of VLAN IDs share the same label in the data plane.

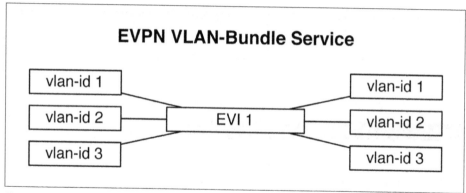

EVPN VLAN-Bundle Service

vlan-id 1

vlan-id 2   EVI 1

vlan-id 3

vlan-id 1

vlan-id 2

vlan-id 3

Figure 6-5. EVPN VLAN Bundle service

The benefit of VLAN Bundling is that it saves on label space, but the drawback is that it has very inefficient flooding because an entire set of VLANs share the same label space. The other drawback is that it cannot support VLAN normalization because of the shared label space. The only way to uniquely identify each VLAN is to read past the label and find the IEEE 802.1Q tag. This means if a frame enters as VLAN ID 1, it must also exit the topology as VLAN ID 1.

The final type of EVPN service is VLAN-Aware, which is a hybrid design of both VLAN Bundle and VLAN-Based, as shown in Figure 6-6. Each VLAN ID is assigned to a single EVI, so it's similar to the VLAN Bundle design with regard to the control plane. All of the VLAN IDs share the same EVI, thus a single route target can handle all of the VLAN IDs.

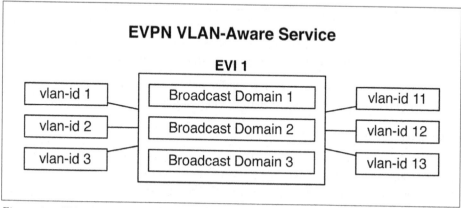

EVPN VLAN-Aware Service

EVI 1

vlan-id 1   Broadcast Domain 1   vlan-id 11

vlan-id 2   Broadcast Domain 2   vlan-id 12

vlan-id 3   Broadcast Domain 3   vlan-id 13

Figure 6-6. EVPN VLAN-Aware Service

However, from a data-plane point of view, each VLAN ID has its own label, which in effect creates its own broadcast domain per VLAN ID. The benefit is that it saves on the number of route targets, supports VLAN normalization, and has efficient flooding.

Table 6-2 concisely summarizes these three services, highlighting the most important attributes for each.

Table 6-2. EVPN services matrix

Attribute	VLAN-Based	VLAN Bundle	VLAN-Aware
VLAN:EVI ratio	1:1	*N*:1	*N*:1
Route target	Per-VLAN	Per-VRF	Per-VLAN
VLAN normalization	Yes	No	Yes
Overlapping MAC addressing	Yes	No	Yes
Juniper support	Yes	Roadmap[a]	Yes

[a] An implicit roadmap item.

Another important design option is whether you need to have overlapping MAC addresses per virtual network. If so, you need to use VLAN-Based or VLAN-Aware, because the VLAN Bundle doesn't support it. This is because VLAN Bundle has a label per VRF and doesn't support a label per VLAN. For example, if you have a label value of "1" for "VRF-1,1" but "VRF-1" has three VLANs all with the same source MAC address, there's no way for the LER to make these overlapping source MAC addresses unique. The LER uses a combination of "label, MAC" in the data plane, so if we have the same label and the same source MAC address, from the perspective of the LER, it's all the same. However, if we use VLAN-Based or VLAN-Aware, the LER now has a label per VLAN. For example, if we have two VLANs, "1" and "2," we can now support overlapping MAC addresses on each LER. Remember that each VLAN has its own label in these services. The LER uses the combination "label, MAC" so for VLAN "1" it looks like "1, MAC" and VLAN "2" looks like "2, MAC." So even though the MAC address is the same, we can create uniqueness with the label.

Now that we understand the high-level differences between the EVPN services, let's walk through how the route targets, labels, and flooding work in each model.

VLAN-Based Service

Let's take a much closer look at how the VLAN-Based model uses the control plane and data plane when it comes to replication of BUM traffic. Recall that VLAN-Based Services has both a route target and service label per VLAN.

Figure 6-7 shows a very simple topology with three PE routers directly attached to one another: PE1, PE2, and PE3. Each PE has two VLANs: VLAN-x and VLAN-y. Below each VLAN are the route target (RT) and label (L) values. For simplicity, we've matched the RT and L values to the VLAN value. VLAN-x has RT-x and L-x. VLAN-y has RT-y and L-y.

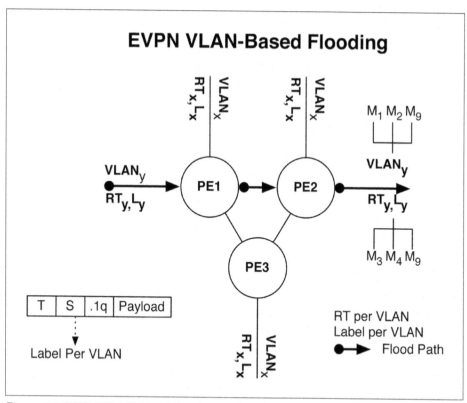

Figure 6-7. EVPN VLAN-Based flooding path and control plane and data plane assignments

The flood path in this figure starts from a host inside of VLAN-y. What we want to do is follow the flood path and logic throughout the topology. The RT is purely a control-plane concept that lets the PEs change routes and build composite next-hops for flood lists. When a set of PE routers share the same RT, this means that they both service traffic that's being advertised through type-2 route updates. The label is a mechanism to keep the data plane synchronized with the control plane. If the control plane agrees on RT-y, typically the data plane will match that with L-y.

PE1 builds perform ingress replication and builds a flood list, which is just an array of other PE routers to which it needs to send the BUM traffic. PE1 builds this list in the control plane with a combination of type-1 and type-3 routes. For VLAN-y to flood traffic from PE1, it needs to find all of the other PE routers that have a matching label. In the case of Figure 6-7, only PE2 has a matching L-y label. Let's walk through the process, step by step:

1. A host on VLAN-y floods traffic.

2. PE1 receives the traffic on VLAN-y.

3. PE1 builds a flood list using members in RT-y and a subset of PE routers with matching L-y labels. In this case, it's only PE2 that also has RT-y and L-y.

4. PE1 floods traffic to PE2.

5. PE2 receives flood traffic from PE1.

6. PE2 has a matching L-y label and floods the traffic to VLAN-y.

7. All hosts on VLAN-y receive the flooded traffic originally from VLAN-y on PE1.

The flood of VLAN-Based service is very efficient, because each VLAN builds its own flood list and sends BUM traffic only to specific PE routers with that particular VLAN. The downside is that as you increase the scale of VLANs, the number of labels required increases, as well.

Figure 6-8 simplifies the RT and label allocations even further. In this example, there are two PE routers and each PE has two routing instances. Each routing instance has a single VLAN. Because there are two routing instances per PE, there are a total of two EVIs between PE1 and PE2.

PE1 and PE2 are performing VLAN normalization because all of the forwarding is performed by the label, which is associated to each VLAN. For example, when PE1 forwards traffic for VLAN-1 to PE 2, it only has to push L-21 and not have to worry about how the VLAN is tagged. PE2 receives the traffic with L-21 and rewrites the IEEE 802.1Q tag from an ID of 1 to 11. The same is true for VLAN-2; PE2 translates it from an ID of 2 to 22.

Within the same PE router, all MPLS labels and VXLAN VNIs must be unique across EVIs, because this is the primary mechanism for tenant and virtual network segmentation. However, between PE routers, MPLS labels can be the same or different because MPLS label namespace is a local operation. If both PE1 and PE2 want to allocate a local label of L-99 for traffic on VLAN-2, it works because only the router in the next-hop has to agree what L-99 means. However, to keep our example simple, Figure 6-8 shows unique label space between all routers.

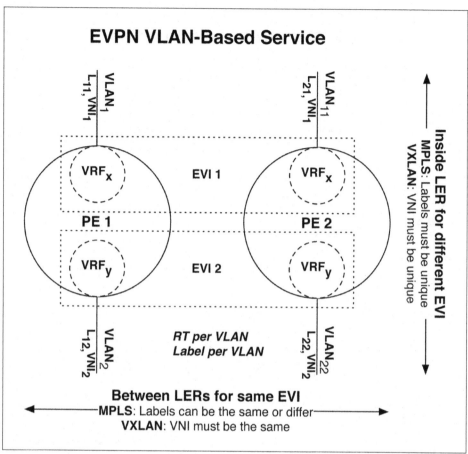

Figure 6-8. EVPN VLAN-Based Service summary

VLAN Bundle service

The topology in Figure 6-9 is exactly the same as that in Figure 6-7, but the difference is that you now see the routing instances, as well. In this case, each PE router has two routing instances, and each routing instance has two VLANs. Because each routing instance has two VLANs, we've named each VLAN instead of saying VLAN-x and VLAN-y.

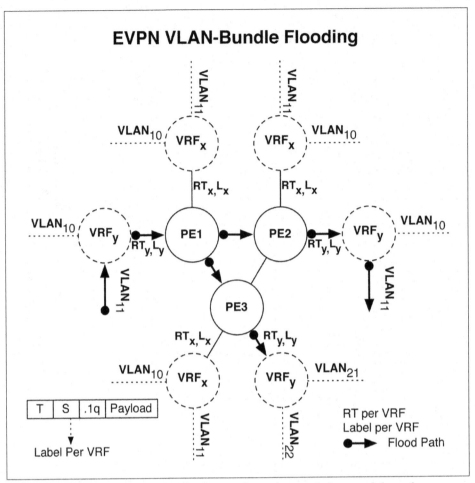

Figure 6-9. EVPN VLAN Bundle flooding paths and control plane and data plane assignments

In our flood example, a host on VLAN-11 sends BUM traffic within VRF-y on PE1. Let's walk through the steps each router takes to flood the traffic in the VLAN Bundle service. Recall that the VLAN Bundle service uses the RT per routing instance and a label per routing instance, as well.

1. A host on VLAN-11 floods traffic.

2. PE1 receives the traffic on VLAN-11 inside the VRF-y routing instance.

3. PE1 builds a flood list using members in RT-y and a subset of PE routers with matching L-y labels. In this case, both PE2 and PE3 have matching RT-y and L-y.

4. PE1 uses ingress replication and floods traffic to PE2 and PE3.

5. PE2 receives the flood traffic from PE1.

6. PE2 has a matching L-y, but L-y is only associated to routing instance VRF-y, which has two VLANs.

7. PE2 looks at the IEEE 802.1Q header to determine the VLAN to which to forward the packet. PE2 has a matching VLAN ID of 11 and forwards the packet to all hosts on VLAN-11.

8. PE3 receives the flood traffic from PE1.

9. PE3 has a matching L-y, but L-y is only associated to routing instance VRF-y, which has two VLANs.

10. PE3 looks at the IEEE 802.1Q header to determine the VLAN to which to forward the packet. PE3 does not have a matching VLAN ID of 11 and drops the packet.

If the egress PE has VLAN-11, the flooding is very efficient. However, if an egress PE doesn't have a matching VLAN-11 in the VRF-y assigned to L-y, the egress PE is forced to drop the packet. In this example, PE2 had VLAN-11 configured and could forward the packet. However, PE3 had the L-y namespace, but didn't have a corresponding VLAN-11, so the bandwidth used was wasted between PE1 and PE3. VLAN Bundling has very inefficient flooding compared to VLAN-Based, but the advantage is that VLAN Bundling requires less label resources in the router. The other disadvantage is that each egress PE must perform extra lookups to determine which egress VLAN to forward the packet to, because the label itself is only associated to the routing instance, which contains multiple VLANs. Therefore, VLAN normalization isn't possible, because the egress PE relies on the VLAN ID for final forwarding.

Now let's take a look at the RT and label assignments in Figure 6-10. There are two PE routers with a single routing instance. However, each routing instance has two VLANs. This is because labels are allocated per routing instance, not VLAN.

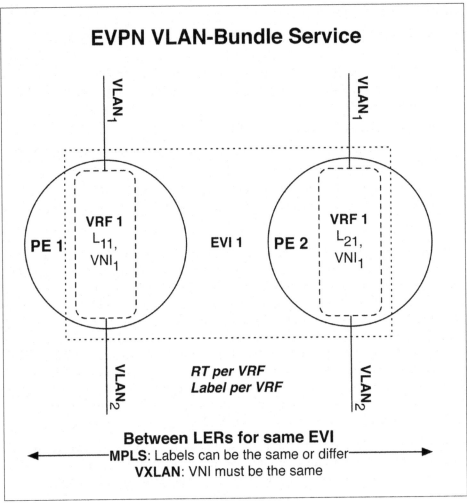

Figure 6-10. EVPN VLAN Bundle Service summary

The VLAN Bundle has the same inter-PE label allocation rules as VLAN-Based. MPLS labels can be the same or be different. However, VXLAN VNIs must match between PE routers for the same EVI.

 As of this writing, Junos doesn't support VLAN Bundle Services, mainly due to the inefficient flooding. In addition, most problems can be solved with either VLAN-Based or VLAN-Aware services.

VLAN-Aware Service

We'll use the same topology and routing instance setup in Figure 6-11 as is depicted in Figure 6-9. This topology uses the same labels, VLAN IDs, and everything else. The only differences are the RT and label allocations. In VLAN-Aware Service, the RT is based per VRF and the labels are allocated per VLAN.

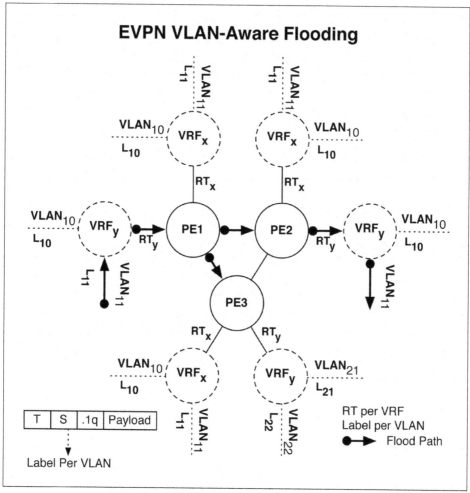

Figure 6-11. EVPN VLAN-Aware flood paths and control-plane and data-plane assignments

Because we have split the control-plane and data-plane allocations, we get a hybrid design with VLAN-Aware. True to its name, it's completely aware of the underlying VLANs within a single EVI and RT. Let's walk through the flood list in detail for VLAN-Aware:

1. A host on VLAN-11 floods traffic.

2. PE1 receives the traffic on VLAN-11 inside the VRF-y routing instance.

3. PE1 builds a flood list using members in RT-y and a subset of PE routers with matching L-y labels. In this case, only PE2 has a matching RT-y and L-y. PE3 has a matching RT-y, but no corresponding L-y, so PE3 is removed from the flood list.

4. PE1 uses ingress replication and floods traffic to only PE2.

5. PE2 receives the flood traffic from PE1.

6. PE2 has a matching L-y which is directly associated with VLAN-11.

7. PE2 forwards the packet to all hosts on VLAN-11.

The benefit to using the VLAN-Aware Service is that it saves on the number of route targets used and provides efficient flooding per VLAN. There's also no need to read into the IEEE 802.1Q header and associate the frame to a particular VLAN, because the label already ties the frame directly to an egress VLAN. This means that each egress PE can perform VLAN normalization because it already knows where to forward the packet to based on the value of the label.

Let's review the label allocation rules for the VLAN-Aware Service in Figure 6-12. There are two PEs with a single EVI; however, each EVI has two VLANs. A single RT is used for the entire routing instance, but a label is assigned for each VLAN.

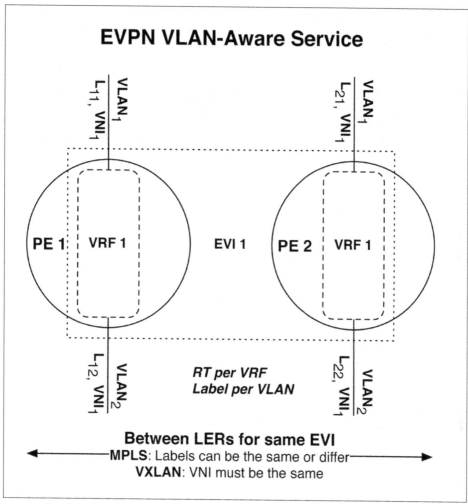

Figure 6-12. EVPN VLAN-Aware Service summary

The VLAN-Aware Service has the same inter-PE label allocation rules as VLAN-Based. MPLS labels can be the same or be different. However, VXLAN VNIs must match between PE routers for the same EVI.

Automatic Route Targets

Junos offers built-in automation for allocating route targets. Traditionally, the route target format was based on three values: 0x02, sub-type, BGP ASN. You generally set these manually on each PE. The general rule of thumb was that you use ASN:n, where n was the same across all PEs interested in that traffic type. However, with EVPN, the number of route targets can increase if you use VLAN-Based or VLAN-Aware Services; it's a label per VLAN. Imagine a scenario in which you have 4,000 VLANs: you would need to manually configure 4,000 route targets as well and make sure they match across all PEs.

Juniper has made a new route target that uses the format (first bit turned on), 0x1, VNID. At least for VXLAN, you can enable automatic route targets. The VNID in VXLAN is required to be the same across a set of PE routers, so the new format will use that VNID value as a base and then append an incremental number for each VLAN. For example, if the VNID were 100 and it had five VLANs, the automatic route targets would be created as:

AS:100:1

AS:100:2

AS:100:3

AS:100:4

AS:100:5

To enable this feature, use the `route-target AS:auto` command in Junos, as shown in the following example:

```
routing-instance FOO
{
    type evpn;
    route-target AS:auto;
    bridge domains {
        BD1 {
            vlan-id 1;
        }
        BD2 {
            vlan-id 2;
        }

    }
}
```

Junos would then use VLAN-Aware Services for `routing-instance FOO` and automatically assign route targets for bridge domains BD1 and BD2.

Split Horizon

Making a loop-free network is very critical when designing an L2VPN service that supports all-active links. It's very easy for BUM traffic to loop back to the source or within the core. One effective method for preventing loops is split horizon. The basic premise is that if you receive BUM traffic, you advertise it out every interface except the interface from which it was learned. Overall, this method works well with single-homed hosts, but as soon as you support multihoming, it becomes more difficult.

Imagine a host multihomed across two routers; how do the routers know if the other router has already sent a copy of the BUM traffic to the host?

Juniper has come up with a few tricks on how to solve this problem. It varies depending on the data-plane encapsulation, but the summary is that the PE routers agree on who should be doing the forwarding of BUM traffic and some loop-detection algorithms to detect and drop duplicate packets. Let's walk through two of the most common examples: MPLS and VXLAN encapsulations.

MPLS data plane

We'll use the topology presented in Figure 6-13 to describe the way loop prevention and split horizon works in an EVPN-MPLS environment. There is a new role in this topology called the designated forwarder (DF); it's responsible for forwarding all BUM traffic for a given ESI. If you recall, ESIs are created when a set of PE routers create a LAG to a CE. For example, Figure 6-13 has two ESIs: one between PE1 and PE2 going to CE2, and another between PE2 and PE3 going to CE3.

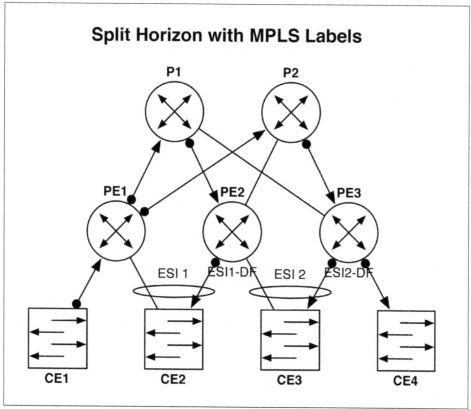

Figure 6-13. Split horizon flooding with MPLS data plane

There are two single-homed CE hubs in this topology: CE1 and CE4. The reason I created such a topology was to have the following scenarios:

- Single-homed CE attached to a PE that is not a DF.
- Single-homed CE attached to a PE that is a DF.
- Dual-homed CE attached to the same PE as single-homed CE which originated the BUM traffic.
- Vanilla dual-homed CE attached to a pair of PE routers.

These different scenarios will affect how BUM traffic is replicated through the network. EVPN-MPLS has the following high-level rules/algorithm when it comes to replicating traffic:

- Ingress PE forwarding a copy to every other interested PE.
- Only DF forwards BUM traffic to CE.
- Split-horizon labels per ESI.
- No split-horizon label for single-homed CEs.
- If egress router receives a split-horizon label from the same ESI, do not forward to that ESI.

Given these simple rules, how can we apply them to Figure 6-13? Will the careful placement of CEs, PEs, DFs, and ESI links in that figure affect how traffic is replicated? Absolutely. Let's walk through what happens at each stage of the replication:

1. CE1 sends BUM traffic to PE1.
2. PE1 receives the BUM traffic.
3. PE1 isn't the DF for ESI 1, so it doesn't forward traffic directly to CE2.
4. PE1 has received type-3 inclusive multicast routes from PE2 and PE3; this is because both PE2 and PE3 are DFs.
5. PE1 learns split-horizon labels from PE2 and PE3 because they're both DFs and have ESIs. In summary, PE1 learned split-horizon labels from PE2 (SH-2) and split-horizon label from PE3 (SH-3).
6. PE1 performs ingress replication. Basically, PE1 makes a local copy for every interested PE.
7. PE1 forwards a copy to PE2 and PE3.
8. PE2 receives a copy from PE1. PE2 is the DF for ESI-1 so forwards the copy to CE2.
9. PE2 is not the DF for ESI 2 and doesn't forward the traffic to CE3.

10. PE3 receives a copy from PE1. PE3 is the DF for ESI-2 and forwards a copy to CE3.

11. PE3 forwards a copy to CE4.

What if the BUM traffic was sourced from CE2 and happened to be hashed to PE1? How does split-horizon labels ensure that PE2 doesn't forward a copy back to CE2, from which it came? In this case, PE1 would receive the traffic from CE2, and because PE1 knows PE2 is part of the same ESI-1, it would add PE2's split-horizon label for ESI-1 to the bottom of the stack and forward it to PE2. When PE2 receives the copy, it would see the split horizon label for ESI-1 and not forward the traffic back to dCE2.

VXLAN data plane

With EVPN-VXLAN, the split horizon follows the same high-level rules as EVPN-MPLS, but with one important difference: it ignores local forwarding rules when it comes to DF. We'll use the same topology again, as depicted in Figure 6-14, but change the names of the device to a data center scheme, instead.

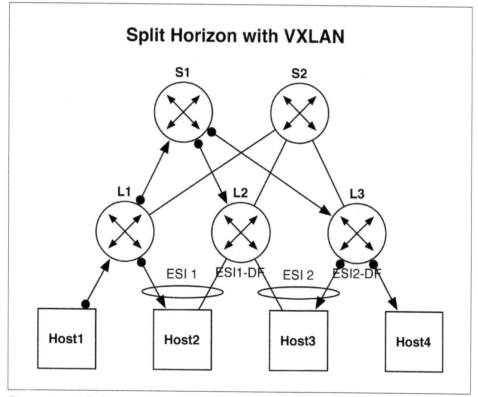

Figure 6-14. Split horizon flooding with VXLAN data plane

The high-level rules for EVPN-VXLAN are as follows:

- Ingress PE forwarding a copy to every other interested PE.
- Always do local flooding unless the source IP of the VXLAN tunnel is from a VTEP that shares the same ESI, then drop the packet.
- DF forwards BUM traffic to CE.

The reason for the change is because VXLAN doesn't support pushing additional labels or metadata into the data plane for the sake of split horizon. So, we need to come up with a different algorithm to accomplish the same result. One piece of additional information we have is the source IP address of the VTEPs that forward BUM traffic. For example, L1 and L2 have the same ESI-1; there is also a VXLAN tunnel between L1 and L2. Therefore, L1 knows the source IP of L2 for that particular VXLAN, and L2 knows the source IP for that particular VXLAN, as well. We can use this piece of information in our split horizon calculations.

We can modify the algorithm to always perform local flooding. For example, Figure 6-14 shows Host1 sending BUM traffic to L1. If we perform local flooding, L1 would send Host2 a copy of that BUM traffic. Now we have to ensure that when L2 receives a copy of the BUM traffic, it would never send it to Host2, as well. Because L2 knows the source IP of VTEP of its ESI-1 peer (L1), it also knows that L1 must have made a local copy and therefore can drop it locally and not forward to Host2.

Let's walk through the BUM traffic replication in Figure 6-14 in more detail:

1. Host1 sends BUM traffic to L1.
2. L1 receives BUM traffic from Host1. L1 makes a local copy to Host2.
3. L1 performs ingress replication to interested VTEPs. L1 sends a copy to L2 and L3.
4. L2 receives a copy from L1.
5. L2 is part of ESI-1 and thus needs to perform split-horizon checks. L2 finds the source IP address of the VTEP that sent the BUM traffic; in this case, it's L1. Because L1 and L2 share the same ESI-1, L2 doesn't forward the traffic to Host2. L2 already knows that L1 must have forwarded a local copy, per EVPN-VXLAN split-horizon rules.
6. L2 isn't the DF for ESI-2 and doesn't send a copy to Host3.
7. L3 receives a copy from L1.
8. L3 is the DF for ESI-2 and forwards a copy to Host3.
9. L3 forwards a copy to Host4.

In summary, EVPN-VXLAN split horizon is exactly the same as EVPN-MPLS, except that it performs local flooding and has to use a different algorithm to perform split-horizon checks with the source IP of the VTEP and ESI. Otherwise, standard DF rules apply.

Mass Withdraw

One of the major design goals of EVPN was to be able to converge as quickly as possible. It's common to have environments with a lot of MAC addresses being learned and changed throughout the network, as demonstrated in Figure 6-15. One area where EVPN can compress the number of MAC addresses learned is behind an ESI.

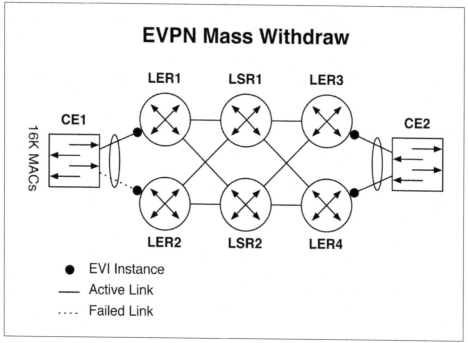

Figure 6-15. EVPN mass withdraw example

For example, in the figure, there are two CEs: CE1 and CE2. Assume that CE1 had 16,000 MAC addresses behind it and those same 16,000 MAC addresses were advertised to LER3 and LER4 so that CE2 could be able to reach them. If there were a link failure between CE1 and LE2, we want to avoid having to withdraw 16,000 MAC addresses with type-2 route updates.

EVPN has optimized failure scenarios to include fast convergence. In the event of a link failure, the corresponding PE can simply invalidate all MAC addresses linked with a single type-1 route update. In the example presented in Figure 6-15, the link between CE1 and LER2 has failed. LER2 would then invalidate all of the 16,000 MAC addresses by withdrawing the corresponding Ethernet A-D type-1 route; then, LER3 and LER3 would invalidate LER2 as a next-hop for the 16,000 MAC addresses.

Anycast Gateways

Traditionally protocols such as VRRP have been used to provide default gateway redundancy. The problem with such designs is that individual secondary addressing is required on each switch, followed by a floating virtual gateway that's shared across the cluster. This creates IP waste because each switch providing gateway redundancy consumes a single IP address in that particular subnet. The other issues are that VRRP isn't an all-active design; only one switch in the cluster can handle gateway processing at any given time. VRRP also requires additional state in the network: frequency timers, dead timers, timeouts, election algorithms, and who's currently the master.

EVPN has helped solve this problem indirectly by natively supporting Layer 2. Figure 6-16 shows a traditional spine-and-leaf architecture in the data center. Instead of using VRRP, you can now directly configure the default gateway on the set of network switches running EVPN. You no longer need to worry about keeping track of timers, state, and individual IP addresses. You simply configure the same IP address/mask on the **irb** interface for each switch participating in providing default gateway services.

The caveat is that you must configure the Anycast default gateway on a switch that natively supports intersubnet routing with MPLS or VXLAN data plane. The Juniper QFX10000 Series supports both, so it's always a safe bet to handle Anycast gateways in the spine. Alternatively, you can configure Anycast gateways in the leaf switches, if they support inter-VXLAN routing. For example, the Juniper QFX5100 Series cannot support inter-VXLAN routing, so you must apply it in the spine with the Juniper QFX10000. However, the Juniper QFX5110 supports inter-VXLAN routing and you can configure it to handle Anycast gateways (shown in the *italics and underline* in Figure 6-16). In summary, EVPN can handle Anycast gateways in either the spine or leaf.

When a host needs to use Address Resolution Protocol (ARP) for its default gateway, one of the spine switches will reply back with a virtual MAC that's shared across all of the spine switches (or leaf switches if using the Juniper QFX5110). The host can then use this virtual MAC address when sending traffic to its default gateway.

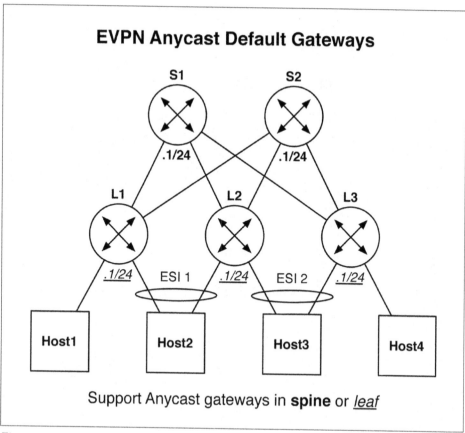

Figure 6-16. EVPN Anycast default gateway architecture options

MAC Mobility

Another consideration of EVPN is that MAC addresses are mobile; they can be moved from one CE to another, as shown in Figure 6-17. Such reasons for MAC mobility could be a virtual machine (VM) migration, mobile backhaul, or any number of other reasons.

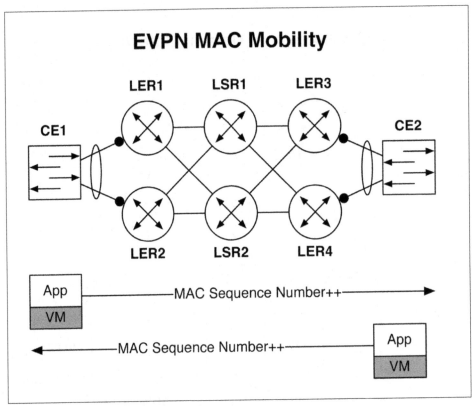

Figure 6-17. EVPN MAC mobility illustration

When a MAC address is learned in the data plane and advertised for the very first time, it's sent as a regular type-2 route. However, if a different PE locally learns the same MAC address, but has an existing type-2 route pointing to a different PE, it will send a new type-2 route with the same MAC address, but include a new extended BGP community called a sequence number. The first time that this happens, the value will be set to 0. All other PEs that receive this new type-2 route with the sequence number community will invalidate previous type-2 routes. For each additional PE that locally learns the same MAC address but has the same MAC address as an existing type-2 route, it will simply increment the extended BGP community value and readvertise the type-2 route along with its extended community to all of the other PEs, which would then invalidate all the previous type-2 routes and use the latest type-2 route with the highest sequence number.

If in the event a MAC moves back and forth very quickly and a set of PE routers advertise the same MAC address with the same sequence number, the PE with the lowest router-ID wins and the other PE routers will flush their local ARP cache.

MAC Aliasing

Due to the nature of where MAC addresses are learned and how other CE devices might hash data into the topology of the network, you can have a scenario in which a CE hashes traffic destined to a remote PE that never locally learned the destination MAC address, as illustrated in Figure 6-18.

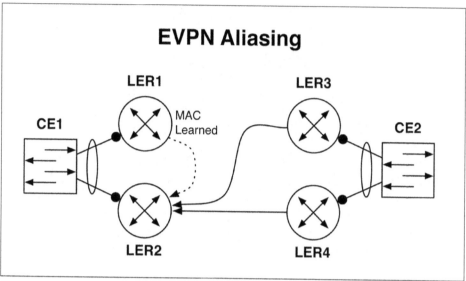

Figure 6-18. EVPN aliasing illustration

The MAC address for CE1 was learned on the data plane of LER1, but it was advertised via EVPN to LER2, LER3, and LER4. CE2 sends traffic to CE1 and happened to hash to both LER3 and LER4. However, LER3 and LER4 have decided to send the traffic to only LER2, which never learned the MAC address of CE1 on the data plane. Because LER1 originally learned the MAC address on the data plane and advertised it via EVPN to all of the other LERs, this means that LER2 already has a type-2 route for the CE2 MAC address and knows it's attached locally to an ESI pointing to CE1.

Load Balancing

When it comes to load balancing the traffic of EVPN, it all depends on the data plane. With MPLS, there's nothing new. You can use a mixture of entropy from the labels, IP, and other things. However, when it comes to EVPN-VXLAN, all of the underlying equipment must rely on IP and UDP for efficient hashing. It gets a bit more complex as IP networks have both L2 *and* L3 hashing that must be accounted for. The originating host flows within the VXLAN encapsulation must be accounted for as well. If Host1 in Figure 6-19 had 100 flows being encapsulated with VXLAN destined to

Host2, how do you ensure that the flows are evenly hashed across both spine switches and to both L3 and L4?

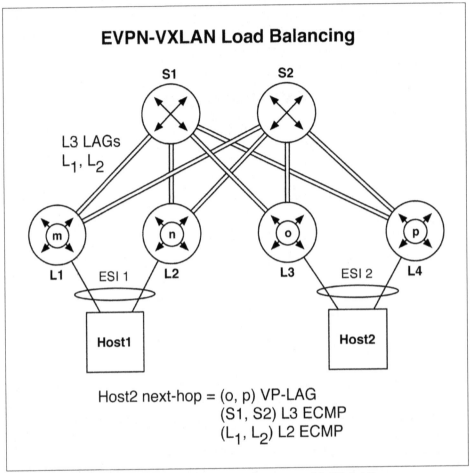

Figure 6-19. EVPN-VXLAN load balancing architecture with VP-LAG

Juniper uses a technology called Virtual Port LAG (VP-LAG) to ensure that flows are efficiently hashed across the network. Figure 6-19 shows a typical spine-and-leaf network with two spines and four leaf switches. This topology is using EVPN-VXLAN and each leaf has a VXLAN tunnel to every other leaf switch in the topology. In other words, it's a full mesh of VXLAN tunnels between all leaf switches. The VTEPs are labeled: m, n, o, and p. Each leaf switch has a VTEP in Figure 6-19 in the center of the switch.

Let's see how traffic is sourced from Host1 and destined to Host2 in this example:

1. Host1 wants to send a frame to Host2.

2. Host1 can send the frame to either L1 or L2. Let's just assume L1 for now.

3. L1 receives the frame destined to Host2.

4. L1 looks at its Ethernet switching table and finds two entries for Host2. The first entry is VTEP-o on switch L3, and the second entry is VTEP-p on switch L4.

5. L1 has a choice to hash to either VTEP-o and VTEP-p. Let's assume VTEP-o for now.

6. L1 encapsulates the frame from Host1 in a VXLAN packet destined to VTEP-o.

7. L1 performs an IP lookup for the VTEP-o address. L1 has a choice to route through either S1 or S2. Let's assume S1 for now.

8. L1 has two forwarding entries for S1 because the link from L1 to S1 is a Layer 3 LAG. That LAG has two interfaces in a bundle: L-1 and L-2. Let's assume L-1 for now.

9. S1 receives the packet.

10. S1 sees the IP packet is destined for VTEP-o.

11. S1 performs an IP lookup for VTEP-o and has two forwarding entries: L-1 and L-2. Let's assume L-1 for now.

12. L3 finally receives the packet. L3 knows it's a VXLAN packet received from L1.

13. L3 pops the VXLAN header and performs a Layer 2 lookup for the destination address in the original Ethernet frame.

14. L3 finds the link attached to Host2 and forwards it along.

A lot has happened for such a simple operation! There are three levels of ECMP for EVPN-VXLAN: VTEP, L3, and L2. The end result is that all the flows from Host2 are equally hashes across the network from leaf to spine.

One advantage to using individual VTEP addressing—as opposed to Anycast VTEP addressing—is that failure scenarios are handled gracefully. Assume that the link between Host2 and L3 failed. Now the next-hop on L1 has changed from "(o, p)" to just "(p)." If you were to use Anycast addressing for VTEPs for both L3 and L4, traffic could be forwarded to a VTEP which has a locally failed link to the host. The leaf switch would be forced to simply drop the traffic, or you have to use interchassis links between L3 and L4.

Inter VXLAN-Routing Modes/EVPN Type-5

Asymmetric and symmetric inter-VXLAN routing. These modes of operation have a funny name because they relate to the number of operations each switch must perform. If you have a pair of switches that are operating in symmetric mode, each switch performs the same number of lookups when performing inter-VXLAN routing. Each switch would perform a different number of forwarding lookups when operating in asymmetric mode. These names come from the number of lookups required on the ingress versus egress PE. For example, asymmetric inter-VXLAN routing requires two lookups on the ingress PE and a single lookup on the egress PE. Symmetric inter-VXLAN routing requires two lookups on both the ingress and egress PE. Unfortunately, these names do not bring to light the actual engineering and design trade-offs behind the scenes.

When EVPN needs to perform inter-VXLAN routing, an EVPN NLRI of type-5 will be used to advertise reachability between the PE switches. If you recall, the NLRI type-2 is used only to advertise MAC addresses; in other words, traffic on the same broadcast domain. In summary, if it's Layer 2 traffic, EVPN uses type-2; and if it's Layer 3 traffic, EVPN uses type-5.

Asymmetric Inter-VXLAN routing

The first option is asymmetric inter-VXLAN routing. The ingress and egress PE will have both source and destination VNIs locally, as demonstrated in Figure 6-20. Let's walk through what's happening in this figure.

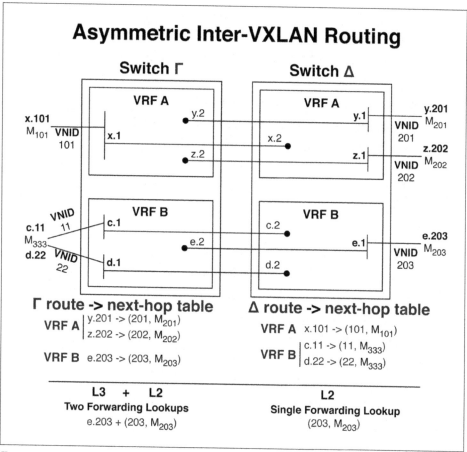

Figure 6-20. Asymmetric inter-VXLAN routing

There are two switches: Gamma and Delta. Each switch has two Virtual Routing and Forwarding (VRF) instances. Each VRF has a variable number of bridge domains and hosts. Let's look at them one by one:

Switch Gamma

- VRF A
  - VNID 101 mapped to VLAN-ID 101 – IRB x.1
    - Single host with MAC address 101 (untagged Ethernet)
      - Host address x.101
  - VNID 201 with IRB y.2
  - VNID 202 with IRB z.2

- VRF B
  - VNID 11 mapped to VLAN-ID 11 – IRB c.1
    - Single host with MAC address 333 (tagged Ethernet)
      - Host address c.11
  - VNID 22 mapped to VLAN-ID 22 – IRB d.1
    - Single host with MAC address 333 (tagged Ethernet)
      - Host address d.22
  - VNID 203 with IRB e.2

Switch Delta

- VRF A
  - VNID 201 mapped to VLAN-ID 201 – IRB y.1
    - Single host with MAC address 201 (untagged Ethernet)
  - VNID 202 mapped to VLAN-ID 202 – IRB z.1
    - Single host with MAC address 202 (untagged Ethernet)
  - VNID 101 with IRB x.2
- VRF B
  - VNID 203 mapped to VLAN-ID 203 – IRB e.1
    - Single host with MAC address 203 (untagged Ethernet)
  - VNID 11 with IRB c.2
  - VNID 22 with IRB d.2

In the example, where x.101 needs to route to y.201, both switch Gamma and Delta need to have both of the corresponding VNIs. In this case, x.101 requires VNID 101 and y.201 requires VNID 201. Therefore, both switch Gamma and Delta need to know about VNID 101 and 201.

Switch Gamma and Delta have two VRFs: A and B. VRF A illustrates how you're able to configure multiple VNIDs per VRF. VRB takes the same concept, but shows the ability to multihome a single host into two VNIDs. For example, the host with MAC address "333" is using IEEE 802.1Q for prefix c.11 and d.22. The c.11 prefix has a VNID of 11 and the d.22 prefix has a VNID of 22.

From the perspective of each host, it only speaks standard Ethernet. There's no concept of VXLAN headers or VNIDs. Keep in mind that VXLAN and VNIDs are only between PE switches.

For example, if c.11 wants to route to e.203, switch Gamma needs to perform two lookups. The first is an L3 lookup to see where e.203 is. Because switch Gamma also has VNID 203 and an IRB e.2, it's able to perform an L2 lookup and forward the frame directly to MAC "333" using VNID 203. When switch Delta receives the frame, it simply needs to perform a single L2 lookup and forward the frame to MAC "333."

The drawback to asymmetric forwarding is that each PE needs to know about all other PE VNIDs, which increases the overall resources and state used per PE.

Symmetric Inter-VXLAN routing

The final mode of inter-VXLAN routing is symmetric mode, as illustrated in Figure 6-21. The big difference is that each PE doesn't need to know about all of the other VNIDs on every other PE. Instead, PE switches are interconnected to one another by using a routed-VNID.

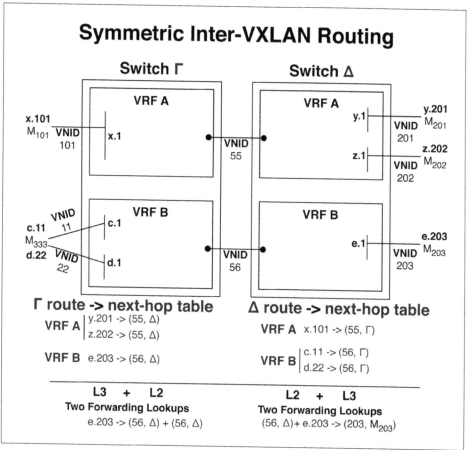

Figure 6-21. Symmetric inter-VXLAN routing

Routed-VNIDs are per VRF. So, for example, VRF A has a routed-VNID of 55 and VRF B has a routed-VNID of 56. Now each ingress and egress PE needs to perform both an L2 and L3 lookup. The benefit is that this accommodates much higher egress PE and VNID scale. For example, you could have a 2,000-egress PE switch with 2,000 VNIDs each, and you only need a single routed-VNID on the ingress PE. Let's again walk both switches, one by one:

Switch Gamma

- VRF A
  — VNID 101 mapped to VLAN-ID 101 – IRB x.1
    — Single host with MAC address 101 (untagged Ethernet)
      — Host address x.101
  — VNID 55 – Routed-VNID for VRF A
- VRF B
  — VNID 11 mapped to VLAN-ID 11 – IRB c.1
    — Single host with MAC address 333 (tagged Ethernet)
      — Host address c.11
  — VNID 22 mapped to VLAN-ID 22 – IRB d.1
    — Single host with MAC address 333 (tagged Ethernet)
      — Host address d.11
  — VNID 56 – Routed-VNID for VRF B

Switch Delta

- VRF A
  — VNID 201 mapped to VLAN-ID 201 – IRB y.1
    — Single host with MAC address 201 (untagged Ethernet)
  — VNID 202 mapped to VLAN-ID 202 – IRB z.1
    — Single host with MAC address 202 (untagged Ethernet)
  — VNID 55 – Routed-VNID for VRF A
- VRF B
  — VNID 203 mapped to VLAN-ID 203 – IRB e.1
    — Single host with MAC address 203 (untagged Ethernet)
  — VNID 56 – Routed-VNID for VRF B

Notice how each ingress PE needs to worry only about its local VNIDs and doesn't have to have a copy of each egress PE VNID. Instead, it has been replaced by a per-VRF routed-VNID. In the case of VRF A, it's VNID 55; for VRF B, it's VNID 56.

Imagine c.11 needs to route to e.203. Switch Gamma needs to do a route lookup for e. 203. It finds it has a route entry for e.203 that points to switch Delta using VNID 55. Now Switch Gamma needs to perform an L2 lookup for switch Delta on VNID 55 as the next-hop. Switch Delta receives the packet from switch Gamma. Switch Delta performs a route lookup for e.203 and sees that it is on VNID 203. Switch Delta performs an L2 lookup and sees that it needs to forward the packet to MAC 203. In summary, switch Delta and Gamma perform the same number of lookups, hence the same symmetric. Also each PE only needs a single routed-VNID per VRF to route traffic between different VNIDs.

EVPN Design

There are a number of design options when it comes to EVPN. We'll begin at a high level and work our way down into the details. The first use case we'll think about is DCI and how EVPN can be applied. The next use case we'll take a look at is a multi-tenant data center. There are various options with engineering trade-offs.

DCI Options

At a high level, DCI is simply connecting any number of data centers together so that traffic can pass between them. However, depending on the existing WAN and protocols, the way in which you can implement EVPN might vary. Let's look at the most common options one by one.

EVPN-VXLAN over L3VPN-MPLS

Let's make the assumption that your company has an MPLS backbone. It doesn't matter whether you manage it in-house or simply buy an L3VPN service from a carrier. What matters is that you have simple L3 connectivity between your data centers and it's encapsulated by MPLS, as shown in Figure 6-22.

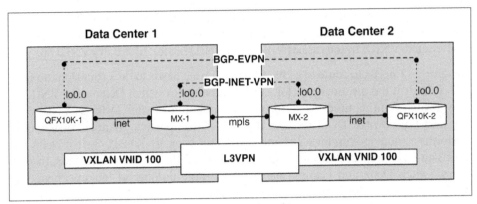

Figure 6-22. EVPN-VXLAN over L3VPN-MPLS architecture

Imagine that QFX10K-1 and MX-1 are in data center "1" and QFX10K-2 and MX-2 are in data center "2." Obviously, you would want redundant nodes and links, but for the sake of simplicity, I've drawn the simplest form of moving traffic from one data center to another.

There are two Juniper MX Series routers that connect the two data centers together and are running a simple MPLS network with an L3VPN. The control plane for L3VPN is MP-BGP running family inet-vpn; the data plane would be MPLS labels.

Figure 6-22 shows that the two Juniper QFX10000 switches set up an EVPN-VXLAN tunnel across the existing L3VPN in the WAN. The control plane is terminated only on the pair of Juniper QFX10000 switches; the Juniper MX routers have no idea about the EVPN control plane. From the perspective of the Juniper MX routers, all the traffic looks like basic L3 traffic. The Juniper QFX10000 switches use MP-BGP family evpn for the control plane and VXLAN for the data plane.

This option is very easy to use because the technical requirements are very easy to meet: simply have L3 connectivity between the two Juniper QFX10000 switches. Most companies today already have a WAN in place and can easily set up EVPN-VXLAN over the top. You can also apply basic traffic engineering to the EVPN-VXLAN tunnel, but because it's encapsulated with VXLAN, the Juniper MX routers can only see the outer IP of the encapsulation, and not all of the flows inside the tunnel. So in summary, you can apply traffic engineering to the VXLAN tunnel itself but not the flows inside.

EVPN-VXLAN to EVPN-MPLS Stitching

To enable per-flow traffic engineering in the WAN, you can use EVPN-VXLAN to EVPN-MPLS stitching. The idea is that the Juniper MX routers participate in the EVPN control plane instead of blindly passing L3 traffic back and forth. The Juniper

QFX10000 switches operate EVPN-VXLAN just like before. There is an EVPN-VXLAN tunnel between the Juniper QFX10000 and MX, as depicted in Figure 6-23.

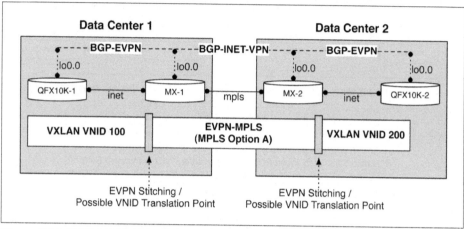

Figure 6-23. EVPN-VXLAN to EVPN-MPLS stitching architecture

The Juniper MX will translate the VXLAN encapsulation into MPLS. During this translation point, it's possible to classify traffic and put it into different QoS profiles or even different MPLS tunnels that are subject to traffic engineering.

The EVPN-VXLAN tunnels are only between the Juniper QFX10000 and Juniper MX; there is no single EVPN-VXLAN tunnel between the Juniper QFX10000 switches any longer. Every time there is a data-plane encapsulation change, there's an opportunity to apply data-plane translations. Figure 6-23 shows two VNID translation points on each Juniper MX router. It's possible to use VNID 100 for data center "1" and VNID 200 for data center "2."

As MAC addresses are exchanged between QFX10K-1 and QFX10K-2, the two Juniper MX routers in the middle participate in the control plane. In the previous example, the Juniper MX routers didn't participate in EVPN at all, but simply forwarded traffic based on the outer IP labels. Because the Juniper MX routers participate in the control plane, it's possible for you to apply control-plane policy at every point between the two data centers.

EVPN-VXLAN over-the-top

Imagine a scenario in which you simply need to transport EVPN-VXLAN over the top (OTT) of an existing network. This is very similar to EVPN-VXLAN over an existing L3VPN in our first example. The first distinction here is the use case. Imagine the network between the two Juniper MX routers is the Internet instead of a private L3VPN, as shown in Figure 6-24.

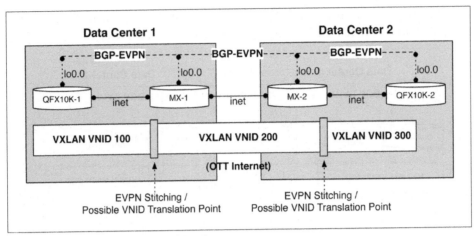

Figure 6-24. EVPN-VXLAN OTT architecture

The next distinction is that the Juniper MX routers are terminating a new EVPN-VXLAN tunnel. Obviously, the Internet isn't very secure, so another option could be to build an encrypted tunnel between the two Juniper MX routers and then transport EVPN-VXLAN.

Regardless of the transport network between the two Juniper MX routers, we're showing an end-to-end EVPN-VXLAN control plane from each data center but with two VNID transition points in the data plane, because the Juniper MX routers are terminating VXLAN.

The other benefit to this design is that you could have multiple EVPN-VXLAN tunnels between the Juniper MX routers, each going over a different transport network for resiliency. One could be over an encrypted tunnel on the Internet, the other tunnel over an internal L3VPN, and so on.

EVPN-VXLAN over dark fiber

The last option is to simply remove the Juniper MX routers from the picture and directly terminate the fiber into each of the Juniper QFX10000 switches, as demonstrated in Figure 6-25.

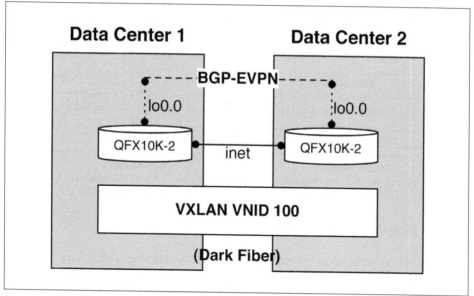

Figure 6-25. Architecture for EVPN-VXLAN over dark fiber

Because the EVPN-VXLAN tunnel is terminated on each switch, there's no opportunity for a VNID translation point.

EVPN-VXLAN Fabric Options

There are also a number of design options when using EVPN within a data center. First, we need to break down how multitenancy is handled. The next design options are the physical network topology, the control-plane design, and finally the placement of VXLAN gateway placement in the topology.

Multitenant fundamentals

There are two basic options for designing multitenancy with the Juniper QFX10000 and EVPN (Figure 6-26). However, each option uses the same fundamental building blocks: virtual switches (VS), VRF instances, and bridge domains (BD). For each tenant to have overlapping IP namespaces, we need to separate them into different VRFs, as illustrated in Figure 6-26. The first tenant is labeled as T1 and the second tenant as T2. For example, if each tenant has its own VRF, T1 and T2 can share the same IP space 192.168/16.

The next namespace to think about is VLAN-ID values. Do you need to use the same VLAN-ID across multiple tenants? If so, you need a VS per tenant. However, if you can use a unique VLAN-ID for each tenant, there's no need for a VS per tenant, as is demonstrated on the left side of Figure 6-26.

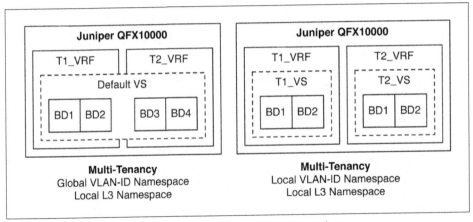

Figure 6-26. Juniper QFX10000 multitenancy namespace options

The first option is the most common and easiest to configure; with it, you can create a global VLAN-ID namespace. For example, all VLAN-IDs in the default virtual switch must be unique, as shown at the far left in Figure 6-26. Each tenant has its own set of unique VLAN-IDs: 1, 2, 3, and 4.

 A default virtual switch requires that each tenant has a unique VLAN-ID. We are talking only about VLAN-ID namespace, not IP or MAC namespace. It's still possible to have overlapping IP addresses between tenants because they're separated with a unique VRF. You can also have overlapping MAC addresses between BDs. For example, MAC address 11:22:33:44:55:66 can exist in both BD1 and BD2 at the same time because each BD represents its own MAC address name space. In summary, all a VS allows you to do is have overlapping VLAN-ID namespaces. For example, if T1 and T2 both require VLAN-ID 444, each tenant needs its own VS.

With the second option, each tenant can have its own virtual switch. Basically each tenant can have overlapping VLAN-ID namespaces. Generally, this is the least common configuration option, because it requires you to keep track of additional VLAN-ID state in the switch at the expense of having the same VLAN-ID across multiple tenants.

 As of this writing, the Juniper QFX10000 series supports only a global VLAN-ID namespace. Check with your account team or Juniper product management to get an update for virtual switch support.

Underlay and overlay BGP design

When designing an EVPN-VXLAN fabric, you must think about the underlay and overlay as two separate networks with completely different control planes. Decisions you make in the underlay affect how the overlay operates. From an underlay point of view, there is only a single core requirement: export switch loopbacks so that all switches are reachable via IP. We could just build a large Layer 2 domain with IRBs for the underlay, but that takes us back to some of the very problems we're trying to solve with EVPN-VXLAN: simple, no chance of Ethernet-based loops, easily scalable, and fast convergence. *The general wisdom is that the underlay should be built using pure Layer 3 with either an IGP or BGP.*

That leads to this question: should you use an IGP or BGP for the underlay? The short answer is that both options work just fine; however, there are trade-offs that you need to consider. To properly evaluate the underlay options, you must first consider the overlay options, as well. EVPN requires MP-BGP to operate, so the natural question is should you use external BGP (eBGP) or internal BGP (iBGP)? Because EVPN is only used in the overlay, consider how the default rules of eBGP and iBGP would affect the way MAC address learning occurs between two PEs. By default, eBGP will change the next-hop to the switch's own interface, whereas iBGP does not. Of course, you can use knobs to change this default behavior, but we'll put that aside.

Imagine a scenario in which you have PE-1 and PE-2 connected only to a P router; in other words, PE-1 and PE-2 are not directly connected and are only reachable through the P router. If PE-1 advertised an EVPN prefix to PE-2 via eBGP, the P router in the middle would change the next-hop to its own interface IP address. This means that whenever PE-1 wants to send traffic destined to PE-2's VTEP address, the forwarding entry will be the P switch, instead. The P router will receive the traffic and see that it's destined to itself, and as it inspects the packet, it needs to remove the VXLAN header and look at the original Ethernet payload to determine where it should be forwarded. In this case, the P router will see the Ethernet frame is destined to PE-2, and it must encapsulate the Ethernet frame yet again and forward it to PE-2.

The other scenario is to imagine EVPN using iBGP, instead; the next-hop will never be changed. PE-1 sends traffic to PE-2, the EVPN forwarding address is PE-2, but the underlay destination IP address is PE-2. PE-1 knows it needs to go to the P switch in order to reach PE-2, so it forwards the traffic to the P switch. The P switch receives the IP packet, sees that it is destined to PE-2 and simply forwards it along, instead of having to remove the VXLAN header. In summary, it's recommended to use iBGP for EVPN, because the default behavior is not to change the next-hop. We could make eBGP work with EVPN, but we need to begin modifying the default behavior of the protocol.

Now let's get back to the underlay. We know we want to use iBGP for the overlay/EVPN. How does this affect the underlay design? If we use BGP For the underlay, the link cost and number of hops will not be communicated back into iBGP/overlay. So, if you have a symmetric topology or other VXLAN L3 Anycast Gateways elsewhere in the network, it can cause problems with EVPN. Imagine both a local and remote VXLAN L3 gateway advertising the same prefix/mask. How does a PE know which VXLAN L3 gateway is closer? If you're using iBGP for the overlay, you need to use standard BGP best path selection in order to determine which gateway is the closest. This means that you need to use a standard IGP in the underlay so that link values are copied into iBGP in the overlay. If your topology is symmetric (spine-and-leaf) and you do not need local and remote VXLAN L3 gateways sharing the same prefix/mask, you can generally get away with using just BGP for the underlay. The benefit being that you can run a single protocol in the underlay, overlay, and WAN. The downside is that you can get some asymmetric traffic during a link failure unless you apply some specific BGP import and export policies to the spine-and-leaf switches.

In summary, I recommend that you use an IGP for the underlay and iBGP for the overlay. Whether it's Open Shortest Path First (OSPF) or Intermediate System to Intermediate System (IS-IS), that decision is up to you. Both work equally well for the underlay. Now the overlay can take into account link failures and link values when ingress PE routers are sending traffic to VXLAN L3 gateways.

VXLAN gateway placement

Inter-VXLAN routing is a big functional requirement with EVPN-VXLAN. Figure 6-27 demonstrates that there are many options for the placement of a VXLAN gateway in the topology.

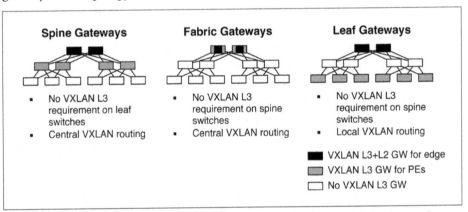

Figure 6-27. Common options for VXLAN L3 gateway placement within a network topology

One thing to note is that we always need VXLAN L3 and L2 gateways on the edge of the network as shown by the black switch in Figure 6-27; this is so we can leave the EVPN-VXLAN bubble and talk to the real world. The big point is that Figure 6-27 is showing three different options for VXLAN L3 gateways when it comes to inter-VXLAN routing between PE switches.

The first option is to put the VXLAN L3 gateways in the spine of the network, as shown on the far left of of the figure, using gray switches. The big benefit is that you can use older leaf switches that do not support VXLAN routing in an EVPN-VXLAN network. The drawback is that all VXLAN routing must happen in the spine of the network.

The second option is very interesting, because it shows both the VXLAN L3 gateways in the fabric or edge of the topology. Recall that we always need VXLAN routing in the edge so that we can talk to the real world. In this example, the VXLAN L3 gateway is performing double duty for both the edge and inter-VXLAN routing between PE switches. The big benefit here is that the spine switches only need to be configured as part of the underlay; there's no requirement for the spine switches to participate in the overlay. One scenario where this will come in handy is during a migration from an older environment where you have existing spine switches and you do not want to replace them immediately.

The third option shows VXLAN L3 gateways in the leaf of the topology using newer Juniper QFX switches. For example, these could be Juniper QFX10002 or QFX5110 switches. The benefit is that all inter-VXLAN traffic is routed locally on the switch and doesn't need to go to the spine or fabric.

BGP route reflector options

Recall that the recommendation for the overlay is to use iBGP. With iBGP comes the typical default behavior of not readvertising prefixes to neighbors with the same Autonomous System (AS) from which it was learned. For all of the switches to learn MAC addresses, we need a full mesh or some form of BGP route reflection (RR), as shown in Figure 6-28.

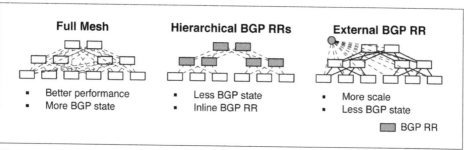

Figure 6-28. BGP RR options

A full mesh of BGP sessions between all PE switches will generally result in faster performance but less overall scale due to the high number of BGP sessions required.

Full mesh generally works well for less than 20 PE switches, otherwise it's recommended to either use hierarchical BGP RRs or external BGP RRs.

Hierarchical BGP RRs work by creating a BGP RR cluster per point of delivery (POD); the spine switches are the BGP RR cluster and the POD leaf switches are the BGP clients. The fabric switches act as another BGP RR, and the spine switches in each POD are the BGP clients.

The other option is to use eBGP RRs. The configuration is a bit simpler and provides more scale. Each switch in the topology peers with external BGP RRs for all EVPN advertisements.

Case Study

Now that we have learned all about EVPN, architecture, and different design options, let's walk through a case study and learn how to configure and verify EVPN-VXLAN in our lab. To kick things off, we'll use the equipment presented in Figure 6-29. The fabric switches are Juniper QFX5200s, because all we need for a simple lab is IP connectivity. We'll use the Juniper QFX10002 switches in the spine and the Juniper QFX5200 switches as the leaf.

Although I recommend an IGP-based underlay for EVPN-VXLAN, we'll take a look at how to implement a pure BGP-based underlay and overlay in this case study. We'll review the specific BGP import and export policies to account for remote VXLAN L3 gateways and failure scenarios to ensure traffic stays local and symmetric.

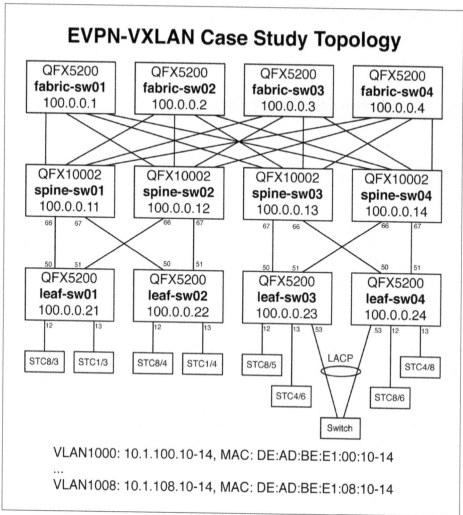

Figure 6-29. EVPN-VXLAN case study topology

We'll also use a testing appliance to generate Ethernet frames and IP packets so that we can verify that EVPN-VXLAN is working properly. The tester ports are plugged in to the leaf switches.

Configuration

There are a lot of moving parts to the EVPN-VXLAN configuration. It begins with the definition of EVPN attributes such as route targets and VNI definitions. We also have to map the VNIs to VLAN-IDs. There is also routing policy that must be present so that each PE learns the MACs from remote PEs in which it's interested.

Loopback and BGP ASN assignments

Table 6-3 lists how the interfaces and BGP AS Numbers (ASNs) are assigned in our test topology.

Table 6-3. Case study loopback and BGP assignments for switches

Switch	Loopback	Underlay BGP ASN	Overlay BGP ASN
fabric-sw01	10.0.0.1	60001	N/A
fabric-sw02	10.0.0.2	60002	N/A
fabric-sw03	10.0.0.3	60003	N/A
fabric-sw04	10.0.0.4	60004	N/A
spine-sw01	10.0.0.11	60011	65200
spine-sw02	10.0.0.12	60012	65200
spine-sw03	10.0.0.13	60013	65200
spine-sw04	10.0.0.14	60014	65200
leaf-sw01	10.0.0.21	60021	65200
leaf-sw02	10.0.0.22	60022	65200
leaf-sw03	10.0.0.23	60023	65200
leaf-sw04	10.0.0.24	60024	65200

Note that the fabric switches have no need to participate in the overlay, as they're just transit IP switches that blindly forward the VXLAN traffic to its final destination. Also be aware this only happens for inter-POD traffic and never within a single POD.

All of the switches are using standard eBGP to create an IP fabric for the underlay. Each link is a /31 point-to-point interface. The eBGP sessions are created by using the interface IP addresses.

EVPN assignments

Let's take a look at how we put together EVPN. We need to specify the encapsulation, VNI list, and replication options for each switch. Table 6-4 lays it all out.

Table 6-4. EVPN Assignments

Switch	Encapsulation	VNI List	Replication
spine-sw01	vxlan	1000–1008	Ingress replication
spine-sw02	vxlan	1000–1008	Ingress replication
spine-sw03	vxlan	1000–1008	Ingress replication
spine-sw04	vxlan	1000–1008	Ingress replication
leaf-sw01	vxlan	1000–1008	Ingress replication
leaf-sw02	vxlan	1000–1008	Ingress replication
leaf-sw03	vxlan	1000–1008	Ingress replication
leaf-sw04	vxlan	1000–1008	Ingress replication

Now we need to assign a route target to each VNI, as shown in Table 6-5. You can optionally use automatically generated route targets as well, but in this test topology, I elected to use manually defined route targets because it's easier to understand as we take a look at the route table and other show commands.

Table 6-5. EVPN VNI assignments

VNI	Route Target	BGP community
1000	target:1:1000	com1000
1001	target:1:1001	com1001
1002	target:1:1002	com1002
1003	target:1:1003	com1003
1004	target:1:1004	com1004
1005	target:1:1005	com1005
1006	target:1:1006	com1006
1007	target:1:1007	com1007
1008	target:1:1008	com1008

The next step is to assign a BGP community used for learning Ethernet Segment Identifier (ESI) memberships across the topology. This can be the same across all PEs and doesn't need to be unique. In our test topology, we'll use the assignment shown in Table 6-6.

Table 6-6. BGP community for EVPN ESI

BGP community name	Value
comm-leaf_esi	target:9999:9999

The comm-leaf_esi community is used on both the spine and leaf for EVPN ESI. As leaf switches are configured for ESI, this community is used to signal other PEs the existence and location of each ESI.

Overlay RRs

In our test topology, each POD served as its own BGP RR; for example, spine-sw01 and spine-sw02 were part of a BGP RR cluster, and spine-sw03 and spine-sw04 were part of another BGP RR cluster. All of the spine switches simply had a full mesh of BGP sessions between each other for EVPN.

Following is the EVPN BGP RR configuration:

```
group overlay-evpn {
    type internal;
    local-address 100.0.0.11;
    family evpn {
        signaling;
```

```
    }
    cluster 2.2.2.2;
    local-as 65200;
    multipath;
    neighbor 100.0.0.21;
    neighbor 100.0.0.22;
}
group overlay-evpn-rr {
    type internal;
    local-address 100.0.0.11;
    family evpn {
        signaling;
    }
    local-as 65200;
    multipath;
    neighbor 100.0.0.12;
    neighbor 100.0.0.13;
    neighbor 100.0.0.14;
}
```

What you see is that each of the spine switches peer with one another by using vanilla iBGP with family EVPN in the group called overlay-evpn-rr. Take note that all spine switches are forming a BGP full mesh in the group overlay-evpn-rr. The overlay-evpn group defines the BGP RR cluster 2.2.2.2 and peers with the leaf switches.

Tenant assignments

We'll have four tenants in our topology: TENANT_10, TENANT_20, SQUARE, and TRIANGLE. The tenant namespace is partitioned so that each POD has both unique and matching tenants as shown in Table 6-7.

Table 6-7. EVPN tenant assignments

Switch	Tenant assigned	POD	IP namespace
spine-sw01	TENANT_10	POD1	10.1.100-104.0/24
spine-sw02	TENANT_10	POD1	10.1.100-104.0/24
spine-sw03	TENANT_10	POD2	10.1.100-104.0/24
spine-sw04	TENANT_10	POD2	10.1.100-104.0/24
spine-sw01	TENANT_20	POD1	10.1.105-108.0/24
spine-sw02	TENANT_20	POD1	10.1.105-108.0/24
spine-sw03	TENANT_20	POD2	10.1.105-108.0/24
spine-sw04	TENANT_20	POD2	10.1.105-108.0/24
spine-sw01	SQUARE	POD1	10.255.99.0/24
spine-sw02	SQUARE	POD1	10.255.99.0/24
spine-sw03	TRIANGLE	POD2	10.255.100.0/24
spine-sw04	TRIANGLE	POD2	10.255.100.0/24

Both PODs share TENANT_10 and TENANT_20; EVPN will use type-2 advertisements between these tenants. However, note that each POD also has its own unique tenant assigned. POD1 has SQUARE and POD2 has TRIANGLE. This was done intentionally to illustrate the point of EVPN type-5. POD1 and POD2 will use EVPN type-5 to learn the prefix/mask of SQUARE and TRIANGLE.

Let's take a look at the VRF configuration for the tenants on spine-sw01 and spine-sw02:

```
routing-instances {
    VRF_TENANT_10 {
        instance-type vrf;
        interface irb.100;
        interface irb.101;
        interface irb.102;
        interface irb.103;
        interface irb.104;
        interface lo0.10;
        route-distinguisher 100.0.0.11:10;
        vrf-target target:10:10;
    }
    VRF_TENANT_20 {
        instance-type vrf;
        interface irb.105;
        interface irb.106;
        interface irb.107;
        interface irb.108;
        interface lo0.20;
        route-distinguisher 100.0.0.11:20;
        vrf-target target:10:20;
    }
    SQUARE {
        instance-type vrf;
        interface irb.999;
        interface lo0.999;
        route-distinguisher 100.0.0.11:999;
        vrf-target target:10:999;
    }

}
```

The spine-sw03 and spine-sw04 have the same configuration, but instead have configuration for the TRIANGLE tenant instead of SQUARE.

Now let's take a look at the VLAN configuration on spine-sw01 and spine-sw02:

```
vlans {
    bd1000 {
        vlan-id 100;
        l3-interface irb.100;
        vxlan {
            vni 1000;
```

```
            ingress-node-replication;
        }
    }
    < ... truncated ... >
    bd1008 {
        vlan-id 108;
        l3-interface irb.108;
        vxlan {
            vni 1008;
            ingress-node-replication;
        }
    }
    SQUARE {
        vlan-id 999;
        l3-interface irb.999;
        vxlan {
            vni 999;
            ingress-node-replication;
        }
    }
}
```

Yet again, spine-sw03 and spine-sw04 have the same configuration, except the SQUARE VLAN is replaced with the TRIANGLE VLAN.

EVPN configuration

The spine and leaf have the same protocols evpn configuration, as shown here:

```
evpn {
    vni-options {
        vni 1000 {
            vrf-target export target:1:1000;
        }
        vni 1001 {
            vrf-target export target:1:1001;
        }
        vni 1002 {
            vrf-target export target:1:1002;
        }
        vni 1003 {
            vrf-target export target:1:1003;
        }
        vni 1004 {
            vrf-target export target:1:1004;
        }
        vni 1005 {
            vrf-target export target:1:1005;
        }
        vni 1006 {
            vrf-target export target:1:1006;
        }
```

```
            vni 1007 {
                vrf-target export target:1:1007;
            }
            vni 1008 {
                vrf-target export target:1:1008;
            }
        }
        encapsulation vxlan;
        extended-vni-list [ 1000 1001 1002 1003 1004 1005 1006 1007 1008 ];
        multicast-mode ingress-replication;
}
```

Both the spine and leaf have the following switch-options configuration, as well:

```
switch-options {
    vtep-source-interface lo0.0;
    route-distinguisher 100.0.0.21:1;
    vrf-import LEAF-IN;
    vrf-target target:9999:9999;
}
```

The only difference is that each switch has its own route-distinguisher, which is a combination of its loopback address appended with :1.

Let's take a look at the default switch import policy on the spine-and-leaf switches:

```
policy-statement LEAF-IN {
    term import_vni1000 {
        from community com1000;
        then accept;
    }
< ... truncated ... >
    term import_vni1008 {
        from community com1008;
        then accept;
    }
    term import_leaf_esi {
        from community comm-leaf_esi;
        then accept;
    }
    term default {
        then reject;
    }
}
```

What's happening here is that we're allowing all of the route targets associated with VNI 1000 through 1008. We're also allowing the global route target that handles EVPN ESIs. Finally, we reject anything else.

Anycast Gateway address configuration

We'll want to use Anycast Gateways across all of the spine switches, using the same IP address. That way, the leaf switches can hash to any of its local spine switches and get a default gateway in an all-active configuration, Here's how to do it:

```
irb {
    unit 100 {
        description " * TENANT 10 - vlan 100 - vni 1000 ";
        family inet {
            address 10.1.100.211/24 {
                virtual-gateway-address 10.1.100.1;
            }
        }
    }
< ... truncated ... >
    unit 108 {
        description " * TENANT 20 - vlan 108 - vni 1008 ";
        family inet {
            address 10.1.108.211/24 {
                virtual-gateway-address 10.1.108.1;
            }
        }
    }
}
```

As of Junos 15.1X53D30.16, the Juniper QFX10000 requires the use of a unique IP address (10.1.100.211/24) in addition to the virtual Anycast Gateway address (10.1.100.1). This is to prevent asymmetric traffic when the spine sends an ARP request to a leaf switch and it comes back on another interface. You can probably expect some software updates in the future to support Anycast Gateways without having to use a unique IP address. Ask your account team for more information.

Access port configuration

The leaf switches have two interfaces plugged in to our testing tool: xe-0/0/12 and xe-0/0/13. We also set up a special switch that connects via LACP to leaf-sw03 and leaf-sw04 on ports et-0/0/53:

```
interfaces {
    xe-0/0/12 {
        description "to STC";
        unit 0 {
            family ethernet-switching {
                interface-mode trunk;
                vlan {
                    members 100-108;
                }
            }
        }
    }
```

```
    xe-0/0/13 {
        description "to STC";
        unit 0 {
            family ethernet-switching {
                interface-mode trunk;
                vlan {
                    members 100-108;
                }
            }
        }
    }
    et-0/0/50 {
mtu 9192;
        unit 0 {
            family inet {
                mtu 9000;
                address 172.16.0.43/31;
            }
        }
    }
    et-0/0/51 {
mtu 9192;
        unit 0 {
            family inet {
                mtu 9000;
                address 172.16.0.47/31;
            }
        }
    }
    et-0/0/53 {
        ether-options {
            802.3ad ae0;
        }
    }
    ae0 {
        esi {
            00:01:01:01:01:01:01:01:01:01;
            all-active;
        }
        aggregated-ether-options {
            lacp {
                active;
                system-id 00:00:00:01:01:01;
            }
        }
        unit 0 {
            family ethernet-switching {
                interface-mode trunk;
                vlan {
                    members 100-108;
                }
            }
```

```
        }
      }
    }
```

The ports xe-0/0/12 and xe-0/0/13 are standard, tagged access ports. The et-0/0/53 is configured for IEEE 802.3ad and assigned to interface ae0. The ae0 interface is configured for LACP. We need to hardcode the system-id so that it matches on both leaf-sw03 and leaf-sw04. We also need to assign an ESI to ae0 that matches on leaf-sw03 and leaf-sw04. However, recall that each ESI must be unique; so if you add another ESI, it needs to have a different ID. The configuration for leaf-sw04 looks the same, minus the et-0/0/50 and et-0/0/51 IP addresses going to the spine switches.

BGP policy

Because we opted to use BGP for the underlay, we need to include some BGP policy to prevent using remote VXLAN L3 gateways and asymmetric traffic during link failures. Let's take a closer look at a specific link failure and how the overlay would respond (Figure 6-30).

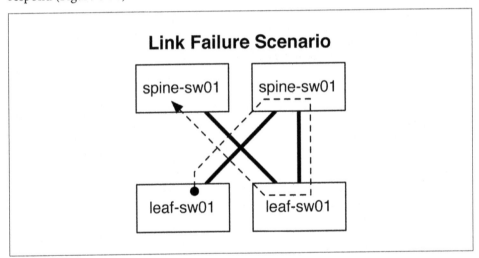

Figure 6-30. Link failure and asymmetric traffic

Imagine that the physical link between spine-sw01 and leaf-sw01 went down, as shown in the figure. Because iBGP is peering using loopback addresses, the overlay BGP connection will still be active because it will follow the dotted line to find the loopback address of spine-sw01. Obviously, this isn't a desired result, so we need to add some underlay BGP policy to prevent this behavior.

Recall that all the spine switches have the same VXLAN L3 gateway address for TENANT_10 and TENANT_20. How does leaf-sw01 know which gateway is local?

Remember that iBGP has all of the link metrics because we aren't using an IGP. We'll need to make some policy to prevent remote VXLAN L3 gateways from being used, as well.

Spine switches. One way to solve the link failure problem is to tag all local prefixes with a POD-based community. Each spine switch adds a POD-specific community to each prefix advertised in the underlay, as shown here:

```
policy-statement bgp-ipclos-out {
    term loopback {
        from {
            protocol direct;
            route-filter 100.0.0.11/32 orlonger;
        }
        then {
            community add MYCOMMUNITY;
            next-hop self;
            accept;
        }
    }
    term as-path {
        from {
            as-path asPathLength2;
            community MYCOMMUNITY;
        }
        then reject;
    }
}
```

The second term handles the link failure scenario. It simply says that any prefix that has more than two as_path attributes that's within its own community shall be dropped. Therefore, the iBGP session shown in Figure 6-30 as the dotted line wouldn't be able to exist.

Leaf switches. To handle the remote VXLAN L3 gateway problem, you can create a policy on the leaf switch that looks for EVPN type-1 and type-2 advertisements from remote spines in other PODs and drop them. Therefore, leaf switches only accept local VXLAN L3 gateways from within the POD:

```
policy-statement OVERLAY-IN {
    term reject-remote-gw {
        from {
            family evpn;
            next-hop [ 100.0.0.13 100.0.0.14 ];
            nlri-route-type [ 1 2 ];
        }
        then reject;
    }
    term accept-all {
        then accept;
    }
}
```

We do not want the leaf switches acting as transit routers in the underlay, so we need to add a `reject` at the end of the BGP export policy:

```
policy-statement bgp-ipclos-out {
    term loopback {
        from {
            protocol direct;
            route-filter 100.0.0.22/32 orlonger;
        }
        then {
            next-hop self;
            accept;
        }
    }
    term reject {
        then reject;
    }
}
```

Verification

There are a lot of moving parts to building an EVPN-VXLAN fabric. We'll use a lot of show commands and walk you through how everything comes together. Let's take a look.

BGP neighbors

The first thing you want to do is ensure that we have full BGP sessions in both the underlay and overlay:

```
dhanks@spine-sw01> show bgp summary
Groups: 3 Peers: 11 Down peers: 0
Table          Tot Paths  Act Paths Suppressed    History Damp State    Pending
bgp.evpn.0
                     721        542          0          0        0          0
inet.0
                      76         44          0          0        0          0
Peer             AS        InPkt    OutPkt    OutQ   Flaps Last Up/Dwn State|#Active/Received/
Accepted/Damped...
100.0.0.12        65200     35409     34294       0      12  3d 4:13:50 Establ
  bgp.evpn.0: 57/57/57/0
  default-switch.evpn.0: 55/55/55/0
  __default_evpn__.evpn.0: 0/0/0/0
  SQUARE.evpn.0: 2/2/2/0
100.0.0.13        65200     94846     94763       0       0 1w0d 8:39:51 Establ
  bgp.evpn.0: 235/235/235/0
  default-switch.evpn.0: 232/232/232/0
  __default_evpn__.evpn.0: 0/0/0/0
  SQUARE.evpn.0: 1/1/1/0
100.0.0.14        65200     94945     94763       0       0 1w0d 8:39:34 Establ
  bgp.evpn.0: 56/235/235/0
  default-switch.evpn.0: 55/232/232/0
  __default_evpn__.evpn.0: 0/0/0/0
  SQUARE.evpn.0: 1/1/1/0
100.0.0.21        65200       200       713       0       3    42:44 Establ
  bgp.evpn.0: 98/98/98/0
```

```
        default-switch.evpn.0: 98/98/98/0
        __default_evpn__.evpn.0: 98/98/98/0
100.0.0.22         65200        929        2003        0        1    3:35:44 Establ
    bgp.evpn.0: 96/96/96/0
        default-switch.evpn.0: 96/96/96/0
        __default_evpn__.evpn.0: 96/96/96/0
172.16.0.0         60001        485        485         0        1    3:35:51 Establ
    inet.0: 8/25/22/0
172.16.0.8         60002        10598      10598       0        1  3d 9:05:00 Establ
    inet.0: 8/13/10/0
172.16.0.16        60003        23023      23024       0        0 1w0d 8:40:26 Establ
    inet.0: 13/18/15/0
172.16.0.24        60004        23014      23017       0        0 1w0d 8:40:26 Establ
    inet.0: 13/18/15/0
172.16.0.33        60021        96         106         0        3      42:48 Establ
    inet.0: 1/1/1/0
172.16.0.35        60022        479        485         0        1    3:35:51 Establ
    inet.0: 1/1/1/0
```

Both the underlay and overlay look great. All sessions are "Established" and we're learning prefixes on each session.

Ethernet switching table

Now let's take a look at the switching table to see what MAC addresses we have learned and where they came from:

```
dhanks@spine-sw01> show ethernet-switching table | no-more

MAC flags (S - static MAC, D - dynamic MAC, L - locally learned, P - Persistent static, C - Control MAC
          SE - statistics enabled, NM - non configured MAC, R - remote PE MAC, O - ovsdb MAC)


Ethernet switching table : 406 entries, 406 learned
Routing instance : default-switch
    Vlan         MAC                MAC          Age    Logical        NH       RTR
    name         address            flags               interface      Index    ID
    bd1000       00:00:5e:00:01:01  DR,SD               esi.1852       0        0
    bd1000       00:31:46:79:e4:9a  D                   vtep.32772     0        0
    bd1000       00:31:46:7a:04:9a  D                   vtep.32775     0        0
    bd1000       de:ad:be:e1:00:20  D                   vtep.32769     0        0
    bd1000       de:ad:be:e1:00:21  D                   vtep.32769     0        0
    bd1000       de:ad:be:e1:00:22  D                   vtep.32769     0        0
    bd1000       de:ad:be:e1:00:23  D                   vtep.32769     0        0
    bd1000       de:ad:be:e1:00:24  D                   vtep.32769     0        0
```

:vxlan.0 RIB

The vxlan.0 is a very special route table. Junos doesn't use the default routing table when looking up the next-hop for a VTEP. Instead, Junos will use the vxlan.0 routing instance:

```
dhanks@spine-sw01> show route routing-instance :vxlan.0

:vxlan.inet.0: 20 destinations, 20 routes (20 active, 0 holddown, 0 hidden)
+ = Active Route, - = Last Active, * = Both

100.0.0.11/32      *[Direct/0] 3d 22:43:55
```

```
                         > via lo0.0
100.0.0.12/32            *[Static/1] 3d 22:40:37, metric2 0
                            to 172.16.0.0 via et-0/0/58.0
                         > to 172.16.0.8 via et-0/0/59.0
100.0.0.13/32            *[Static/1] 2d 19:18:26, metric2 0
                            to 172.16.0.0 via et-0/0/58.0
                         > to 172.16.0.8 via et-0/0/59.0
100.0.0.14/32            *[Static/1] 2d 19:18:21, metric2 0
                            to 172.16.0.0 via et-0/0/58.0
                         > to 172.16.0.8 via et-0/0/59.0
100.0.0.22/32            *[Static/1] 3d 22:40:38, metric2 0
                         > to 172.16.0.35 via et-0/0/67.0
100.0.0.23/32            *[Static/1] 2d 19:18:26, metric2 0
                         > to 172.16.0.0 via et-0/0/58.0
                            to 172.16.0.8 via et-0/0/59.0
100.0.0.24/32            *[Static/1] 2d 19:18:26, metric2 0
                            to 172.16.0.0 via et-0/0/58.0
                         > to 172.16.0.8 via et-0/0/59.0
< ... truncated ... >
```

VXLAN L3 gateways

The first step we want to do is check to see if we can find our VXLAN L3 gateways from the leaf switch:

```
dhanks@leaf-sw01> show ethernet-switching vxlan-tunnel-end-point esi
ESI                             RTT                  VLNBH INH  ESI-IFL   LOC-IFL   #RVTEPs
00:01:01:01:01:01:01:01:01:01 default-switch         1765  131081 esi.1765  esi.1765  2
    RVTEP-IP        RVTEP-IFL       VENH    MASK-ID    FLAGS
    100.0.0.23      vtep.32773      1788    1          2
    100.0.0.24      vtep.32770      1764    0          2
ESI                             RTT                  VLNBH INH  ESI-IFL   LOC-IFL   #RVTEPs
05:00:00:00:00:00:00:03:e8:00 default-switch         1762  131078 esi.1762  esi.1762  2
    RVTEP-IP        RVTEP-IFL       VENH    MASK-ID    FLAGS
    100.0.0.11      vtep.32774      1790    1          2
    100.0.0.12      vtep.32769      1753    0          2
ESI                             RTT                  VLNBH INH  ESI-IFL   LOC-IFL   #RVTEPs
05:00:00:00:00:00:00:03:e9:00 default-switch         1761  131077 esi.1761  esi.1761  2
    RVTEP-IP        RVTEP-IFL       VENH    MASK-ID    FLAGS
    100.0.0.11      vtep.32774      1790    1          2
    100.0.0.12      vtep.32769      1753    0          2
< ... truncated ... >
```

The first ESI 00:01:01:01:01:01:01:01:01:01 is located on leaf-sw03 and leaf-sw04 as part of the LACP bundle going to our switch CE device. The next two ESIs begin with 05:, which tells us that it's a virtual MAC (vMAC) address used by the spine switches for VXLAN L3 gateway. We can see that the remote VTEPs are the two spine switches: spine-sw01 and spine-sw02. For each remote VTEP, a logical interface (IFL) is created locally that keeps track of traffic statistics and other data.

We can verify on spine-sw01 that 05:00:00:00:00:00:00:03:e8:00 belongs to it:

```
dhanks@spine-sw01> show evpn database | match e8
  1000  00:00:5e:00:01:01  05:00:00:00:00:00:00:03:e8:00  Mar 01 22:39:15  10.1.100.1
```

The MAC 05:00:00:00:00:00:00:03:e8:00 is bound to the IP address 10.1.100.1, which is configured on both spine-sw01 and spine-sw02:

```
dhanks@spine-sw01> show interfaces irb terse | match 10.1.100
irb.100                 up      up    inet    10.1.100.211/24
dhanks@spine-sw01> show configuration interfaces irb.100
description " * TENANT 10 - vlan 100 - vni 1000 ";
family inet {
    address 10.1.100.211/24 {
        virtual-gateway-address 10.1.100.1;
    }
}
```

Of course, you can verify that we're advertising these vMACs from the spine by using the following command:

```
dhanks@spine-sw01> show route advertising-protocol bgp 100.0.0.21

bgp.evpn.0: 612 destinations, 803 routes (612 active, 0 holddown, 0 hidden)
  Prefix                    Nexthop              MED    Lclpref   AS path
  1:100.0.0.11:0::0500000000000003e800::FFFF:FFFF/304
*                          Self                         100       I
  1:100.0.0.11:0::0500000000000003e900::FFFF:FFFF/304
*                          Self                         100       I
```

EVPN type-2

The next step is to make sure you're seeing all of the MAC addresses in POD2 that were originally learned from POD2. For example, we had a set of MAC addresses learned on leaf-sw01 and leaf-sw02 that should now appear on leaf-sw03 and leaf-sw04:

```
dhanks@leaf-04> show ethernet-switching vxlan-tunnel-end-point remote mac-table | match de:ad:be
  de:ad:be:e1:00:20   D     vtep.32772      100.0.0.22
  de:ad:be:e1:00:21   D     vtep.32772      100.0.0.22
  de:ad:be:e1:00:22   D     vtep.32772      100.0.0.22
  de:ad:be:e1:00:23   D     vtep.32772      100.0.0.22
  de:ad:be:e1:00:24   D     vtep.32772      100.0.0.22
  de:ad:be:e1:00:10   D     vtep.32773      100.0.0.21
  de:ad:be:e1:00:11   D     vtep.32773      100.0.0.21
< ... truncated ... >
```

We have a lot of EVPN type-2 advertisements installed on leaf-sw04. We can see that the "DEADBEEF" MACs are pointing to a remote VTEP with the IP address 100.0.0.21 (leaf-sw01) and 100.0.0.22 (leaf-sw02).

Let's take a closer look at the remote end-point 100.0.0.21 (leaf-sw01) from the perspective of leaf-sw04:

```
dhanks@leaf-sw04> show ethernet-switching vxlan-tunnel-end-point remote ip 100.0.0.21

MAC flags (S -static MAC, D -dynamic MAC, L -locally learned, C -Control MAC
           SE -Statistics enabled, NM -Non configured MAC, R -Remote PE MAC)
```

```
Logical system    : <default>
Routing instance : default-switch
 Bridging domain : bd1000+100, VLAN : 100
 VXLAN ID : 1000, Multicast Group IP : 0.0.0.0
 Remote VTEP : 100.0.0.21, Nexthop ID : 1785
   MAC              MAC      Logical        Remote VTEP
   address          flags    interface      IP address
   de:ad:be:e1:00:10  D       vtep.32773     100.0.0.21
   de:ad:be:e1:00:11  D       vtep.32773     100.0.0.21
   de:ad:be:e1:00:12  D       vtep.32773     100.0.0.21
   de:ad:be:e1:00:13  D       vtep.32773     100.0.0.21
   de:ad:be:e1:00:14  D       vtep.32773     100.0.0.21
   fa:ce:b0:01:00:10  D       vtep.32773     100.0.0.21
   fa:ce:b0:01:00:11  D       vtep.32773     100.0.0.21
   fa:ce:b0:01:00:12  D       vtep.32773     100.0.0.21
   fa:ce:b0:01:00:13  D       vtep.32773     100.0.0.21
   fa:ce:b0:01:00:14  D       vtep.32773     100.0.0.21
< ... truncated ... >
```

Now we can filter all of the EVPN type-2 advertisements pointing to leaf-sw01. The MAC addresses match the original test topology, as shown in Figure 6-30. Let's see how much traffic this remote VTEP has processed:

```
dhanks@lead-sw04> show interfaces vtep.32772
  Logical interface vtep.32772 (Index 562) (SNMP ifIndex 529)
    Flags: Up SNMP-Traps Encapsulation: ENET2
    VXLAN Endpoint Type: Remote, VXLAN Endpoint Address: 100.0.0.22, L2 Routing Instance:
    default-switch, L3 Routing Instance: default
    Input packets : 1585
    Output packets: 998840826
    Protocol eth-switch, MTU: Unlimited
      Flags: Trunk-Mode
```

Let's break down the EVPN type-2 advertisement even more by looking into the global EVPN BGP route table:

```
dhanks@leaf-sw04> show route table bgp.evpn.0 evpn-mac-address de:ad:be:e1:00:10

bgp.evpn.0: 528 destinations, 1056 routes (436 active, 0 holddown, 184 hidden)
+ = Active Route, - = Last Active, * = Both

2:100.0.0.21:1::1000::de:ad:be:e1:00:10/304
                    *[BGP/170] 02:16:04, localpref 100, from 100.0.0.13
                      AS path: I, validation-state: unverified
                    > to 172.16.0.42 via et-0/0/50.0
                      to 172.16.0.46 via et-0/0/51.0
                     [BGP/170] 02:16:04, localpref 100, from 100.0.0.14
                      AS path: I, validation-state: unverified
                    > to 172.16.0.42 via et-0/0/50.0
                      to 172.16.0.46 via et-0/0/51.0
```

We have a very curious string: 2:100.0.0.21:1::1000::de:ad:be:e1:00:10/304. What do these values mean?

Table 6-8. Breakdown of EVPN NLRI from RIB

Key	Value
2	EVPN type
100.0.0.21	Route distinguisher
de:ad:be:e1:00:10	MAC address
/304	The length required to mask entire EVPN type-2 NLRI

In addition to having a global EVPN route table, Junos also breaks down the route table per virtual switch. Because we have only a single virtual switch configured, its contents are identical to the global EVPN route table.

```
dhanks@leaf-sw04> show route table default-switch.evpn.0 evpn-mac-address de:ad:be:e1:00:10

default-switch.evpn.0: 590 destinations, 1117 routes (498 active, 0 holddown, 184 hidden)
+ = Active Route, - = Last Active, * = Both

2:100.0.0.21:1::1000::de:ad:be:e1:00:10/304
                   *[BGP/170] 02:16:19, localpref 100, from 100.0.0.13
                      AS path: I, validation-state: unverified
                    > to 172.16.0.42 via et-0/0/50.0
                      to 172.16.0.46 via et-0/0/51.0
                    [BGP/170] 02:16:19, localpref 100, from 100.0.0.14
                      AS path: I, validation-state: unverified
                    > to 172.16.0.42 via et-0/0/50.0
                      to 172.16.0.46 via et-0/0/51.0
```

If we had lots of virtual switches configured, each specific route table would show only EVPN NLRIs relevant to that particular virtual switch.

It's important to note that all EVPN routes are dumped into the bgp.evpn.0 route table. BGP will determine if the route is valid, reachable, and other things. If the route is invalid, it will be marked as hidden and remains in bgp.evpn.0. All routes that are validated are processed by the destination route table's BGP import policy. If the route is accepted by the destination's route table import policy, it will be installed into that route table.

Let's double check that we can ping some of our host POD1 MAC addresses from POD2. We'll log in to leaf-sw03 this time and try to ping some MAC addresses that are advertised from leaf-sw01:

```
dhanks@leaf-sw03> ping overlay tunnel-src 100.0.0.23 tunnel-dst 100.0.0.21 mac deadbee10010

ping-overlay protocol vxlan

        vni 1000
        tunnel src ip 100.0.0.23
        tunnel dst ip 100.0.0.21
        mac address de:ad:be:e1:00:10
        count 5
        ttl 255

Request for seq 1, to 100.0.0.21, at Feb 22 2016 23:12:44.965 PST
Response for seq 1, from 100.0.0.21, at Feb 22 2016 22:45:15.332 PST, rtt 12 msecs
```

```
    Overlay-segment present at RVTEP 100.0.0.21

        End-System Present
```

Now that was cool! Ping a host inside of a VXLAN tunnel. What about traceroute? Yup. That works, too:

```
dhanks@leaf-sw04> traceroute overlay tunnel-src 100.0.0.23 tunnel-dst 100.0.0.21 mac deadbee10010

traceroute-overlay protocol vxlan

        vni 1000
        tunnel src ip 100.0.0.23
        tunnel dst ip 100.0.0.21
        mac address de:ad:be:e1:00:10
        ttl 255

ttl  Address   Sender Timestamp              Receiver Timestamp          Response Time
  1  172.16.0.40   Feb 22 2016 23:13:17.367 PST          *                 11 msecs
  2  172.16.0.4    Feb 22 2016 23:13:17.379 PST          *                 11 msecs
  3  172.16.0.3    Feb 22 2016 23:13:20.391 PST          *                 11 msecs
  4  100.0.0.21    Feb 22 2016 23:13:20.403 PST   Feb 22 2016 22:45:50.774 PST   11 msecs

    Overlay-segment present at RVTEP 100.0.0.21

        End-System Present
```

For leaf-sw03 to reach the MAC address DE:AD:BE:E1:00:10, it had to travel through spine-sw03, fabric-02, and leaf-01, as shown by `traceroute`.

EVPN type-5

The next type of advertisement in EVPN is prefix/mask, which uses a type-5 NLRI. In the case of spine-sw01 and spine-sw02, it has the SQUARE tenant that uses the prefix 10.255.99.0/24 and advertises it to spine-sw03 and spine-sw04. Let's take a look at the IP prefix database on spine-sw01 and see if we can find our type-5 advertisements:

```
dhanks@spine-sw01> show evpn ip-prefix-database
L3 context: SQUARE

IPv4->EVPN Exported Prefixes
Prefix                                       EVPN route status
10.255.99.0/24                               Created
10.255.99.2/32                               Created

EVPN->IPv4 Imported Prefixes
Prefix                                Etag     IP route status
10.255.99.0/24                        0        Created
  Route distinguisher   VNI/Label  Router MAC        Nexthop/Overlay GW/ESI
    100.0.0.12:999      999        ec:3e:f7:89:15:1a 100.0.0.12
10.255.99.3/32                        0        Created
  Route distinguisher   VNI/Label  Router MAC        Nexthop/Overlay GW/ESI
    100.0.0.12:999      999        ec:3e:f7:89:15:1a 100.0.0.12
10.255.100.0/24                       0        Created
  Route distinguisher   VNI/Label  Router MAC        Nexthop/Overlay GW/ESI
```

```
100.0.0.13:30          999          00:31:46:79:e4:9a  100.0.0.13
100.0.0.14:30          999          00:31:46:7a:04:9a  100.0.0.14
```

As suspected we have two EVPN type-5 prefixes: 10.255.9.0/24 and a more specific 10.255.99.2/32, which is the IRB address. We can find more information about each prefix by using the extensive option:

```
dhanks@spine-sw01> show evpn ip-prefix-database ethernet-tag extensive | no-more
L3 context: SQUARE

IPv4->EVPN Exported Prefixes

Prefix: 10.255.99.0/24
  EVPN route status: Created
  Change flags: 0x0
  Forwarding mode: Symmetric
  Encapsulation: VXLAN
  VNI: 999
  Router MAC: 00:31:46:7b:e1:18

Prefix: 10.255.99.2/32
  EVPN route status: Created
  Change flags: 0x0
  Forwarding mode: Symmetric
  Encapsulation: VXLAN
  VNI: 999
  Router MAC: 00:31:46:7b:e1:18

EVPN->IPv4 Imported Prefixes

Prefix: 10.255.99.0/24, Ethernet tag: 0
  IP route status: Created
  Change flags: 0x0
  Remote advertisements:
    Route Distinguisher: 100.0.0.12:999
      VNI: 999
      Router MAC: ec:3e:f7:89:15:1a
      BGP nexthop address: 100.0.0.12

Prefix: 10.255.99.3/32, Ethernet tag: 0
  IP route status: Created
  Change flags: 0x0
  Remote advertisements:
    Route Distinguisher: 100.0.0.12:999
      VNI: 999
      Router MAC: ec:3e:f7:89:15:1a
      BGP nexthop address: 100.0.0.12

Prefix: 10.255.100.0/24, Ethernet tag: 0
  IP route status: Created
  Change flags: 0x0
  Remote advertisements:
```

```
          Route Distinguisher: 100.0.0.13:30
            VNI: 999
            Router MAC: 00:31:46:79:e4:9a
            BGP nexthop address: 100.0.0.13
          Route Distinguisher: 100.0.0.14:30
            VNI: 999
            Router MAC: 00:31:46:7a:04:9a
            BGP nexthop address: 100.0.0.14
```

To wrap it up, let's review a nice summary command for all of the type-5 NLRIs in the SQUARE routing instance:

```
dhanks@spine-sw01> show evpn ip-prefix-database l3-context SQUARE
L3 context: SQUARE

IPv4->EVPN Exported Prefixes
Prefix                                        EVPN route status
10.255.99.0/24                                Created
10.255.99.2/32                                Created


EVPN->IPv4 Imported Prefixes
Prefix                              Etag       IP route status
10.255.99.0/24                      0          Created
    Route distinguisher   VNI/Label Router MAC      Nexthop/Overlay GW/ESI
    100.0.0.12:999        999       ec:3e:f7:89:15:1a  100.0.0.12
10.255.99.3/32                      0          Created
    Route distinguisher   VNI/Label Router MAC      Nexthop/Overlay GW/ESI
    100.0.0.12:999        999       ec:3e:f7:89:15:1a  100.0.0.12
10.255.100.0/24                     0          Created
    Route distinguisher   VNI/Label Router MAC      Nexthop/Overlay GW/ESI
    100.0.0.13:30         999       00:31:46:79:e4:9a  100.0.0.13
    100.0.0.14:30         999       00:31:46:7a:04:9a  100.0.0.14
```

Summary

This chapter reviewed EVPN in depth. We began with the basics of EVPN and how it's able to handle both L2 and L3 VPNs. We walked through all of the forwarding and broadcast replication modes of each service. We then looked at all of the major features of EVPN such as MAC mobility, aliasing, and mass withdraw. There are many design options when it comes to EVPN; we took a look at the major options for both DCI and multitenant data centers. We wrapped up the chapter with an in-depth case study that shows how to set up a multitenant data center by using MP-BGP with EVPN.

Chapter Review Questions

1. Which EVPN NLRI handles MAC prefixes?

   a. Type-1

b. Type-2

c. Type-3

d. Type-5

2. Which combination of RT and labels does VLAN-Aware Service use?

a. RT=VRF and LABEL=VRF

b. RT=VLAN and LABEL=VLAN

c. RT=VRF and LABEL=VLAN

d. RT=VLAN and LABEL=VRF

3. Does split horizon with VXLAN allow for local replication even when the PE isn't the DF?

a. Yes

b. No

4. What's an example of EVPN stitching?

a. EVPN-MPLS to EVPN-VXLAN

b. EVPN-VXLAN to IP

c. EVPN-MPLS to IP

d. EVPN-VXLAN to EVPN-NVGRE

Chapter Review Answers

1. **Answer: B.** The type-2 NLRI handles all MAC address advertisements in EVPN.

2. **Answer: C.** The VLAN-Aware Service uses the VRF as the route target and a label per VLAN. This lets you save on the number of route targets used, but have efficient flooding because each VLAN has its own label.

3. **Answer: A.** Yes. When using split horizon with VXLAN, the PEs are smart enough to know if the traffic is sourced locally, and if so, they can flood it locally, even when it isn't the DF. This is because the other PE will look at the remote VTEP address of the replication traffic, and if it matches a common ESI, it will not flood and prevent loops.

4. **Answer: A and D.** EVPN stitching is when a switch or route takes one EVPN encapsulation and translates it to another EVPN encapsulation.

EVPN Configuration

In Chapter 6, we reviewed the details of EVPN-VXLAN. In the case study we had a laboratory with fabric, spine, and leaf switches. Here are the full configurations for each switch. For brevity, we have only included a single switch from each tier. Other switches in the same tier have similar configurations, but allowing for IP address changes.

Spine Configuration

```
## Last changed: 2016-02-23 00:43:56 PST
version 15.1X53-D30.17;
system {
    services {
        ssh;
        netconf {
            ssh;
        }
    }
    syslog {
        user * {
            any emergency;
        }
        file messages {
            any notice;
        }
        file cli-commands {
            interactive-commands any;
            explicit-priority;
        }
        time-format millisecond;
    }
}
interfaces {
```

```
et-0/0/58 {
    mtu 9192;
    unit 0 {
        family inet {
            mtu 9000;
            address 172.16.0.1/31;
        }
    }
}
et-0/0/59 {
    mtu 9192;
    unit 0 {
        family inet {
            mtu 9000;
            address 172.16.0.9/31;
        }
    }
}
et-0/0/60 {
    mtu 9192;
    unit 0 {
        family inet {
            mtu 9000;
            address 172.16.0.25/31;
        }
    }
}
et-0/0/61 {
    mtu 9192;
    unit 0 {
        family inet {
            mtu 9000;
            address 172.16.0.17/31;
        }
    }
}
et-0/0/66 {
    mtu 9192;
    unit 0 {
        family inet {
            mtu 9000;
            address 172.16.0.32/31;
        }
    }
}
et-0/0/67 {
    mtu 9192;
    unit 0 {
        family inet {
            mtu 9000;
            address 172.16.0.34/31;
        }
```

```
            }
        }
        irb {
            unit 100 {
                description " * TENANT 10 - vlan 100 - vni 1000 ";
                family inet {
                    address 10.1.100.211/24 {
                        virtual-gateway-address 10.1.100.1;
                    }
                }
            }
            unit 101 {
                description " * TENANT 10 - vlan 101 - vni 1001 ";
                family inet {
                    address 10.1.101.211/24 {
                        virtual-gateway-address 10.1.101.1;
                    }
                }
            }
            unit 102 {
                description " * TENANT 10 - vlan 102 - vni 1002 ";
                family inet {
                    address 10.1.102.211/24 {
                        virtual-gateway-address 10.1.102.1;
                    }
                }
            }
            unit 103 {
                description " * TENANT 10 - vlan 103 - vni 1003 ";
                family inet {
                    address 10.1.103.211/24 {
                        virtual-gateway-address 10.1.103.1;
                    }
                }
            }
            unit 104 {
                description " * TENANT 10 - vlan 104 - vni 1004 ";
                family inet {
                    address 10.1.104.211/24 {
                        virtual-gateway-address 10.1.104.1;
                    }
                }
            }
            unit 105 {
                description " * TENANT 20 - vlan 105 - vni 1005 ";
                family inet {
                    address 10.1.105.211/24 {
                        virtual-gateway-address 10.1.105.1;
                    }
                }
            }
            unit 106 {
```

```
                    description " * TENANT 20 - vlan 106 - vni 1006 ";
                    family inet {
                        address 10.1.106.211/24 {
                            virtual-gateway-address 10.1.106.1;
                        }
                    }
                }
                unit 107 {
                    description " * TENANT 20 - vlan 107 - vni 1007 ";
                    family inet {
                        address 10.1.107.211/24 {
                            virtual-gateway-address 10.1.107.1;
                        }
                    }
                }
                unit 108 {
                    description " * TENANT 20 - vlan 108 - vni 1008 ";
                    family inet {
                        address 10.1.108.211/24 {
                            virtual-gateway-address 10.1.108.1;
                        }
                    }
                }
            }
        lo0 {
            unit 0 {
                family inet {
                    address 100.0.0.11/32;
                }
            }
            unit 10 {
                family inet {
                    address 100.10.0.11/32;
                }
            }
            unit 20 {
                family inet {
                    address 100.20.0.11/32;
                }
            }
        }
    }
}
routing-options {
    router-id 100.0.0.11;
    forwarding-table {
        export pfe-ecmp;
        ecmp-fast-reroute;
    }
}
protocols {
    bgp {
        log-updown;
```

```
graceful-restart;
bfd-liveness-detection {
    minimum-interval 350;
    multiplier 3;
    session-mode automatic;
}
group overlay-evpn {
    type internal;
    local-address 100.0.0.11;
    family evpn {
        signaling;
    }
    cluster 2.2.2.2;
    local-as 65200;
    multipath;
    neighbor 100.0.0.21;
    neighbor 100.0.0.22;
}
group overlay-evpn-rr {
    type internal;
    local-address 100.0.0.11;
    family evpn {
        signaling;
    }
    local-as 65200;
    multipath;
    neighbor 100.0.0.12;
    neighbor 100.0.0.13;
    neighbor 100.0.0.14;
}
group underlay-ipfabric {
    type external;
    mtu-discovery;
    import bgp-ipclos-in;
    export bgp-ipclos-out;
    local-as 60011;
    bfd-liveness-detection {
        minimum-interval 350;
        multiplier 3;
        session-mode automatic;
    }
    multipath multiple-as;
    neighbor 172.16.0.0 {
        peer-as 60001;
    }
    neighbor 172.16.0.8 {
        peer-as 60002;
    }
    neighbor 172.16.0.16 {
        peer-as 60003;
    }
    neighbor 172.16.0.24 {
```

```
                    peer-as 60004;
                }
                neighbor 172.16.0.33 {
                    peer-as 60021;
                }
                neighbor 172.16.0.35 {
                    peer-as 60022;
                }
            }
        }
    evpn {
        encapsulation vxlan;
        extended-vni-list [ 1000 1001 1002 1003 1004 1005 1006 1007 1008 ];
        multicast-mode ingress-replication;
        vni-options {
            vni 1000 {
                vrf-target export target:1:1000;
            }
            vni 1001 {
                vrf-target export target:1:1001;
            }
            vni 1002 {
                vrf-target export target:1:1002;
            }
            vni 1003 {
                vrf-target export target:1:1003;
            }
            vni 1004 {
                vrf-target export target:1:1004;
            }
            vni 1005 {
                vrf-target export target:1:1005;
            }
            vni 1006 {
                vrf-target export target:1:1006;
            }
            vni 1007 {
                vrf-target export target:1:1007;
            }
            vni 1008 {
                vrf-target export target:1:1008;
            }
        }
    }
    lldp {
        interface all;
    }
}
policy-options {
    policy-statement LEAF-IN {
        term import_vni1000 {
            from community com1000;
```

```
                then accept;
        }
        term import_vni1001 {
            from community com1001;
            then accept;
        }
        term import_vni1002 {
            from community com1002;
            then accept;
        }
        term import_vni1003 {
            from community com1003;
            then accept;
        }
        term import_vni1004 {
            from community com1004;
            then accept;
        }
        term import_vni1005 {
            from community com1005;
            then accept;
        }
        term import_vni1006 {
            from community com1006;
            then accept;
        }
        term import_vni1007 {
            from community com1007;
            then accept;
        }
        term import_vni1008 {
            from community com1008;
            then accept;
        }
        term import_leaf_esi {
            from community comm-leaf_esi;
            then accept;
        }
        term default {
            then reject;
        }
}
policy-statement bgp-ipclos-in {
    term loopbacks {
        from {
            route-filter 100.0.0.0/16 orlonger;
        }
        then accept;
    }
}
policy-statement bgp-ipclos-out {
    term loopback {
```

```
                from {
                    protocol direct;
                    route-filter 100.0.0.11/32 orlonger;
                }
                then {
                    community add MYCOMMUNITY;
                    next-hop self;
                    accept;
                }
            }
        }
        term as-path {
            from {
                as-path asPathLength2;
                community MYCOMMUNITY;
            }
            then reject;
        }
    }
    policy-statement pfe-ecmp {
        then {
            load-balance per-packet;
        }
    }
    community MYCOMMUNITY members target:12345:111;
    community com1000 members target:1:1000;
    community com1001 members target:1:1001;
    community com1002 members target:1:1002;
    community com1003 members target:1:1003;
    community com1004 members target:1:1004;
    community com1005 members target:1:1005;
    community com1006 members target:1:1006;
    community com1007 members target:1:1007;
    community com1008 members target:1:1008;
    community comm-leaf_esi members target:9999:9999;
    as-path asPathLength2 ".{2,}";
}
routing-instances {
    VRF_TENANT_10 {
        instance-type vrf;
        interface irb.100;
        interface irb.101;
        interface irb.102;
        interface irb.103;
        interface irb.104;
        interface lo0.10;
        route-distinguisher 100.0.0.11:10;
        vrf-target target:10:10;
    }
    VRF_TENANT_20 {
        instance-type vrf;
        interface irb.105;
        interface irb.106;
```

```
            interface irb.107;
            interface irb.108;
            interface lo0.20;
            route-distinguisher 100.0.0.11:20;
            vrf-target target:10:20;
        }
}
switch-options {
        vtep-source-interface lo0.0;
        route-distinguisher 100.0.0.11:1;
        vrf-import LEAF-IN;
        vrf-target target:9999:9999;
}
vlans {
        bd1000 {
            vlan-id 100;
            l3-interface irb.100;
            vxlan {
                vni 1000;
                ingress-node-replication;
            }
        }
        bd1001 {
            vlan-id 101;
            l3-interface irb.101;
            vxlan {
                vni 1001;
                ingress-node-replication;
            }
        }
        bd1002 {
            vlan-id 102;
            l3-interface irb.102;
            vxlan {
                vni 1002;
                ingress-node-replication;
            }
        }
        bd1003 {
            vlan-id 103;
            l3-interface irb.103;
            vxlan {
                vni 1003;
                ingress-node-replication;
            }
        }
        bd1004 {
            vlan-id 104;
            l3-interface irb.104;
            vxlan {
                vni 1004;
                ingress-node-replication;
```

```
        }
    }
    bd1005 {
        vlan-id 105;
        l3-interface irb.105;
        vxlan {
            vni 1005;
            ingress-node-replication;
        }
    }
    bd1006 {
        vlan-id 106;
        l3-interface irb.106;
        vxlan {
            vni 1006;
            ingress-node-replication;
        }
    }
    bd1007 {
        vlan-id 107;
        l3-interface irb.107;
        vxlan {
            vni 1007;
            ingress-node-replication;
        }
    }
    bd1008 {
        vlan-id 108;
        l3-interface irb.108;
        vxlan {
            vni 1008;
            ingress-node-replication;
        }
    }
}
```

Leaf Configuration

```
## Last changed: 2016-02-23 00:31:30 PST
version 14.1X53-D30.3;
system {
    services {
        ssh;
        netconf {
            ssh;
        }
    }
    syslog {
        user * {
            any emergency;
        }
        file messages {
```

```
                any notice;
            }
            file cli-commands {
                interactive-commands any;
                explicit-priority;
            }
            time-format millisecond;
        }
    }
}
chassis {
    aggregated-devices {
        ethernet {
            device-count 4;
        }
    }
}
interfaces {
    xe-0/0/12 {
        unit 0 {
            family ethernet-switching {
                interface-mode trunk;
                vlan {
                    members 100-108;
                }
            }
        }
    }
    xe-0/0/13 {
        unit 0 {
            family ethernet-switching {
                interface-mode trunk;
                vlan {
                    members 100-108;
                }
            }
        }
    }
    et-0/0/50 {
        mtu 9192;
        unit 0 {
            family inet {
                mtu 9000;
                address 172.16.0.33/31;
            }
        }
    }
    et-0/0/51 {
        mtu 9192;
        unit 0 {
            family inet {
                mtu 9000;
                address 172.16.0.37/31;
```

```
                }
            }
        }
        lo0 {
            unit 0 {
                family inet {
                    address 100.0.0.21/32;
                }
            }
        }
    }
    routing-options {
        router-id 100.0.0.21;
        forwarding-table {
            export pfe-ecmp;
        }
    }
    protocols {
        bgp {
            log-updown;
            graceful-restart;
            group overlay-evpn {
                type internal;
                local-address 100.0.0.21;
                import OVERLAY-IN;
                family evpn {
                    signaling;
                }
                local-as 65200;
                bfd-liveness-detection {
                    minimum-interval 350;
                    multiplier 3;
                    session-mode automatic;
                }
                multipath;
                neighbor 100.0.0.11;
                neighbor 100.0.0.12;
            }
            group underlay-ipfabric {
                type external;
                mtu-discovery;
                import bgp-ipclos-in;
                export bgp-ipclos-out;
                local-as 60021;
                bfd-liveness-detection {
                    minimum-interval 350;
                    multiplier 3;
                    session-mode automatic;
                }
                multipath multiple-as;
                neighbor 172.16.0.32 {
                    peer-as 60011;
```

```
            }
            neighbor 172.16.0.36 {
                peer-as 60012;
            }
        }
    }
    evpn {
        vni-options {
            vni 1000 {
                vrf-target export target:1:1000;
            }
            vni 1001 {
                vrf-target export target:1:1001;
            }
            vni 1002 {
                vrf-target export target:1:1002;
            }
            vni 1003 {
                vrf-target export target:1:1003;
            }
            vni 1004 {
                vrf-target export target:1:1004;
            }
            vni 1005 {
                vrf-target export target:1:1005;
            }
            vni 1006 {
                vrf-target export target:1:1006;
            }
            vni 1007 {
                vrf-target export target:1:1007;
            }
            vni 1008 {
                vrf-target export target:1:1008;
            }
        }
        encapsulation vxlan;
        extended-vni-list [ 1000 1001 1002 1003 1004 1005 1006 1007 1008 ];
        multicast-mode ingress-replication;
    }
    lldp {
        interface all;
    }
}
policy-options {
    policy-statement LEAF-IN {
        term import_leaf_esi {
            from community comm-leaf_esi;
            then accept;
        }
        term import_vni1000 {
            from community com1000;
```

```
            then accept;
    }
    term import_vni1001 {
        from community com1001;
        then accept;
    }
    term import_vni1002 {
        from community com1002;
        then accept;
    }
    term import_vni1003 {
        from community com1003;
        then accept;
    }
    term import_vni1004 {
        from community com1004;
        then accept;
    }
    term import_vni1005 {
        from community com1005;
        then accept;
    }
    term import_vni1006 {
        from community com1006;
        then accept;
    }
    term import_vni1007 {
        from community com1007;
        then accept;
    }
    term import_vni1008 {
        from community com1008;
        then accept;
    }
    term default {
        then reject;
    }
}
policy-statement OVERLAY-IN {
    term reject-remote-gw {
        from {
            family evpn;
            next-hop [ 100.0.0.13 100.0.0.14 ];
            nlri-route-type [ 1 2 ];
        }
        then reject;
    }
    term accept-all {
        then accept;
    }
}
policy-statement bgp-ipclos-in {
```

```
                term loopbacks {
                    from {
                        route-filter 100.0.0.0/16 orlonger;
                    }
                    then accept;
                }
            }
            policy-statement bgp-ipclos-out {
                term loopback {
                    from {
                        protocol direct;
                        route-filter 100.0.0.21/32 orlonger;
                    }
                    then {
                        next-hop self;
                        accept;
                    }
                }
                term reject {
                    then reject;
                }
            }
            policy-statement pfe-ecmp {
                then {
                    load-balance per-packet;
                }
            }
            community com1000 members target:1:1000;
            community com1001 members target:1:1001;
            community com1002 members target:1:1002;
            community com1003 members target:1:1003;
            community com1004 members target:1:1004;
            community com1005 members target:1:1005;
            community com1006 members target:1:1006;
            community com1007 members target:1:1007;
            community com1008 members target:1:1008;
            community comm-leaf_esi members target:9999:9999;
        }
        switch-options {
            vtep-source-interface lo0.0;
            route-distinguisher 100.0.0.21:1;
            vrf-import LEAF-IN;
            vrf-target target:9999:9999;
        }
        vlans {
            bd1000 {
                vlan-id 100;
                vxlan {
                    vni 1000;
                    ingress-node-replication;
                }
            }
```

```
bd1001 {
    vlan-id 101;
    vxlan {
        vni 1001;
        ingress-node-replication;
    }
}
bd1002 {
    vlan-id 102;
    vxlan {
        vni 1002;
        ingress-node-replication;
    }
}
bd1003 {
    vlan-id 103;
    vxlan {
        vni 1003;
        ingress-node-replication;
    }
}
bd1004 {
    vlan-id 104;
    vxlan {
        vni 1004;
        ingress-node-replication;
    }
}
bd1005 {
    vlan-id 105;
    vxlan {
        vni 1005;
        ingress-node-replication;
    }
}
bd1006 {
    vlan-id 106;
    vxlan {
        vni 1006;
        ingress-node-replication;
    }
}
bd1007 {
    vlan-id 107;
    vxlan {
        vni 1007;
        ingress-node-replication;
    }
}
bd1008 {
    vlan-id 108;
    vxlan {
```

```
                vni 1008;
                ingress-node-replication;
            }
        }
}
```

Fabric Configuration

```
## Last changed: 2016-02-22 16:46:35 PST
version 14.1X53-D30.3;
system {
    services {
        ssh;
        netconf {
            ssh;
        }
    }
    syslog {
        user * {
            any emergency;
        }
        file messages {
            any notice;
        }
        file cli-commands {
            interactive-commands any;
            explicit-priority;
        }
        time-format millisecond;
    }
}
interfaces {
    et-0/0/12 {
        mtu 9192;
        unit 0 {
            family inet {
                mtu 9000;
                address 172.16.0.6/31;
            }
        }
    }
    et-0/0/13 {
        mtu 9192;
        unit 0 {
            family inet {
                mtu 9000;
                address 172.16.0.4/31;
            }
        }
    }
    et-0/0/14 {
        mtu 9192;
```

```
            unit 0 {
                family inet {
                    mtu 9000;
                    address 172.16.0.2/31;
                }
            }
        }
        et-0/0/15 {
            mtu 9192;
            unit 0 {
                family inet {
                    mtu 9000;
                    address 172.16.0.0/31;
                }
            }
        }
        lo0 {
            unit 0 {
                family inet {
                    address 100.0.0.1/32;
                }
            }
        }
    }
routing-options {
    router-id 100.0.0.1;
    forwarding-table {
        export pfe-ecmp;
    }
}
protocols {
    bgp {
        log-updown;
        graceful-restart;
        group underlay-ipfabric {
            type external;
            mtu-discovery;
            import bgp-ipclos-in;
            export bgp-ipclos-out;
            local-as 60001;
            bfd-liveness-detection {
                minimum-interval 350;
                multiplier 3;
                session-mode automatic;
            }
            multipath multiple-as;
            neighbor 172.16.0.1 {
                peer-as 60011;
            }
            neighbor 172.16.0.3 {
                peer-as 60012;
            }
```

```
                neighbor 172.16.0.5 {
                    peer-as 60013;
                }
                neighbor 172.16.0.7 {
                    peer-as 60014;
                }
            }
        }
        lldp {
            interface all;
        }
    }
    policy-options {
        policy-statement bgp-ipclos-in {
            term loopbacks {
                from {
                    route-filter 100.0.0.0/16 orlonger;
                }
                then accept;
            }
        }
        policy-statement bgp-ipclos-out {
            term loopback {
                from {
                    protocol direct;
                    route-filter 100.0.0.1/32 orlonger;
                }
                then {
                    next-hop self;
                    accept;
                }
            }
        }
        policy-statement pfe-ecmp {
            then {
                load-balance per-packet;
            }
        }
    }
}
```

Index

About the Author

Douglas Richard Hanks, Jr. is Director of Product Line Management and Strategy with Juniper Networks and focuses on next-generation hardware and software solutions and corporate strategy. He works in the Juniper Development and Innovation (JDI) organization, which is responsible for all Juniper hardware, software, and solutions.

Douglas is certified with Juniper Networks as JNCIE-ENT #213 and JNCIE-SP #875. His interests are network engineering and architecture for enterprise and service provider technologies. He is also the author of the *Juniper QFX5100* and *Juniper MX Series* books published by O'Reilly Media, and several *Day One* books published by Juniper Networks Books.

Douglas is the cofounder of the Bay Area Juniper Users Group (BAJUG). When he isn't busy with networking, he enjoys computer programming and photography.

You can reach Douglas on Twitter *@douglashanksjr*.

About the Lead Technical Reviewers

Damien Garros is a senior technical marketing engineer with Juniper Networks. Damien works with Juniper's largest customers and is recognized as one of the top network automation experts. Damien has appeared at Network Field Day, Packet-Pushers, and various network conferences, speaking about Juniper technology and network automation. For the past two years, he has been working closely with the Juniper QFX10000 platform. Damien created the Junos Fusion packet walk-through collateral in Chapter 5.

Damien was a professor at CPE in France for two years, teaching data center and cloud computing. He is also very active in the open source community and contributes code to Ansible modules; he is the author of the EVPN-VXLAN Ansible project, and coauthor of Juniper's OpenNTI monitoring project. You can check out Damien's work at *https://github.com/dgarros*, and you can contact him on Twitter *@damgarros*.

Michael Pergament joined Juniper in 2005. In the past 10 years, he has worked as a consulting sales engineer in EMEA Center of Excellence and technical marketing engineer in JDI. Michael holds JNCIE-ENT #23 and JNCIE-SP #512. Michael is the coauthor of Juniper's OpenNTI and Ansible EVPN-VXLAN project. He has also been working with Damien for the past two years bringing the Juniper QFX10000 Series to market.

About the Technical Reviewers

Many Junos engineers reviewed this book. They are, in the authors' opinion, some of smartest and most capable networking people around. They include but are not limited to: Lakshmi Namboori, Masum Mir, Sathish Shenoy, Praful Lalchandani, Najeeb Haddad, Suresh Krishnan, Krisna Karanam, Aldrin Isaac, Muralidhar Devarasetty, Ravi Shekar, Bruno Rijsman, Colby Barth, Sam Rajarathinam, Wen Lin, Kumaraguru Radhakrishnan, Prabakaran A, and Avi Godbole.

Colophon

The animal on the cover of *Juniper QFX10000 Series* is a rook (*Corvus frugilegus*). Its species name, *frugilegus*, is Latin for "food-gathering."

Rooks are similar in size to carrion crows at 45–47 cm in length. They have black legs, feet, and feathers, which show blue or purple in the sunlight. Feathers on the head, neck, and shoulders are dense and silky. Their bills are grey-black. Rooks are distinguishable from other crows by the gray-white skin bared in front of the eyes around the base of the adult rook's bills.

Rooks are found in Great Britain, Ireland, and north and central Europe. They are also found in parts of Iceland and Scandinavia in open agricultural areas. They tend to move south during autumn. Rooks nest in rookeries, usually in the very tops of trees. To build nests, they break off branches and twigs or steal them from nearby nests. Adults lay 3–5 eggs in February or early March and incubate them for 16–18 days. In autumn, the young birds collect into large flocks along with unpaired birds from previous seasons. During this season, incredible aerial displays can be seen by adult birds.

Rooks probe the ground with their strong bills to feed on earthworms and insect larvae. They also feed on cereal grain, small amounts of fruit, small mammals, acorns, small birds, eggs, and carrion. Their call is often described as *kaah*, similar to the call of the carrion crow.

When confronted with problems in captivity, rooks are one of several species of birds capable of using tools, as shown in experiments. One rook figured out how to get a worm floating out of its reach. The water level was too low to reach the worm, so the rook placed some nearby rocks into the water until the level was high enough. They've been known to use sticks and wire, bending the wire into a hook to reach an object. Rooks' cleverness with tools has been likened to a chimpanzee's dexterity with its hands.

Many of the animals on O'Reilly covers are endangered; all of them are important to the world. To learn more about how you can help, go to *animals.oreilly.com*.

The cover image is from *British Birds*. The cover fonts are URW Typewriter and Guardian Sans. The text font is Adobe Minion Pro; the heading font is Adobe Myriad Condensed; and the code font is Dalton Maag's Ubuntu Mono.

Lightning Source UK Ltd.
Milton Keynes UK
UKOW04f1955270417

300066UK00003B/7/P